PROBLEM OF INDIAN NATIONALITY

Problem of Indian Nationality

Sukumar Dutt

LOW PRICE PUBLICATIONS
Delhi-110052

Distributed by
D.K. Publishers Distributors (P) Ltd.
4834/24, Ansari Road, Darya Ganj,
New Delhi-110002
Phones: 23278584, 23278368, 23261465
e-mail: dkpd@del3.vsnl.net.in
url: www.dkpd.com

First Published 1926

Reprinted in **LPP** 2004

ISBN 81-7536-322-3

Published by
Low Price Publications
A-6, Nimri Commercial Centre,
Near Ashok Vihar Phase-IV,
Delhi-110052
Phones: 27401672, 27452453
e-mail: lpp@nde.vsnl.net.in
url: www.lppindia.com

Printed at
D K Fine Art Press P Ltd.
Delhi-110052

PRINTED IN INDIA

University Jubilee Research Prize-Thesis, 1922

PROBLEM OF INDIAN NATIONALITY

By

SUKUMAR DUTT, M.A., B.L.

Principal and Senior Professor of English Literature, Ramjas College, Delhi; sometime Professor of English Literature, Ripon College, Calcutta; Griffith Memorial Prize-winner, 1919, and Jubilee Research Prize-winner, 1922, of the University of Calcutta; Author of 'Early Buddhist Monachism.'

PUBLISHED BY THE
UNIVERSITY OF CALCUTTA
1926

To

The Blessed Memory of

My Deeply Revered Uncle

Who was more than a Father to me

ASWINI KUMAR DUTT OF BARISAL

One of the foremost of Nation-Builders of India

whose name has passed into a household word in Bengal

For the purest Patriotism that works and suffers in silence

For Devotion to God and Truth, fixed as the polar star

For Love of Humanity knowing no barriers of creed or caste

For Dedicated Life lived in the Task-Master's eye

The following pages are humbly inscribed by one

who has most need of his Blessings from Above

His Unworthy Nephew.

CONTENTS

PREFACE

The subject of the present thesis has a living interest. The last word upon it cannot be said yet and I do not pretend to be able to say it.

Indian nationality is a topic of current politics, and has been casually discussed as such in several magazines, journals and hand-books on India. Bevan's *Indian Nationality*, Besant's *India —A Nation*, Pannikar's *Indian Nationalism* do not rise above the topical quality. An attempt is made in Risley's *People of India* to understand the problem in the light of history and political philosophy. A similar attempt, more systematic, is Gilchrist's *Indian Nationality*. The last-mentioned work contains valuable suggestions, opinions and views which I have often had occasion to refer to in the following pages. I am indebted to Prof. Gilchrist specially for the convenient and compendious expression, 'Unities of Nationality,' which I have adopted and used frequently in this work.

All discussions about Indian nationality, as it appears to me, have proceeded hitherto on wrong lines. The conception of nationality itself is wrapped up in a confusion of ideas. I hope my exposition of Nationality in the present work will help a little towards clearing up this confusion.

I have tried to look at the whole problem from a new point of view. The prevailing misconceptions about the relation of the 'unities' to nationality have been, to my mind, largely responsible for the current erroneous views on Indian nationality. The historical back-ground has never been sufficiently regarded and scrutinised. But in my opinion the key to the whole problem lies hidden there. Whether my point of view is right or wrong is not for me to say, but it has at any rate the refreshing virtue of originality.

In reading this historical back-ground of Indian nationality, I have availed myself of the latest researches of scholars in the field of ancient Indian social life and polity. These researches, as it appears to me, lay the basis for a new view of ancient Indian society as an aggregation of several autonomous units---a view which has an important bearing on the interpretation of Indian life as it was and as it is to-day.

But the subject, as I have repeatedly said in these pages, is not one for historical research only. History becomes important in as-much as it helps in the interpretation of present conditions. While therefore maintaining my base in history, I have advanced into the latest times and the existing Indian social and political phenomena. The main significance of these phenomena in relation to our subject lies in the manner of their psychological reaction, *i.e.*, how they affect the mind of the people. In considering this, I have had to go into current politics and political literature. The writings specially of Aurobindo Ghosh and Rabindra Nath Tagore and the speeches of Bal Gangadhar Tilak have been for this purpose often laid under contribution. The Non-co-operation Movement, the activities of the Indian National Congress, debates in Parliament on India, utterances of Indian Governors—all these are very delicate ground, but it lay across my appointed path and had to be trodden. I only hope that in controversial matters the reader will cover with charity all differences of opinion.

The scope of the present work necessarily admitted certain topics of contemporary history and politics. The author does not claim to be a political prophet and his treatment of these topics has therefore become a little out of date in some places with the lapse of a few years taken by the publication. The reader is asked to bear in mind that the following pages were written between January and June of 1922 when the echoes of the last Great European War had not died down and the re-adjustment of national life in Europe had just begun ; the Free State of Ireland had recently been established, Czecho-Slavia and Poland had been asserting their right to a 'place in the sun' and the Austrian and the German Empires had gone to pieces. In India, the Non-co-operation Movement and the allied Khilaphat Movement were at their height, centring round the Indian National Congress. The subsequent developments of these two movements and the subsequent activities of the Indian National Congress, divided into political parties with different political programmes, have not been touched upon. Should the work reach a second edition, it will be brought up to date.

As the manuscript was set up in a lino-type machine, it was not possible to use diacritical marks in the transliterated Sanskrit words and passages. Some typographical errors also have crept into them which are pointed out in the Errata, kindly prepared for me by Pundit H. Sarma of Ramjas College, Delhi, as a labour of love.

In conclusion, I venture to express the hope that my work may be of some little help to all those who are honestly striving to understand a unique and intricate problem of political philosophy, *viz.*, the evolution of Nationality in the Indian continent.

BARISAL (Bengal) : S. DUTT.

June, 26, 1922.

INTRODUCTION

The approaches to the subject of the present thesis are mainly beset with two-fold difficulties. In the first place, it rests on an assumption or postulate which has not yet been universally accepted; in the second place, it is so hedged round with thorny political passions and prejudices that a detached academic perspective becomes difficult of attainment. It is necessary therefore to grasp and comprehend these difficulties clearly and firmly at the very threshold of our treatment.

If we had to deal with the problem of nationality in a country like Germany, France or England, our task would be comparatively easy. For in most of the European countries, nationality is an accomplished fact,—it is the palpable evolved product of a long course of historical circumstances. An enquiry into its basis, meaning and development would, under this condition, resolve itself more or less into an historical enquiry. It would be necessary only to pursue the clue steadily through the unfolding chapters of history. But with regard to the problem of Indian nationality, the case is altogether different. Here the certitude of historical facts and circumstances is wholly wanting. We have to grope our way, often blindly enough, through the tangled promiscuity of causes, conditions and tendencies, some of which make a fitful appearance in Indian history, others find expression in Indian philosophy and literature, while still others have to be fished out of the obscure depths of what MacDougall calls the 'group mind.' But these are difficulties inherent in the treatment of the problem of nationality in relation to India. The difficulties enumerated above are of another order and they affect the very fundamentals of our treatment.

Any treatment of the subject of Indian nationality must needs proceed on the assumption of the possibility or probability of such a political entity as Indian nationality. Yet this very possibility has been strenuously assailed on two sides—from the ground of abstract theory and from that of social and historical experience. The question—whether such a political entity can ever arise—has been emphatically answered in the negative. It behoves us to examine this denial before we proceed any further.

The attack from the ground of abstract theory has been dealt by a school of political thought, which has come specially to the fore on the conclusion of the recent European War and of which the Indian exponent is Rabindranath Tagore. Political thoughts are said to emerge out of the material results of history. In Europe since the Middle Ages, the progress of history has established a certain order of political aggregates known as Nations, and out of this historical result again has emanated a course of political thinking which has become painfully self-conscious, since Mazzini during the thirties of the last century. It is needless for us to follow all the turns and complications of this political thinking from its first passionate articulation by Joseph Mazzini, through its exaggerated emphasis in the militant principle of Nationalism, its recent ordeal of fire, as Prof. Ramsay Muir points out,[1] in the last European War, to its last technical formulation in the Doctrine of Self-determination. But what concerns us here is that from the beginning there has existed a political school side by side which has distrusted nationality and its objective manifestation in the principle of nationalism. To this school for example belonged Lord Acton. Since the thunder of guns has been hushed and the smoke of the battlefields laid and the death-grip of nations, triumphing in nationalism, over, this school has re-asserted its influence. As a writer in the *Round Table* says, "Two schools of thought and sentiment dominate the politics of modern Europe,—the liberal and the national,"[2]

[1] See Prof. Ramsay Muir's *Nationalism and Internationalism* (1919). Prof. Muir regards the last great European War as a conflict between peoples who repudiate the Nation-idea and peoples who staunchly uphold it. "While Germany and her allies, Austria and Turkey, stand now, and long have stood, as the supreme opponents of the national cause, there are ranged against them Britain and France, the two most ancient of the European nation-states, and the steadiest friends of the national principle; Italy, the most perfect example of the true national spirit; * * * Russia, * * * Japan, the only purely national state in the non-European world; Belgium and Serbia: * * * And this group of nation-states has formally declared that it is fighting for the national principle" (p. 126). "The Great War is the last, and the greatest, and the most definite and decisive challenge and defiance of the national cause in Europe," (p. 125).

[2] See the *Round Table* (December, 1914)—Article on *Nationalism and Liberty*, p. 18.

and at the present day the liberal school is represented by the somewhat pathetic and solitary figure of Romain Rolland in Europe. The tendency of this liberal school in short is "to appeal from existing states and structures to a universal code of political principle."[3] It does not believe in nationality as a necessary or inevitable stage in the evolution of human aggregation. To it, the existing order of nation-states in Europe is a special product of history, and it is not necessary to the political perfection of a people or community to attain to or pass through this stage.

Of this school, Rabindranath Tagore is the typical Indian exponent. The exclusiveness which nationality implies is abhorrent to him, and the geographical segregation of humanity into different nations is to him futile and meaningless under modern conditions of progressive scientific intercommunication. "During the evolution of the Nation," says Tagore, "the moral culture of brotherhood was limited by geographical boundaries, because at that time those boundaries were true. Now they have become imaginary lines of tradition divested of the qualities of real obstacles. So the time has come when man's moral nature must deal with this great fact with all seriousness or perish."[4] Hence he condemns the nation-idea. "I am not against one nation in particular, but against the general idea of all nations."[5] Being a champion of the liberal school and an avowed enemy of nationalism, Tagore foresees for his country a destiny that should transcend and defeat the barren exclusiveness of mere nationality. In his reading, the whole history of India is at bottom the complicated history of racial harmonisation. The problem of India is the Race-problem—"her problem is the problem of the world in miniature."[6] Hence at no period of her history, however distant, can the internal organisation and adjustment of her life be considered complete. The India of his dream—the 'Greater India' that the poet envisages—is one not cribbed, cabined and confined within the narrowing bounds of

[3] *Ibid*, p. 23.
[4] Tagore's *Nationalism* (1918), pp. 101-102.
[5] *Ibid*, p. 110.
[6] *Ibid*, p. 114.

nationality. To him India is and will ever remain 'a country of the No-Nation.' "In India, the history of humanity is seeking to elaborate a specific ideal, to give to general perfection a special form which shall be for the gain of all humanity."[7] Further on Tagore says, "This new India belongs to humanity. What right have we to say who shall and who shall not find a place therein? Who is this 'we'? Bengali, Marathi or Punjabi, Hindu or Mussalman? Only the larger *we* in whom all these,—Hindu, Moslem and Englishman, and whosoever else there be,—may eventually unite shall have the right to dictate who is to remain and who is to leave."[8] The poet's exhortation to his countrymen is therefore to aim at this cosmopolitanism. He considers that the insistence on the ideal of nationalism in India is tantamount to "damning up the true course of our historical stream and borrowing power from the sources of other people's history." His conclusion of the whole matter and his own conviction are thus clinched and summed up: "India has never had a real sense of nationalism. Even though from childhood, I had been taught that idolatry of the Nation is almost better than reverence for God and humanity, I believe I have outgrown that teaching, and it is my conviction that my countrymen will truly gain their India by fighting against the education which teaches them that a country is greater than ideals of humanity."[9] It will be observed how near the poet stands to the mental attitude of Herbert Spencer who exposes in his brief essay on *Patriotism* the hollow mock-sentiment that rings in the cry—'Our country, right or wrong.'[10] He owns also intimate spiritual kinship with Romain Rolland whose hero Clerambault says, echoing distinctly the author's own sentiment, "I belong to life as a whole; I have brothers in every nation, enemy or ally. The families of our souls are scattered throughout the world. Let us re-unite them. Our task is to undo these chaotic nations, and in their places to bind together more harmonious groups."[11] But

[7] Tagore's *Greater India* (The East and West in Greater India), p. 82.
[8] *Ibid*, p. 86.
[9] *Nationalism*, p. 106.
[10] See Herbert Spencer's *Facts and Comments* (1902), p. 89.
[11] See R. Rolland's *Clerambault* (A story of an Independent Spirit during the War).

it will be further observed that Rabindranath agrees with a difference. Herbert Spencer brings to the matter the acid test of pure abstract morality. To him patriotism or the inner spirit of nationality is a colourless thing, neither to be shunned nor sought after, till it is viewed in the dry light of moral reason. Romain Rolland on the other hand considers the principle of nationality to be an inherently wrong principle of human aggregation; the true principle, in his view, is the bond of spiritual kinship which breaks up the political and hence chaotic groups and re-unites them more harmoniously. Rabindranath puts his case in a somewhat different way. He finds the root-principle of human life in synthesis and harmony, and in his view nationalism tends to sterilise it by segregating politically one group of humanity from another. This, according to him, has been the woful fate of Europe where the Nation has starved humanity. But in the history of India this principle of synthesis and harmony has been inherent. Hence "her problem is the problem of the world in miniature. India is too vast in its area and too diverse in its races. It is many countries packed in one geographical receptacle. It is just the opposite of what Europe truly is, namely, one country made into many."[12] Thus the tendency of India has never been and will never be towards the segregation of herself within the four walls of nationality from the rest of humanity at large.

The Liberal School, therefore, represented by Rabindranath Tagore, challenges on the ground of abstract theory the very assumption that underlies the subject of the present thesis, *viz.*, the possibility of Indian nationality. But another challenge is more commonly thrown down from a more commonplace plane, *viz.*, the social and historical experience of Indian life. This challenge has been mostly made by foreigners who have travelled or lived in or helped in the administration of India. They have in most instances found India no country at all, but only an extensive tract of Asia, where a remarkable variety of different races with different cultures and creeds have come to settle through the lapse of centuries, and who are kept together at the present day

[12] *Nationalism*, p. 114.

within the geographical boundaries of India by the pressure of *Pax Britannica*, established by British rule. They cannot see at the end of their vista, however long it may extend, the historical miracle of a nation being built out of these wholly unsuitable and unmatchable materials.

There can be no gain-saying the fact that all the outward appearances of Indian life and history lend strong colour to the view of this school, which we may term, for the sake of brevity, the Anglo-Indian School. To all outward seeming, the political history of India has been, despite vast attempts at empire-building and political federation by Chandragupta, Asoka, Samudragupta, Akbar and Sivaji, a complicated history without a trace of that unity of movement, characteristic of the histories of different peoples of Europe since, to adopt the words of Pollard, 'vertical lines' of nationality began to traverse the 'horizontal lines' of common mediæval culture.[13] Such unity of movement has been gained by Indian history only in recent times when this insoluble problem has been led to a *deus ex machina* denouement by the instrumentality of British rule. Yet this unity of movement is apparent only, a wholly external one, constituted by and consisting in the imperial acts and measures of British viceroys and provincial governors. It is not such historical unity as is the measure and manifestation of an inner psychological unity among the inhabitants of the land themselves.

It cannot moreover be said, judging by the external appearances of Indian life and society, that history's 'long tale of consummating circumstances,' has synthesised the wonderful varieties of race, cult, culture and living in India. The fact stares one in the face from the pages of the Census Reports, and one rises from the perusal of such a work as Risley's on *The People of India* with a bewildering sense of India as the epitome of the world.

These external appearances of Indian history and Indian life are constantly insisted upon by a school of writers whom I have designated as the Anglo-Indian School, since it consists mostly of Britishers, connected with India through the work of political administration. Sir John Strachey, ex-lieutenant-governor of

[13] See A. F. Pollard's *Factors of Modern History* (1919), pp. 10 ff

the United Provinces, may be taken as the central exponent of this school. "This is the first and most essential thing to learn about India," says Strachey,[14] "that there is not, and never was an India, or even any country of India, possessing, according to European ideas, any sort of unity, physical, political, social and religious; no Indian nation, no 'people of India' of which we hear so much." With regard to the possibility of the growth of Indian nationality, Strachey is equally emphatic. Such a prospect is to him an unthinkable impossibility. "We might with as much reason," says he,[15] "look forward to a time when a single nation will have taken the place of the various nations of Europe." The views expressed by Sir John Strachey have been echoed and re-echoed by nearly all Anglo-Indian writers and administrators down to Lord Ronaldshay, ex-Governor of Bengal:[16] they have almost been reduced by all too frequent repetition to the easy virtue of a truism. But the later writers of this school, while always assenting to the major premise, the existence of hopelessly anti-national characteristics in Indian life, have felt somewhat shaky in drawing the conclusion which Sir John Strachey so boldly draws, *viz.*, that Indian nationality must be an utterly impossible entity. Writing in 1890, Sir Charles Wentworth Dilke, with a certain amount of caution said as follows:[17] "There are two commonplaces in the discussion of Indian problems upon which, though much has been said, much remains to be said. The one is that general observations upon India are invariably mistaken, because India is a continent rather

[14] Sir John Stratchey's *India* (1903), p. 5.

[15] *Ibid*, p. 8.

[16] See the Earl of Ronaldshay's *An Eastern Miscellany* (1911), pp. 191-193. "Any one seeking to understand the problems with which British statesmanship is confronted in India is foredoomed to failure unless he first learns to think of India not as a country, but as a continent, and of the Indian people not as a nation, but as a vast and complex mosaic of peoples, differing from one another as widely as do the countries in which they dwell. To think of India as one would think of Great Britain or of France is to think of a purely imaginary India which has no existence in fact; if an analogy from Europe were drawn at all, it is to be found in Europe itself, and not in any one of its component parts. The reason is simple. The elements necessary for the creation of a homogeneous nation—common language, common faith, common institutions—have never been found in India. Successive waves of invasion through centuries of time have left upon her soil fragments of many of the races of mankind, widely differing in speech, in religion, in custom, in tradition—races which have never fused but remain to this day peoples apart."

[17] Sir Charles Wentworth Dilke's *Problems of Greater Britain* (1890), p. 403.

than a single country; and the second that while India is in many matters stationary beyond the possibility of European comprehension, it is in other matters a country of rapid changes." These 'rapid changes,' adumbrated by Dilke, have cast a deep shadow of doubt over the 'dogmatic assertions and burly negations' of the Anglo-Indian school. "It is the glimmering of the idea of nationality that some find in India at the present time," said Dilke in 1890.[18] Since then this glimmering has gained light so steadily as to become unmistakable even to the Anglo-Indians. In fact, the views of this school have with the lapse of years tended to become 'a child's puzzle still unsolved.' This baffling aspect of the problem, the incongruity between all the appearances and the unmistakable reality, so struck Sir Herbert Risley that, after bringing to the matter all the light vouchsafed by historical analogies, he confessed that he had been "left with the uncomfortable feeling that he has by no means got to the root of the matter."[19] He had therefore to release the problem into the twilight of mysticism, remarking that "analysis has its limits, and a people, like an individual, is something more than a bundle of tendencies. The mysterious thing called personality, the equally mysterious thing called national character, has in either case to be reckoned with."[20] Risley's remark would remind one irresistibly of the words of Prof. Pollard who quotes Maitland to say that national character "is a wonder-working spirit at the beck and call of every embarrassed historian, a sort of *deus ex machina*, which is invoked to settle any problem which cannot readily be solved by ordinary methods of rational investigation. The rule of the game seems to be—when in doubt play National Character." [21]

It is unnecessary for us to discuss at length at this stage the views of this Anglo-Indian school from which however has emerged a poser that may be stated as follows. All the normal 'unities' of nationality are absolutely lacking in India which really is a welter of all kinds of anti-national diversities, yet a

18 *Ibid*, p. 406.
19 Sir Herbert Risley's *The People of India* (Ed. 1915), p. 299.
20 *Ibid*, p. 299.
21 A. F. Pollard's *Factors of Modern History* (1919), p. 12.

common sentiment of nationality is emerging out of this hopeless welter; how could this be possible in the teeth of all experience of history? Finding no satisfactory answer to this poser, the writers of this school have from time to time called in aid such dubious factors as the use of English learning and the English language, uniformity of laws and regulations under British rule, oneness of British administration, etc., little understanding the extent of the bearing of these factors on the psychology of the people.

As a matter of fact a unique problem of political science like Indian nationality can hardly be comprehended by bringing to bear upon it preconceived notions drawn from the history of the growth of European nations. Its complications reach far into the history and traditions of India and spread by such delicate filaments into the mental constitution of the Indian peoples that a western mind finds it impossible to grasp and co-ordinate them. Nationhood, as MacDougall has pointed out, is essentially a psychological conception. "To investigate the nature of national mind and character and to examine the conditions that render possible the formation of the national mind and tend to consolidate national character, these are the crowning tasks of psychology."[22] Indian nationality, in fact, has to be studied and understood in this psychological perspective and not viewed through the coloured glasses of such western conceptions as 'unity of race,' 'unity of language,' 'unity of religion,' etc. The simple fact should be constantly borne in mind that the connotations of all such facile terms, as race, language and religion, differ in India vastly from their connotations in the west. The point will be made clearer in a later portion of this work. Hence, the secret of the failure and self-contradiction of the views of the Anglo-Indian school lies in interpreting the phenomena of Indian life and history in terms of western conception as well as mistaking outward appearances for inward psychological realities. It is no surprise therefore that foreigners regard the problem of Indian nationality as an insoluble crux: while all their knowledge and experience of India tend to disprove the possibility of Indian nationality almost

22 McDougall's *Group Mind* (1920), p. 100.

to demonstration, it nonetheless makes its appearance in Indian life like some strange god out of the machine.

Having reviewed in brief the views of the two schools which deny from two divergent grounds the very possibility of Indian nationality, we shall pass on to other fundamental difficulties that beset treatment of the subject. These difficulties are of another order and they obtrude on the treatment irresistibly to derange clear perspective. Academic discussion of a subject should always be, like the dignity of English royalty, above politics. But unfortunately current political controversies, in which it is next to impossible for a contemporary to keep himself from taking sides, interpenetrate the subject to the very core. We shall presently see how these political controversies start up spontaneously all round our subject.

During the last three decades or so, there has been going on a political controversy between the British administrators of India who believe in the indefinite continuation of British rule over the country and the educated intelligentsia who as emphatically controvert that belief. The controversy has during the last few years reached an acute and almost critical stage. The main plank in the platform of the first party has always been the impossibility of India ever becoming a nation and hence her needing, for untold ages to come, the strong hand of a foreign power, the pressure of some external force in the shape of a neutral foreign government, to keep her from automatic disintegration. The opposite party argues with as great vehemence that such disintegration cannot follow, as India has either become or is on a fair way to becoming a united nation to which external pressure of a strong foreign government is not only needless, but a positive oppression. This party has, acting on this belief, set up an organised assembly to represent and bespeak this united nation (either made or in the making) and christened it 'The Indian National Congress.'[23] This controversy is not a mere war of words only, but bears a real political significance, for, to quote the

[23] There are two handbooks on the growth and development of the Indian National Congress—Annie Besant's *How India wrought for Freedom* (1915), which gives the history of the Congress down to the 27th session, and Amvika Charan Mazumdar's *Indian National Evolution* (2nd Ed. 1917) which is a collection of essays on different aspects of the Congress movement.

words of Bluntschli, the Indian Empire of the English "might be endangered by too strong an insistence on nationality." [24]

More than three decades ago, Sir John Seeley discussed from the standpoint of political science the phenomenon of British rule in India, from the chair of Modern History in the University of Cambridge. British rule in India has certainly some special characteristics. "With a handful of British civilians, and an army of 76,000 Europeans and 159,000 Indian troops, Great Britain governs and secures against invasion a population of 231,000,000 people, scattered over 983,000 square miles of territory, while she also maintains close relations with the great ruling chiefs of feudatory states, whose joint population amounts to 63,000,000 and whose area totals 6,56,000 square miles." [25] This fact is certainly a striking phenomenon in history. As Dr. Crozier says, with a touch of patriotic exaggeration, "It is a phenomenon, unique in the history of the world; for if we compare it with Imperial Rome, who came nearest to us in the ease of her administration of subject-nations, we shall find that whereas during the period of Roman imperial supremacy, the temple of Janus was for centuries rarely shut; with us in India, on the contrary, it has rarely been open. It looks, therefore, as if we must have been peculiarly favoured by the gods *somewhere* in this our easy domination." [26] Now this is a phenomenon well worthy of being accounted for by the political scientist. The first attempt in this direction was made by Sir John Seeley in his illuminating lectures on the *Expansion of England.* It has been obvious even to superficial thinkers on the subject for a long time that British supremacy in India cannot be accounted for by military prowess,—the true cause of it is to be searched for not in the might of British rule itself, but in the political condition of people who unresistingly accept it.

According to Sir John Seeley, the strangeness of the phenomenon vanishes if we dissipate from our view two leading misconceptions, 'first, that India constitutes a nationality, and

[24] Bluntschli's *The Theory of the State*, pp. 98-99.
[25] Ronaldshay's *An Eastern Miscellany*, p. 192.
[26] Dr. J. B. Crozier's *Last Words on Great Issues* (1917), p. 165.

second, that this nationality has been conquered by England.'[27] India, in his view, is a congeries of peoples and 'ought not to be classed with such names as England or France, which correspond to nationalities, but rather with such as Europe, marking a group of nationalities which have chanced to obtain a common name owing to some physical separation.'[28] Such being the condition of the country, 'India had no jealousy of the foreigner, because India had no sense whatever of national unity, because there was no India and therefore, properly speaking, no foreigner.'[29] Thus it happened that the establishment of British supremacy was not seriously thwarted by that jealousy of the foreigner which is the necessary correlative of the sense of nationality. It was not therefore a conquest in the ordinary sense, that is, the subordination by a foreign power of a conquered people's nationality. As Sir John pithily says, "India can hardly be said to have been conquered at all by foreigners; she has rather conquered herself."[30] Thus the utter lack of nationality in India was historically the cause of the establishment of British rule in the country, and the cause is a *continuing* one and constitutes the real secret of the continuance of British power. Not only did British rule establish itself by taking advantage of India's want of nationality but it also sustains itself by it. It is based upon a negation of Indian nationality and is bound to continue so long as this basis remains.

On this fundamental thesis, sketched so ably by Sir John Seeley, the whole controversy has turned hitherto. Believers in the indefinite continuation of British rule have justified their position on the ground that, nationality being impossible in India, a foreign rule is a perennial necessity. The opposite party on the other hand without disputing the logic of the position has attacked the major premise. Indian speakers claiming self-government for India from the platform of the Indian National Congress have always laid emphasis on the growing nationality of India and on that ground justified their claim. To cite one instance only, the

27 Seeley's *Expansion of England* (1918), p. 219.
28 *Ibid*. p. 221.
29 *Ibid*. p. 203.
30 *Ibid*. p. 202.

President of the thirty-sixth Indian National Congress, resented as an 'insult offered to India,' the use of the expression, 'Indian peoples,' in the Preamble to the Government of India Act, 1919, regarding it as an 'assertion by Parliament that India is not one, but many.'[31] From the heated political arena of the Indian National Congress, the cry of Indian nationality has sent its echoes into the coolness of academic cloisters. There has recently come into existence a school of thought, represented by Dr. Radhakumud Mookerji, which seeks to demonstrate the fundamental unity of India from literary and historical sources, although this demonstration is chiefly confined to what may be called Hindu India[32] Thus the controversy is one to which British administrators of India are invited by the necessity of self-justification and Indian public men by patriotism and the desire for political self-government. It is all but impossible for an Indian or a Britisher interested in the maintenance of British rule in India from keeping his academic perspective of the subject clear of the dust and turmoil of this controversy. The writer of the present thesis for instance is one of those who would rejoice to see the establishment of complete *Swaraj* or Self-Government in India immediately, and this being the wish of his mind, it may easily affect his thought and lead him, even through bias existing in unconscious cerebration, to exaggerate those aspects of Indian life which make for the growth of nationality. For such unconscious bias, the only corrective is no doubt the scientific spirit which Spinoza brought to the study of politics. "When I applied my mind to politics," says Spinoza, "so that I might examine what belongs to politics with the same precision of mind as we use for mathematics, I have taken my best pains not to laugh at the actions of mankind, not to groan over them, not to be angry with them, but to

[31] See *Young India*, edited by M. K. Gandhi (Vol. IV, No. 2, 12th January, 1922) —Undelivered Presidential Address by C. R. Das, p. 18.

[32] See Radhakumud Mookerji's *Fundamental Unity of India* (1914) and *Nationalism in Hindu Culture* (1921). "It has recently been pointed out by Babu Radhakumud Mookerji in his Essay entitled, 'The Fundamental Unity of India,' that India was recognised as a geographical unit and as a motherland long before the advent of the British Raj. Its history as a unit goes to remote antiquity: the writer gives considerable evidence to prove his point. But his whole treatise is compiled from the Hindu point of view, and his concluding sections on the future contribution of Indian nationality to the sumtotal of the world's good, are vitiated by the fact that he overlooks the present political composition of India."—R. N. Gilchrist's *Indian Nationality* (1920), p. 211.

understand them." "By understanding them, he says, he means looking at the motives of human feeling,—love, hatred, envy, ambition, pity,—not as vices of human nature, but as properties belonging to it, just as heat, cold, storm, thunder, belonging to air and sky." [33] But it is given to few students of politics to be able to rise above the circumambient atmosphere of current political controversies and ascend the rarefied height of Spinoza's scientific temper.

It is however essentially necessary to keep our mental gaze steadily fixed on the abstract subject presented to our study in the following thesis, *viz.*, the basis, meaning and development of Indian nationality. It is not futile to repeat what was said at the beginning of this chapter, *viz.*, that the subject is not one for historical study and research merely. We have not only to look before and after, but also to look around. While Indian nationality is not a *fait accompli*, it would be wrong to say on the one hand that, even admitting its possibility, it exists at such vague and immeasurable distance that the possibility becomes one of extreme tenuity only; it would be equally wrong to say on the other that Indian nationality has already emerged and is functioning in the world of political phenomena, or even that it has become a thoroughly tangible and comprehensible entity. Between these two extreme notions, the true poise of Indian nationality must somewhere lie. Be that as it may, it is clear that this political entity, whether *in esse* or *in posse*, does not lend itself to measurement by the 'two-foot rule.' Those who attempt to measure it by applying the rough and ready tests of the 'unities,' will utterly fail, as the race, language and religion problem of India is altogether on a different footing from that presented by any European country. It is necessary to admit frankly that in political science there are no categorical imperatives. The nuances of significance in respect of political verities change according to history and culture: the manner in which the problem of race for instance presents itself to the European mind is different from the manner in which practically the same problem has presented itself for ages to the Indian, Hindu or Muhammadan mind. The

[33] Lord Morley on *History and Politics*.

same is the case with language and religion. As a matter of fact what is understood to be religion by the Hindu mind is something incomprehensible to the westerner. These unities are thus not the standards of political value at all when applied to India, but they themselves require to be evaluated.

In fact we may go further and say that the idols of the cave, we gather from our study of western political science generalised from the history of Europe, have to be shattered in the very approaches to our subject. If nationality is a 'spirit,' essentially a psychological fact, it may assume different shapes in the histories of different peoples. Europe, as Dr. Tagore has said with the poet's luminous precision, is one country made into many. The common shape which nationality has assumed in the different countries of Europe may be after all of the special moulding of European history. It has taken the shape of the nation-state in Europe. Under a different sun, with different cultural environments, and with a different course of history, the same spirit which has manifested itself in the nation-state in Europe, may assume another appearance, altogether strange to a mind accustomed to the European idea of nationality. The conceptions of political science, as Seeley pointed out long ago,[34] are at bottom generalisations from historical phenomena. There can be no categorical finality about them, for the simple reason that the phenomena which supply their basis are themselves in a continual process of evolution. "For history is not over and in politics we are making it: and even if all human history is only a tragedy of good intentions, the fifth act still remains unwritten."[35] It is therefore necessary, to quote the words of Delisle Burns, 'to conceive politics more greatly and to deprovincialise history.' The conceptions of political science are emptied of all truth and meaning as soon as they are cast into cut-and-dried formulæ. Take this conception of Nationality for instance. After all heroic attempts at analysis and definition, it has not been possible to reduce it to anything more tangible than a mere sentiment. The entire futility of the definition of Nationality is exposed when we have

34 See Seeley's *Introduction to Political Science.*
35 Delisle Burns's *Political Ideals* (1919), p. 27.

to say, in the last resort, 'that a nation is a nation because its members passionately and unanimously believe it to be so.'[36] But even when we have said this, the last word is not said. For there may be various modes of such popular belief, and by one mode of belief a people may attain to the state-ideal, *i.e.*, nationality as functioning itself in political government, while by another mode a people may reach some other ideal far removed from the state-ideal of Europe. The mode of belief is after all determined by history and culture. "Ideals," as Mr. Lindsay truly says,[37] "are born of historical circumstances and fashioned to meet historical problems, and the would-be timeless ideals which political philosophers have put before us have always borne clear marks of the country and time of their origin."

Now the statement is susceptible of historical proof that the idea of India as a whole,—India as a distinct entity,—has actually been present to the mind of the inhabitants of this country. The slow growth and development of this idea through succeeding epochs of Indian history is a study of fascinating interest. It may be traced in somewhat unbroken outline even from the earliest monuments of Aryan literature. In the Vedas an interesting sociological fact is the occurrence of tribal place-names, which leave their sediment in all later literature, and in the Vedas too the king is most frequently referred to as a sort of non-territorial monarch, the king of the *Jana* or *Vis*. But side by side we discover the Vedic bards' love of the soil, due in all probability to their agricultural occupation as well as to the distinctive configuration of the early home of the Aryans in the Punjab. At a very early stage, it seems, this love of the soil linked itself to pride in the spread of Aryan culture: the land, over which Aryan culture projected itself, was regarded not in the light of some external acquisition, but as part and parcel of the original territory of settlement. It was something like territorial assimilation by cultural conquest.

36 "Nationality, then, is an elusive idea, difficult to define. It cannot be tested or analysed by formulæ, such as German professors love. Least of all must it be interpreted by the brutal and childish doctrine of racialism. Its essence is a sentiment; and in the last resort we can only say that a nation is a nation because its members passionately and unanimously believe it to be so."—Ramsay Muir's *Nationalism and Internationalism* (1919), p. 45.

37 Marvin's *Recent Developments in European Thought* (1920), p. 164. (Lindsay on *Political Theory*).

Thus the *patrie* of the original Aryans extended not so much by bringing lands under political subjugation, as by conversion to Aryan culture: it was through religious associations, cultural affinities and community of worship that the mother country was extended and consolidated. Thus what would otherwise be a political or merely geographical idea was interpenetrated by religion, and among the adherents of Aryan culture, who still constitute the overwhelming majority of the Indian population, the idea of Indian unity took a special turn even from the start. The subsequent amplifications of this conception by establishment of shrines, by institution of places of pilgrimage, by sanctification of rivers and places through *Pouranic* traditions, have been dealt with in an able manner by Dr. Radhakumud Mookerji. It is necessary also to observe that into this elastic framework of the conception of a spiritual unity of India all immigrant tribes and races, who could catch up even a veneer of Aryan culture, could find their respective places. For here culture and not race or language was the passport for admission. The only formidable difficulty was about the Mahammadans whose religion of spiritual brotherhood kept them moored to the main body of their co-religionists outside the boundaries of India. It is difficult for a western mind to grasp the order of ideas, unknown in European history, which has evolved this unique conception of the spiritual unity of India,—and which cannot in reality be equiparated with any of the forms of mediæval communism. The old Vedic love of the soil, the impregnable hieratic belief in a special culture directly springing from this soil, exclusive and peculiar to itself, and the faith that its full fruition lies in its victorious extension over the whole extent of this soil blend curiously in this Hindu psychological conception of Indian unity. Therefore when Seeley says that "in Brahmanism India has a germ, out of which sooner or later an Indian nationality might spring,"[38] he fails to understand that if any nationality were to grow out of this germ at all it would not be such nationality as we are familiar with in European history. It would in fact have no potency at all to culminate in the national-state ideal. I refer to this point which will

[38] See Seeley's *Expansion of England* (1918), p. 226.

be elaborated later on only to show at this stage that a mind free from western conceptions of nationality is absolutely necessary to comprehend the problem of Indian nationality. The foreign idols of the cave, as we said at the beginning, have to be ruthlessly discarded at the threshold of our subject.

The venerable, old leaders of the Indian National Congress, who in the first flush of enthusiasm for western learning were inclined to pay almost fetish-worship to western political philosophy, were led astray by this very failing. Committed definitely to the cause of Indian nationality, they accepted unquestioningly the western conception of it as its sole standard and measure. They took consolation from the fact that the existing nations of Europe were mixed races; that in countries like Switzerland and Belgium differences of language and religion did not operate against the growth of nationality; that in Germany extreme religious dissensions did not succeed in killing it and that even in Italy, where, before Mazzini and Garibaldi, nationality had but the glamour of a lost cause, national unity became finally possible.[39] Thus granting the possibility of Indian nationality, they laid emphasis on the altered circumstances of India since the establishment of British rule, specially the adoption by the intelligentsia of the English language as *lingua franca*, the existence of common rights and common grievances, and the extension of sympathy among the different races and peoples of India through increased facilities of intercommunication.[40] Led by their western prepossessions, these nationalists of the old school hailed all movements towards the establishment of a common script or tongue in India, or eclectic religious movements such as the Brahma Samaj or the Theosophical Society or the Sikh Khalsa, or advanced ventures in social reform like inter-dining or intercaste marriage, as contributory to Indian nationality.[41] The logic of their position however

[39] See, for instance, Surendranath Banerjea's Address on *Indian Unity* at a meeting of the Students' Association, held on 16th March, 1878, in the Medical College Theatre, Calcutta (*Speeches of Babu Surendranath Banerjea*, 1876-80, edited by Ramchandra Palit 2nd Ed., Vol. I, pp. 105 ff.).

[40] See *Ibid;* Also Bhupendranath Basu's *Presidential Address* at the Madras Congress, 1914; Mazumdar's *Indian National Evolution*, 2nd Ed., pp. 154-160.

[41] See Annie Besant's *India—A Nation;* Surendranath Banerjea also laid great store by the Brahma Samaj Movement. Says Banerjea—" The Brahma Samaj may also powerfully help to bring about Indian unity. Among the obstacles to national unity,

has been countermanded by the higher, inexorable logic of facts. Though these nationalists will readily admit that nationality in India is growing,—even with the rapidity of a rolling snow-ball, —the factors which they laid their rest upon are steadily dwindling and diminishing. Even the Indian National Congress has begun to cast off the English language as the Indian *lingua franca;* the liberal religious movements which were expected to thin the lines of partition between Hinduism and Mahammadism are by no means flourishing in response to growing nationality; advanced ventures in social reform, barring perhaps the limited question of 'untouchability,' are getting more and more to be isolated phenomena, and the existence of British rule which was believed to foster the growth of Indian nationality, is now widely believed to have a tendency just the opposite.[42]

But even with a mind 'clear of cant,' we may well own a sense of diffidence in dealing with the subject in its almost immeasurable totality. The monumental phrase of Auguste Comte may fitly be employed to describe the amplitude of our subject—'By the past, through the present, to the future.' Any adequate treatment of it must embrace past history, present tendencies and future developments as well. There are countries on the face of the earth the history whereof is known to persons less learned than Macaulay's schoolboy, where one drama after another of human civilization have been played out and done with. After each performance the stage has been cleared and footlights blown out and the curtain has risen on a new one and so on into the present era. Such countries are Egypt, Mesopotamia, Persia, Greece and Italy. But though perhaps equal in age with these countries, where human civilization has enacted itself, drama

difference of religion occupies not wholly an unimportant place. The Brahma Samaj by uniting Indians of varied creeds and beliefs under the bonds of a Common Faith, may help to remove this great difficulty and foster and promote Indian union."—Address on *Indian Unity*, 1878, Palit's Edition of Speeches, 2nd Ed., Vol. I, pp. 116-117.

42 This reversal of belief regarding the nationality-fostering virtues of British rule has become very pronounced recently among Indian Nationalists who are supported in their view by several European sympathisers. Even Dr. W. R. Inge, the Dean of St. Paul's, to whom no bias or prejudice can be attributed, says incidentally in his essay on *Patriotism*, "It would be unfair to say that Rome destroyed nations, for her subjects in the west were barbarous tribes, and in the East she displaced monarchies no less alien to their subjects than her own rule. But she prevented the growth of nationalities, as it is to be feared we have done in India."—*Outspoken Essays* (1920), p. 45.

after drama, India's case is different. Here the whole history has been but one vast and complicated play of which the fifth act is not yet. This marvellous continuity of Indian history clearly marks her off from other countries of equally hoary antiquity and makes every Indian problem so wide and deep in its complications and so difficult of final solution. Traditions, customs, religious and social institutions live by their roots that strike far into the depths of almost prehistoric ages. With the learned labourers in the field of Indian research, it has been the custom hitherto to trace their subjects back to the Vedas, the earliest literary monuments of the Aryans. But a new school of Indian history is at the same time slowly rising which would make even the Aryan invasion of India not the beginning of Indian history, but merely an early episode of it. As the Cretan discoveries of the last two decades have pushed back the beginnings of Greek history beyond Homer, so the recent researches into the non-Aryan and Dravidian elements of Indian history are likely to take its beginnings even beyond the Vedas and the Aryan invasion.[43] Doubts have already been cast on the very theory of Aryan invasion,[44] and attempts have been made to prove the Aryan race autochthonous in India which would put back her history even beyond the storied land of the Nile.[45] In fact the adventurous explorer as he proceeds up the river of Indian history comes gradually to despair of discovering its source and finds himself lost in the cloud-land of theories. But the custom of beginning research at the Vedas seems to be well settled up till now, and it is no doubt an advantageous point of beginning in as much as we can start from the

[43] See the remarks of Vincent Smith in *The Early History of India* (3rd Ed.), p. 8. He quotes approvingly the following dictum of Sundaram Pillai—"The scientific historian of India ought to begin his study with the basin of the Krisna, of the Cauvery, of the Vaigai, rather than with the Gangetic plain, as it has been now long, too long the fashion." Krishnaswami Aiyangar's *Ancient India* is an attempt in this direction.

[44] See for example Srinivas Iyengar's *Life in Ancient India in the Age of the Mantras*. The theory propounded by the learned author is that the Dravidian element is predominant in the Indian population, not only in the South, but also in the North. The Aryan element is an admixture, due to the influx in tribes and clans from time to time of the outside Aryans, and the difference between the Aryans and the Dasyus is really one of cult and not of race.

[45] See Abinash Chandra Das's *Rig-Vedic India*. The theory of Indian autochthony of the Aryan race, discredited by western scholars, is however the orthodox theory held in Brahmanical literature. Durgadas Lahiri, in the first volume of his Bengalee work, *Prithibir Itihās* (The History of the World) has elaborated the theory creditably from the Shastras. But it still remains to be established on the sounder basis of western methods of research.

comparatively solid ground of recorded matters. But as we proceed downwards through epoch after epoch, bright, dim or dark,—we marvel to find that, although the historical relations ramify amazingly, they nowhere break off completely,—there is a vital continuity all through, however complicated, that never stops dead. Forces bear in upon it from outside,—immigrations of races, importations and infiltrations of culture, relations of commerce, invasions by nomadic hordes, conquests by foreign powers,—but they mingle after all in the main stream, and serve to muddle or strengthen or even divert its current, but never to choke it off as in desert sands. Thus even the remote past in its relation to the present, in India, unlike in Egypt, Mesopotamia, Persia, Greece, or Italy, is not a dead hand, but a strongly living and shaping hand.

We have to regard and scrutinise this past in treating of the subject of Indian nationality in respect of its two uses—objective and subjective. Objectively considered, the past transmits to the present formative ideas, tendencies, institutions and various other living forces. As we have already seen, one of these ideas, *viz.*, the conception, from a cultural stand-point, of Indian unity is one which may be traced back to the Vedic age. It determines the mental attitude of the Hindus towards the country of their birth and links them up with the later-coming peoples and races who affiliated themselves to their religious culture. Another idea, as will be pointed out later, is the imperialistic one which marshals in one unbroken order the Vedic Chakravarti **Rājās**, Chandragupta, Asoka, Samudragupta, Akbar, Auranzeb, Shivaji down to the present King-Emperor of India. Still another idea is that of racial harmonisation and affiliation which, as Rabindranath Tagore has pointed out, has embodied and manifested itself in the unique and hoary institution of caste.[46] These ideas are long-descended inheritances from the past, not to speak of others which may be said to be of comparatively late introduction.

But history, besides its contribution of these moral and spiritual factors, has another use—a much subtler one. From the subjective point of view, Indian history is not a closed chapter to

[46] See Tagore's *Nationalism.*

the Indians of to-day. Eucken, speaking of the 'Eternal in History,' says, "Spiritually speaking, the past is by no means a finished stóry. It is always open to the present to discover, to stir up, something new in it. Even the past is still in making." "Thus history, from the human point of view," he continues, "may well seem to be a constant return upon old truth rather than a progressive advance towards new truth."[47] This 'stirring up of something new' in the past of India may become psychologically a potent formative factor in Indian nationality. If the history of India is one vast palimpsest, the past, when spelt out by the Indian mind, carries forward its meaning and significance into later writings on the parchment, and the perception of this continuity is the solvent of all the formidable contradictions that stare out of the census figures. As a well-known Irish writer, who is in deep sympathy with Indian nationality, has said, "The India of the Indians is no more the real India than a house is its occupants; and the Indians of India are not to be put wholly in a census return. When you have put the Indian nation into a string of figures, you are eternities away from the real nation, unless you have reckoned up the contents of the counted heads. The real India hovers over India's head; it is the totality of all that lives in the region of the imagination."[48] It is precisely in this 'region of the imagination' that the past of India lives and works, however dimly it may be. If the past of India were erased and blotted out to the Indian mind, it would find in the present but diversities of race, language, creed, and culture with no hope of any real lasting unity evolving. With the present as the starting point, the goal of Indian nationality may very well seem to be nowhere, a modern political chimera, but not so with the past. Hence Nivedita rightly insists on the 'awakening of a sense of history' for the creation of the national idea.[49]

[47] Eucken's *Christianity and the New Idealism* (translated by Gibson and Gibson), Chapter on Religion and History, p. 54.

[48] James H. Cousin's *The Renaissance in India*. (Ganesh and Co., Madras, June, 1918), p. 25.

[49] "The mind of India may to-day be held to have understood that the most important problem before it is the creation of a national idea. For this there must be the awakening of a sense of history. But we must carefully distinguish between such an awakening, and the process of collecting materials for history."—Sister Nivedita's *Civic and National Ideals* (1918, 2nd Ed.), p. 23.

Indeed it is this very blindness to the sense of history that unfits the writers of the Anglo-Indian school for the appreciation of the possibility of Indian nationality. In regard to our subject, therefore, the past has not only an objective but also a subjective value which, I assert, only an Indian mind is capable of truly appreciating.

But the past must lead us on to the present, and in the appreciation of the present, greater difficulties must needs be experienced. The advantage of dealing with the past is that here time automatically winnows away the accidentals from the essentials of events, tendencies and movements. But a contemporary is faced with the mixed stuff and his judgment is very apt to go wrong. The 'perspective,' which is of supreme value to the historian, is wanting, and when events move on before our very eyes in the mass, we are likely to miss their true import and direction. If these events again move the spectator also, another element of error arises from the inevitable shifting of the intellectual point of vision which must be its consequence. An Indian dealing with the present circumstances of India is thus in a doubly difficult position and he can only aim at second best. Now, there are strong currents in modern Indian life which are manifesting themselves not only in the field of politics, but also in the domains of art and literature. One of the most dominant and puissant of these currents is a political movement, technically called Non-Co-operation, which is of the utmost importance in our study, as will be explained later on. Not only has this movement crystallised the nationalist tendencies in modern India and overtaken and captured the Indian National Congress, but it has also thrown up on its crest a personality which in itself is an asset in national evolution. We have thus not only to evaluate the movement, but also the personality at its head. MacDougall has an instructive chapter in his book on the *Group Mind* on the part of leaders in national life. Speaking of them, MacDougall says, "These men exert a guidance and a selection over the cultural elements which the mass of men absorb. They praise what they believe to be good, and decry what they believe to be bad; and, in virtue of the prestige which their exceptional powers have brought them, their verdict is accepted and moulds popular opinion and sentiment.''[50] Mohandas Karamchand Gandhi, the leader of the Non-Co-operation movement, is an exact type of this class of national leaders,—a man decidedly not of pale hopes and middling expectations.

Round this great political movement of our time, which is still in progress and the upshot of which we can see only darkly through a glass, there is a subtle play and interplay of many political forces which we have got to calculate. Swadeshism or the preference for home-made commodities is one; the change in the whole mental attitude of the Mahammadan population of India towards the country of their birth (for which however, as I shall have occasion to explain later on, the Treaty of Sevres and the mutilation of the Khilapat was not solely responsible) is another; they are indeed material and psychological forces that determine the character of the main political movement. Out of all the bitter and passionate controversies about this political movement, one fact stands out clear, *viz.*, that, in its essence, it is a potent nationality-movement, having famous counterparts in the modern history of Europe.[51]

But the problem of nationality, though essentially political, has a scope that overlaps the area of politics. Nationality, being after all a reflex of the Group Mind in its highest organisation, its activities and manifestations must needs be various and comprehensive. There may possibly be, as a contemporary writer on political ideals has well pointed out, 'a tendency to mythology in the use of such terms as the Crowd Mind or the Soul of a People.'[52] But it is nonetheless true that an awakened sense of nationality shows itself in, while it is at the same time both measured and advanced by, many forms of activities non-political or even extra-political. In Ireland, the Celtic Revival and schemes of economic organisation were forms of national activity; the adoption of the

50 MacDougall's *Group Mind* (1920), p. 138.

51 The analogy between the Non-co-operation movement in India and similar movements in modern Europe is the subject of a brochure by Mr. Fenner Brockway, entitled, *Non-co-operation in Other Lands*. The analogy between the Hungarian Policy, re-named Sinn Fein, in Ireland, and Indian Non-co-operation struck M. Sylvain Briolay, who says in his recently published book, entitled *Ireland in Rebellion* (1922): "Inspired by this example (*i.e.*, of Hungary), he (Arthur Griffith) proposed that Ireland should adopt a programme of pacific non-co-operation similar to that recommended by Gandhi in India," pp. 7-8.

52 Delisle Burns's *Political Ideals*, p. 177.

Hungarian language and of education free from state-control are famous instances from Hungary; even in very recent times Bohemia tries to raise her head above the welter of the Balkan States by insistence on the native language and culture of the Czech, and Ukrania aspires to separate herself nationally by an appeal to the heroic and literary traditions of the Ruthenian Little Russians. There are essentially similar movements and activities current in India at the present time in non-political domains, such as the movement for national education, the encouragement of Hindustani as the Indian *lingua franca*, Bengal School of Painting, etc., which are seeking to realise vaguely what is best expressed by an equally vague expression, *viz.*, the soul of the people. These movements may appear to be quite disparate and unrelated to one another. They will be dealt with in their place. But though from an external point of view they appear to be different and separate currents, their movement is in the same direction and towards one mouth. There is no mistaking the fact that, among the thinking population of the country, there exists a feeling, vague and inchoate it may be as yet, that the principle by means of which the vastly differing tastes and mentalities of the highly mixed population of the United States of America are unified, through education and training, into a common political personality, should govern all public movements and activities in our country too. Just as the heterogeneous immigrants of America are steadily 'Americanised,' so the different and divergent sections of the vast population of India require to be Indianised in order to develop a common nationality. "Acting on the same principle, India must recognise that certain standards of taste, thought and sentiment are necessary to union and should devise and carry out a comprehensive scheme of 'Indianisation' with a view to creating a new type of Indian citizenship and building up an efficient unified Indian nation."[53] It is this feeling for 'Indianisation,'—which at the present day is fully though vaguely conscious of itself, that rationalises and unifies such movements in different directions as we have mentioned above.

53 Sir M. Visweswaraya's *Reconstructing India* (1918).

One standing feature of the situation is sometimes made too much of and about which it is necessary to utter a word of caution. It used to be believed and is still believed though by a constantly dwindling number that British Government, acting like a magician's wand, is awakening sleeping India into a sense of nationality. "The fact remains," asserts Prof. Gilchrist, "that Indian nationality is—or will be when completed—a product of British rule."[54] The argument of the believers in this creed is, briefly, that British rule has brought certain benefits to India which have had their effect in evoking nationality in the country. These benefits are well-known and Indians themselves have shown their glad appreciation of them by ready and unhesitating appropriation. But, while willing to give British rule in India all the credit that is due on this particular score, the only kernel of truth in the above argument seems to us to be that the necessary concomitants of a western system of administration and governance which cannot possibly go on without such modern conveniences as the Railway, the Post and Telegraph the Law-Court with its western tradition of uniform and equal justice, the School and the College, the Legislative and Executive Councils, etc., have made easier the progress of a feeling of nationality in India by facilitating the material ways and means by which it must work. In a country, politically and intellectually dead, all these amenities, increased a hundredfold, would not evoke any feeling of nationality at all. The real fact is that Indian nationality is not and cannot be a product of British rule, but its working and manifestation is facilitated by the amenities of western civilization introduced by it. It is necessary to refer to the topic here in order that the reader, if he happens to belong to the above school of thought, may not assume that in our calculations on Indian nationality in the following pages, we have really counted without the host.

As a matter of fact, the situation, at which India stands at the present time, bristles with numerous points of interest for the student of Indian nationality. Some nationalists are inclined to make of it a political Pisgah. But the student must clear his

[54] R. N. Gilchrist's *Indian Nationality*, pp. 211-212.

mind's eye of the mists of political enthusiasm or optimism. He has to keep his eye, from the angle of vision that his subject determines, on the singular conjuncture of tendencies which the present situation reveals, and estimate them with scrupulous and, if possible, overscrupulous accuracy. Such estimate, it will be found, is a task of extremely delicate difficulty.

Now the scope of our work allows us to project our outlook on the subject even into the future. The temptation of entering the cloud-land and dream-land of political prophecies is a common and at the same time a dangerous one. Political philosophy has not yet ripened into a science of history which would make prevision possible. When therefore the political philosopher, who is not a politician, is called upon to take account of the future, he can do no more than describe the existing tendencies. He can only point to such dispositions of phenomena as have a sort of syllogistic value, leaving the inference to be drawn by that subtle god of human destiny whom the Germans call Time-spirit (*Geitgeist*). Between the premises and the conclusion so many indeterminate factors intervene that social phenomena which include politics can never be resolved by process of logic. Political speculations and forecasts have therefore a hopeless air of unreality about them, and it is enough to be able to read the dim outline of the future in present tendencies, rather than attempt to prefigure it more clearly by driving these tendencies to their logical conclusion. There is perhaps nevertheless a core of truth in the following dictum of Auguste Comte :—

"In the minor arts of life it is generally recognised that principles should be investigated and taught by thinkers who are not concerned in applying them. In the art of Social Life, so far more difficult and important than any other, the separation of theory from practice is of far greater moment."

PART I.

Basic Factors of Indian Life

Race and Nationality

Race is a biological fact. It enters into the composition of different nations and peoples in various degrees, forms and combinations. Thus we have nations composed of a practically homogeneous race (*e.g.*, Iceland, China), nations composed of a sub-race produced by repeated blendings of allied racial stocks (*e.g.* England), nations in which the racial stocks though partially blended have not, owing to some geographical separation, fused so completely as to produce a distinct sub-race (*e.g.*, France), nations in which the races have existed side by side in a more or less loose conglomeration (*e.g.*, Switzerland), nations in which a variety of races has been held together in a sort of mechanical mixture (*e.g.*, the United States of America) and so on. Ethnology has established the fact that in nearly all parts of the world (with the possible exception of the inaccessible parts of Africa and America and distant inhabited islands of tropical oceans), racial purity is only a myth. 'From China to Peru,' races exist in separate geographical groupings in almost untold permutations and combinations. How racial differentiations come about,—whether through the operation of the same agency which the Darwinians believe to be the origin of species or otherwise,—is a problem still awaiting solution, nor is the discussion of this obscure biological problem pertinent to our purpose.

But the problem we have to deal with is the bearing of Race on Nationality. It would no doubt be accurate to say that the two belong to two different ranges of phenomena : while race is properly a question of biology, nationality is a question of psychology. But it is the subtle inter-relation between the biological fact of race and the essentially psychological fact of nationality that we have to consider and ponder over.

Sociological writers of the older school used to ignore or make little of the possibility of such an inter-relation. The then prevailing doctrine of psychology which regarded the human mind as a *tabula rasa* cast its influence on the sociological speculations of such writers as Mill and Buckle. "Of all vulgar modes of escaping from the consideration of the effect of social and moral influences on the human mind," says Mill, "the most vulgar is that of attributing the diversities of conduct and character to inherent natural differences." Thus Mill insisted with laboured overemphasis on the moulding forces of education and social environment, while Buckle on physical environment, in shaping national character. The school of Mill and Buckle still survives, though in recent years the 'inherent natural differences' which they affected to discount have been attracting more and more emphasis in sociological writings.

Before history began, there were the flowing periods of what are called pre-history and proto-history. Their total duration vastly exceeds the properly historical period of the world. Recent researches into anthropology are steadily bringing these obscure periods, but dimly discerned and ill defined till now, into increasing clearness, and so successfully exhibiting their importance and significance in the making of the historical period, that recent historians attempt to include them within the range of their discussion.[1] During these long formative periods, the influences of physical environment and similar biological factors must have exerted a much more potent shaping power than in later periods, since the increase of civilization implies the growing resistance of man to the influences of physical surroundings. Thus, according to MacDougall, the original or primary divergence of mental type between any two peoples must have been due to two fundamental causes, *viz.*, differences of physical environment and spontaneous variations of mental structures.[2] These causes again have operated on human society during its historical period with a force in inverse ratio to the growing power of civilization. Bagehot therefore draws a perfectly intelligible distinction between

[1] H. G. Wells, for instance, in his *Outline of the History of the World* (1920).
[2] MacDougall's *Group Mind*, p. 211.

what he calls the race-making force, 'which has now wholly, or almost, given over acting' and the nation-making force, properly so called, 'which is acting now as much as it ever acted, and creating as much as it ever created.'[3] This 'race-making force,' which no doubt may be ultimately resolved into several component forces and which has almost given over acting during the historical period, has produced those inborn racial qualities that exert such determining influence in history. Now, these racial qualities are thoroughly recognisable: their determinant power in history is also unmistakable. But while writers of the old school sought to explain them on the historical basis of differences of political and religious institutions, writers of the new school ascribe them to biological factors long operating during pre-historic periods, regarding all political and religious differences between two peoples (such as the English and the French for example) as being not primary, but secondary only.[4] Thus at the threshold of history we stand with well-defined peoples whose minds are not at all like *tabula rasa*, but are already written and scribbled over an infinite number of times. 'Motley was the wear of the world when Herodotus first looked on it,' and so it has continued down to date.

Now in social sciences every effect tends to become ultimately an operating cause. While on the one hand the biological forces, operating during the long period of pre-history, have produced innate differences of race, these differences themselves in their turn have produced during historical periods distinct differences of social and moral environment. Their operation has followed the lines of biological evolution. As Mac Dougall says, "We may in fact regard each distinctive type of civilization as a species, evolved largely by selection; and the selective agency, which corresponds to and plays a part analogous to the part of the physical environment of an animal species, is the innate mental constitution of the people. The sum of innate qualities is the environment of the culture-species, and it effects a selection among all culture-variations, determining the survival and further evolution

[3] Bagehot's *Physics and Politics*, pp. 86-87 (Kegan Paul's Ed.).
[4] MacDougall's *Group Mind*, pp. 226-232.

of some, the extermination of others. And, just as animal species (especially men) modify their physical environment in course of time, and also devise means of sheltering themselves from its selective influence, so each national life, each species of civilization, modifies very gradually the innate qualities of the people and builds up institutions which, the more firmly they are established and the more fully they are elaborated, override and prevent the more completely the direct influence of innate qualities on national life."[5] The analogy drawn so fully by MacDougall contains a profound truth which may be illustrated from the political, religious and social institutions of different nations.

Thus it has been held by leading European ethnologists like Ripley and Fleure[6] that of the three main racial stocks which are distributed among the diverse peoples of Europe, viz., *Homo Europœus*, *Homo Alpinus*, *Homo Mediterraneus*, the first is distinguished by greater individualism, independence and initiative of character, while the second and third by greater tendency to be guided by and depend upon authority. These seem to be essentially racial qualities, as they exhibit themselves in all concerns of life and are clearly perceptible even in personal intercourse. A traveller in France—a country where all the three racial stocks are represented—can easily pick off a representative of the Nordic race from the Southern. "A Norman, as you may see by looking at him, is of the north, a Provencal is of the south, of all that there is most southern."[7] Now these racial qualities, the existence of which is so palpable and note-worthy, have wide-spread and far-reaching consequences. They work themselves out in history in the political, religious and social institutions of the European peoples in accordance with the pre-dominance of one or another of these racial stocks in them. It is a well-known fact that individualistic forms of political and social organisation hold sway among peoples where the Nordic type prevails. In this respect, England and France are often contrasted. "Thus France,

[5] MacDougall's *Group Mind*, p. 113.
[6] See Ripley's *Races of Europe* and Fleure's *Human Geography in Western Europe* (1919).
[7] Bagehot's *Physics and Politics*, p. 70.

in becoming a republic, did not overthrow the centralised system perfected by Henry IV, Louis XIV, Richelieu and Napolean; for that system was congenial to the innate qualities of the mass of the people." But across the Channel, England has always favoured and developed popular and individualistic forms of political government. With regard to religious institutions also, it is found that the Protestant variety of Christianity with its emphasis on individual conscience prevails and flourishes exactly in those regions of Europe where the Nordic type predominates, while the Catholic variety with its reliance on authority covers and coincides with the other regions. In the Netherlands, for example, the line of racial division runs clearly along the line that divides Protestant Holland from Roman Catholic Belgium. The outstanding institutions of society also exhibit the same racial differences. Thus the Feudal system of France—a direct result of what Buckle calls 'the dominance of the protective spirit in France'—being transplanted by William the Conqueror in England rapidly underwent dissolution in the course of about three to four centuries, mainly because it went counter to 'the spirit of independence in England,' as Buckle terms it. We cannot indeed lay our finger on the real secret of the different fates of the Feudal system in England and in France unless we are prepared to take into account the operation of these differences in innate racial qualities.

Race then is a selective agency in national life. It evolves congenial types of political, religious and social institution and depresses or kills out types uncongenial to it. It thus plays the same part in the collective life of a people as physical environment does in animal life. Yet as this very collective life develops itself and expands into an organised type of civilisation, the racial factor ceases to operate directly, though "giving a constant bias to the evolution of the social environment." This operation of race by way of a sort of natural selection in the life of a people is comparatively easy to understand. But the difficulty comes in where this race factor is not a simple or integral one.

We have said at the beginning that a people descended from a single racial stock is an extremely rare exception. In most cases races exist in different permutations and combinations within definite geographical groupings. We use the phrase, 'geographical groupings,' advisedly so as to include peoples and nations in different stages of corporate organisation. Three such typical geographical groupings, *viz.*, England, France, and United States of America may be considered. The original population of England consisted probably of a mixture in some unascertained proportion of the fair-complexioned Nordic *Homo Europœus* and the darker Southern races, *Homo Mediterraneus* and *Homo Alpinus*. The predominant type was probably Nordic of the Celtic variety. The colonisation of the Angles, Saxons and Jutes led to a diffusion of some closely-allied stocks of the Nordic race all over the island, and since that age, there have been further diffusions of the same race through the Danes and the Normans with the result that the Nordic type has come to prevail. For long centuries, among these allied stocks there has gone on free crossing and fusion till the process has evolved a distant race. In the innate mental qualities of this sub-race, there are several strains blended in complete harmony, and a proof of this harmonious blending is found in the fact that though the celtic element in it stands in the far back-ground of its history, it still shows itself, as Matthew Arnold has pointed out, in certain characteristics of English literature—in its turn for style, its turn for melancholy and its turn for natural magic.[8] In France all the three principal racial stocks of Europe are largely represented. But they exist in a condition different from what we find in England. They remain more or less separated geographically in three belts running east and west and there is no such intimate fusion of stocks as in England. Consequently no such distinct sub-race has been produced in France and the expression, 'French race,' would hence be scientifically inaccurate. In the mental qualities of the French people too, wide divergences will be found from the north to the south which are perceptibly represented in mediæval French literature,—in the Chansons, for example, which were sung in the north in the *langue d'oc* dialects and those sung in the south in

[8] Matthew Arnold on *The Study of Celtic Literature*, p. 104 (*Everyman's Library Series*).

the *langue d'oil*. In the United States of America the racial conditions are different altogether from those in England and in France. In a huge geographical receptacle are held together the representatives of all the races and sub-races of Europe. They are neither separated in different localities nor fused into an organic whole. The blending and crossing of stocks is not considerable and the mixture of races there can best be described as a mechanical mixture. Yet out of the diverse mental qualities of these casually mixed races, there has been emerging even in our time a recognisable type, namely, the American. Now there can be no denying the fact that in all these three geographical groupings we have distinct nations. England, France, and the United States have each its characteristic organisation of corporate life, its peculiar social and political institutions, in short its particular nationality. Yet the racial factors in all these three nations are combined in three different and various ways. The selective agency of race in these cases must have been a highly complicated one.

In each of these cases, however, we may discover a certain stability and harmony of the co-existing racial elements. In England, as we have seen, it is produced by fusion, in France by a long-established centralised government, and in the United States by a prevailing democratic atmosphere which has enormous absorbing power. In fact it is only in countries where this harmony exists that race can exert undisturbed its selective power over culture-variation or its constant bias on the social environment, and thus define the distinctive nationality of a people. In all cases where this racial stability and harmony has not been secured, by whatever means it may be, the mixed people held in a geographical grouping has tended towards disruption. It would be a commonplace to say that when races mix in a geographical receptacle they bring together their innate mental qualities; if these mental qualities are harmonious, they can operate together and evolve by combined selective power a culture-species, a palpable type of nationality. But where there are mixed races who bring together discordant and mutually jarring mentalities, the process of accordant selection is disturbed and the evolution of nationality becomes impossible. We are thus in a position to understand the true bearing of race on nationality. But the factor of race is rarely simple or integral : hence its operation in almost all cases is bound to be greatly complicated, and becomes possible only where no conflict of tendencies or jarring of mentalities arises from racial complications ; in other words, the process to be successful in evolving nationality has to work under one condition, *viz.*, the stable harmony of racial elements. Where this condition has been absent or has broken down, either no nationality has been evolved or its appearance has vanished at the first hard touch of reality. The last European War gave this touch of reality to the peoples of Europe and its disintegrating results have been gradually unfolding themselves during recent years before our eyes with all the ringing passionateness of post-Elizabethan tragedy.

We have not yet reached such a stage of perfection in historical generalisation and political science as to be able to lay down laws which operate to bring about racial harmony in a mixed and diverse people. On taking a broad survey of the facts of history, it will appear that the condition of racial harmony where it exists has been brought about in various ways, sometimes mainly through natural physical causes independent of human effort and sometimes by artificial means such as a centralised government, monarchy or republic, which people have consciously devised. Of the former, Switzerland is a perfect example. The small Swiss confederation is as well safe-guarded as any nation from racial conflict or disruption and the bulwark of Swiss nationality is the natural and physical environments of life in their beautiful mountain-girt country. "Reduced from of old for all means of communication with the world to the mountain-paths or the difficult navigation of a stormy lake, this sort of seclusion has naturally drawn them close together among themselves. From this spirit of association and of mutual aid, which they possess in a high degree, accompanied as it is by isolation of the individual—a natural result of the pastoral life—there develops in each one of them a courageous independence. It is thus by the configuration of the land as well as by the habits of the people that these little valleys seem to have been providentially destined to become, in the centre of Europe, the cradle and one of the fortresses of liberty.''[9]

We may on the other hand cite from contemporary history alone examples of peoples that have suffered disintegration and artificial groupings that have gone to pieces, for lack of racial harmony and stability :

Great Britain and Ireland—It was in 1800 that this artificial group was formed by the Act of Union forced through Parliament by Pitt and Castlereah. It was expected at that time that the group thus formed by a *coup de grace* of legislation would attain an organic unity, and this fond expectation was symbolised on the New Year's Day of next year by a new imperial standard which was exhibited on London Tower and on the Castles of Dublin and Edinburgh combining the three crosses of St. George, St. Patrick and St. Andrew, popularly known as the Union Jack. But students of history know that this wished-for and looked-for unity was never attained, that the Irish always insisted on remaining Irish, and that after bitter struggles lasting for nearly a century and a quarter, as these lines are being penned, the news is cabled that the Irish Treaty Bill has received Royal Assent on 31st March, 1922. By this Act, the artificial group formed in 1800, though not finally broken up, is loosened almost to the point of disruption and there is reason to think from the recent activities of De Valera and his party that the Treaty does not spell the last word in Irish politics.

The affairs of Ireland are part history and part current politics. But those who have kept a steady eye on the growth of what has been called 'the sacred egoism of Sinn Fein'[10] cannot have failed to notice how definitely this 'egoism' has crystallised round the nucleus of race. Throughout the 19th century, attempts were made to eliminate it from the national life of Ireland, but with no result at all. The linguistic and literary movements, embodied by the Gaelic League and the Cuman an Gaedheal, started in 1893 and 1902 respectively, which shaped the Sinn Fein

[9] *Historian's History of the World* (Switzerland), Vol. XVI, p. 545.

[10] Sinn Fein is a Gaelic expression for 'Ourselves.' '*The Sacred Egoism of Sinn Fein*' is the title of a Sinn Fein pamphlet by Gnathai Gan Iarraidh (Mannunsel and Co., Ltd., Dublin and London, 1918—As passed by the Censor).

egoism, ran on definitely racial lines: they sought to separate the Gaelic mentality and its resultant culture from the Anglo-Saxon.[11] Language, the supposed badge of race, was made the rallying point of the resurgent Irish nation. As embodying the literature, the history, the ideal, the social ensemble of the Irish, it was considered to be the strongest bulwark and safeguard of its historic egoism. "Our frontier is twofold," says MacSwinney, one of the purest-minded of the numerous martyrs to the Sinn Fein cause, "the language and the sea." [12] His dream was the foundation of an Ireland, "full of the music of her olden speech and caught by the magic of her encircling sea." [13] Both MacSwinney and Pearse emphasised the spiritual aspect, symbolised by insistence on the Gaelic language and the Gaelic culture, of Thomas Davis's nationalism. "Davis," says the former, "caught up the great significance of the language when he said, 'It is a surer barrier, and more important frontier, than fortress or river." Similarly Pearse in his Tract on *The Spiritual Nation* analyses Davis's teachings the core of which he finds to be the conception of spiritual nationality as the sum of the facts, spiritual and intellectual, which mark off one nation from another, the language, the folklore, the literature, the music, the art, the social customs.[14]

Thus Ireland has stood to Sinn Fein nationalists as the visible image of the great Gaelic language and culture over which the Anglo-Saxon seeks in vain to cast its hated mantle. The loud and distinct ring of racialism in the Sinn Fein conception of 'ourselves,' can be heard with more or less distinctness through all the noise and storm of the political history of Ireland. The word, 'Gaelic,' with its full racial implication, is writ large on all the clamorous nationalist movements of the country. Under the outward appearance of political agitation, they yearn in their souls for and hark passionately back to

"The old memorials
Of the noble and the holy,

[11] A brief summary of the main incidents and their interpretation will be found in a well-written pamphlet, entitled, '*Sinn Fein—An Illumination.*'

[12] MacSwinney's *Principles of Freedom* (1921), p. 131.

[13] *Ibid*, p. 133.

[14] See Henri's *The Evolution of Sinn Fein* (Modern Ireland in the Making Series —Talbot Press), p. 208.

> Of the chiefs of ancient lineage,
> Of the saints of wondrous virtues,
> Of the Ollamhs and the Brehons,
> Of the bards and the betaghs." [15]

We all know how this racial rift between England and Ireland has widened with the lapse of time till political separation between the countries, averted for the time by the recent Treaty, has become almost inevitable.

The Austro-Hungarian Empire—The clearest case of racial disharmony and consequent disintegration is provided by the now defunct Austro-Hungarian Empire. For centuries racial conflict had been the key-note of this so called ' ram-shackle empire ' of Central Europe. The age-long conflict between the Teutonic Austrians of Austria proper, Tyrol, Styria and Corinthia and the Hunnish Magyars inhabiting the central Danubian plain is now a matter of history and centres round the honoured name of Louis Kossuth. But since the separation of Austria from Hungary, a pre-existing though subordinate racial conflict had been gradually coming to a head, *viz.*, the conflict between the Magyars on one hand and the Czechs of Bohemia, Moravia and Silesia together with the Slovaks of Northern Hungary with whom they are bound by common cause and racial affinities, on the other. Shortly before and during the last European War, " Rumania Irridenta had become almost as familiar a phrase as Italia Irridenta." [16] Among the medley of races and potential nations in Austro-Hungary, " The national idea suddenly began to produce a great fermentation during the forties; it culminated in the amazing and confusing Revolution of 1848, which broke out simultaneously among all these conflicting peoples, and most fiercely among the Magyars." [17] During the seventy odd years that have elapsed since then, the conflicts between the traditions of Teutonic hegemony, of the old independent kingdom of Hungary, the passionate lingering

[15] See *Poems* by D. F. MacCarthy. The lines are taken from the quotation at p. 66 of Cusack's *A History of the Irish Nation*.

[16] See Article on The Future of Bohemia II, by Francis Gribble in The *Nineteenth Century and After*, March, 1917, p. 583.

[17] Muir's *Nationalism and Internationalism*, p. 101.

memories of the ancient greatness and glory of the defunct Bohemian kingdom, which had centred in the fifteenth century round John Hus the Prophet and Ziska the General, produced a racial jar of protentious magnitude. The dismemberment of the old empire into the Austrian Republic, the Hungarian Republic and the Czecho-Slovak State, as a result of the War, is an inevitable denouement of the racial complications of centuries.

Race in India

Having sketched in brief outline the bearing of race on nationality, we shall now turn to the vexed subject of race in India. India covers a vaster area than any geographical division of Europe, or of any other continent, which corresponds to a well-defined nation. Its history covers a longer duration than that of any country in Europe with the possible exception of Greece, which has been latterly proved by the Cretan discoveries of Schliemann, Evans, Halbherr, Hawes and others to be co-eval in antiquity with hoary Egypt and Phœnicia. India therefore has offered ampler possibilities for the mixture of races both in point of time and of space. European writers, accustomed to shorter views and smaller scales, have not inaptly called India a museum of races. The expression may be taken in a double sense, to indicate the enormous number of races held together within its boundaries as also the clean-cut distinctions that still subsist among them.

A running view of the distribution of peoples and races in India is supplied by the following summary presentation by a recent writer.[18] "In Beluchistan, to begin with, we have two distinct peoples, not, however, differing very markedly in physical appearance, which is usually handsome in both men and women. There are the Beluch tribes speaking one or more languages of the Persian type,—being in fact like the Afgans, Armenians, Ossets and Kurds, little more than an outlying extension of the ancient

[18] Sir Harry Johnston's *The Backward Peoples and our Relations with them* (The World of To-day Series, 1920).

Persian empire; there are the descendants of former Arab invasions and colonisations (though these seem to have lost their Semitic speech); and there are the Brahuis. * * * East of the Indus river and right up into the Western Himalayas and Kashmir, across North Central India to Bengal and Orissa, we have perhaps 200,000,000 Indians speaking Aryan languages, but nevertheless differing a good deal in physical type. The Brahmin caste among the Hindus, most of the Sikhs, Punjabis and Sindhis, the descendants of Afgan and Persian invaders, the peoples of Western Kashmir and adjacent states vary in complexion from dusky white to yellow and even brown; but in lineaments and head-form resemble the Southern Europeans or the Arabs. In Bengal and Assam, we find a strong Mongolian strain which results in little hair on the face and a rather rounded countenance. In central and southern India, the skin-colour is much darker, in some places almost becoming black. The aboriginal strain is strongest here, and the more savage types recall the black Australian. In Ceylon there is a mixture of the Negroid Tamil with the aristocratic Aryan Hindu type resembling that of Northern India, together with a Mongolian element evidently derived from Malaysia. On the coasts of Southern India and Ceylon, there are also turbulent people like the Moplas, seemingly descended from colonies of sea-faring Arabs. There are also dark-skinned Jews, and further north in the great coast-towns and trading centres, Parsis. The Parsis are descended from the Persians of the old fire-worshipping religion who fled to India when Persia was conquered by Arab armies and converted to Mahomedism. Add to these, many diverse types of Asiatics, the million of Portugese half-castes (' goanese '), the English-speaking Eurasians, the Dutch half-castes of Ceylon, the French half-castes from Pondicherry, and it will be realised how little uniformity there is in the inhabitants of the vast Indian Empire." This is a pretty complete picture, though slightly inaccurate in some of the details, of the amazing mixture of races in India, and those who concentrate only on this external aspect of Indian life

[19] See Risley's *The People of India* (2nd Ed. by W. Crook, 1915), pp. 35-47.

are apparently justified in holding the view of Sir John Strachey and his school that India is no country, but a mere geographical expression.

These ethnic data have been collated and classified, specially by Risley and Gait, in connection with the decennial census of India. By applying to them the well-known anthropometric tests of cephalic index, nasal index and facial angle, Risley has classified Indian races into seven physical types—(*i*) Turko-Iranian, (*ii*) Indo-Aryan, (*iii*) Scytho-Dravidian, (*iv*) Ayro-Dravidian, (*v*) Mongolo-Dravidian, (*vi*) Mongoloid, and (*vii*) Dravidian. This standard classification however has been vigorously attacked on its own ground, and the difficulties which beset Risley's method and render its results dubious have been well pointed out by his editor, W. Crooke, in the Introduction to his work.[20] It is beside our purpose to take a hand in the thorny controversies that make the subject of Indian ethnology so fascinating and perplexing at the same time. But there is a general agreement among experts about the component racial elements, as pointed out by Risley, whatever may be their distribution, composition and ultimate analysis. West and east, we have two outlying racial groups, *viz.*, the Turko-Iranian and the Mongoloid, and so far as the internal evolution of Indian history is concerned they may be dismissed from consideration with a very short notice. In the main body of India itself and forming integral factors in the age-long evolution of its history, we have autocthonous racial elements like the Dravidian (which some scholars resolve into two, *viz.*, Kolarian and Munda), elements derived long centuries back from outside like the Aryan (which also, according to some scholars, were not racially homogeneous), elements infiltrating much later on in history like the Hun, Bactrian and Scythian, elements invading the country still later like the Tartar, Afgan and Mongol, whose governing genius upreared the Peacock Throne at Delhi and held the rod of power till the advent of other races from the west. Thus chronologically arranged, it may appear to superficial observers that a procession of races runs right

[20] See *Ibid*, XVIII-XIX. See also Rama Prasad Chanda's *The Indo-Aryan Races*, Part I (1916), pp. 62-78.

6

down the vast field of Indian history. But it is not so in reality, for the races that drifted into India lost sooner or later their outside affinities, mingled their blood with the surrounding population, evolved new types of sub-races and complicated further the racial diversities of the population. They did not merely pass and repass over the stage of Indian history. This statement would perhaps require a little modification in respect of some later-coming elements which will be dealt with in its proper place. Racial elements in India do not thus simply co-exist in mechanical mixture in the way, we have seen, the races exist in the United States of America, but mingle in a sort of molecular fashion to form distinct racial types—which Risley and Gait notably have attempted to distinguish and classify. Now a glance at any ethnological map of India will show that the Dravidian type has the widest distribution in India and, according to some scholars, it had a still wider distribution in the earliest age of Indian history and its displacement has been only gradually effected. This in short is the external appearance of the racial conditions in India at the present time. In order however to understand in what way these racial conditions subsist, we shall have to go further afield and pass on into Indian history.

But in dealing with Indian races from the historical point of view, it is necessary to use the utmost caution. The present distribution and composition of races may not after all supply us with the key to their original distribution and composition. There are certain laws in ethnics the operation of which though obscure is unmistakable. What is called selective birth-rate and death-rate brings about changes through centuries in the distribution of races. It has been proved by a mass of anthropological observations by ethnologists like De Lapouge, Ammon and Hensen that even at the present day the racial elements in Germany and France are being modified by internal selections. The Nordic racial type is being steadily weeded out in these countries, and the type of Homo Alpinus is gaining ground on the Homo Europœus.[21] It is extremely unsafe to ignore these ethnic laws and rely solely

[21] See McDougall's *Group Mind*, pp. 252-253.

on the data of history. Risley in fact falls into this trap in assigning Scythian origin to the Marhattas, and it is necessary for us to exercise the greatest caution while dealing historically with the racial problems of India.

Making however the minimum assumptions, we have to understand clearly in what relation the races stood to each other in the past and to what extent this relation has been modified in the course of Indian history. In traversing the highly speculative field covered by this question, all that we can do is to fix our attention on the leading features of history and pass with long rapid strides from epoch to epoch.

It is, as we have already said, the custom of workers in the field of Indian research to begin from the age which is represented by the *mantras* of the Vedas and which has been compendiously called by Srinivas Iyengar ' the age of the Mantras.' [22] We know however that it is possible to discover even in these *mantras* several stratifications of culture. Thus many of the *mantras* of the Rig-veda demonstrably belong to an age earlier and more primitive than the age represented by several *mantras* of the Atharva-veda, and *vice-versa*. But one fact stands out, that throughout this age or during a greater part of it, there were certain clear and definite racial conflicts in India—that between the Aryans and the non-Aryans, and subordinately among the Aryans themselves.[23]

There is a ringing note of conflict in several hymns of the Vedas between the Aryas and the Dasyus. These latter were, of a certainty, not Aryan in race, though it is difficult to define exactly what tribes or races were comprehended under the name Dasyu or Dasa. The word is sometimes used to indicate war-captives as opposed to the Aryan free-men and sometimes of people warring against the Aryans. Where the word is used in the latter sense we notice unmistakably in some of the hymns a

[22] See Iyenger's *Life in Ancient India in the Age of the Mantras.*

[23] See Macdonell and Keith's *Vedic Index* (1912), Vol. I, p. 65. " Aryan foes (Vritra) are referred to beside Dasa foes, and there are many references to war of Aryan *versus* Aryan, as well as to war of Aryan against Dasa. From this it can be fairly deduced that, even by the time of the Rig-veda, the Aryan communities had advanced far beyond the stage of simple conquest of the aborigines. In the later *Samhitas* and *Brahmanas* the wars alluded to seem mainly Aryan wars, no doubt in consequence of the fusion of Arya and Dasa into one community."

racial and physiological difference implied. But in most cases the reference is to the differences of cult and culture. Thus the Dasyus are called *Avrata* (without religious rites),[24] *Abrahma* (without hymns),[25] *Ayajyu* (without sacrifice),[26] *Mridhra-vac* (of lying speech),[27] *Akarman* (without ceremonial rites),[28] *Adevyam* (without gods),[29] *Anasa* (of unintelligible speech),[30] etc. Srinivas Iyengar, by stressing such epithets applied to the Dasyus, indicative of differences in cult and culture, has propounded the view that the enemies of the composers of these hymns, thus described, were probably not racially different. The conflict between the Arya and the Dasyu was essentially not a racial one, but a conflict between the adherents of an imported Aryan culture and the opponents of it.[31] This view however is one-sided, for we have proofs in other hymns that the conflict was as much a racial as a cultural one.

Thus in the Rig-veda, III, 34, 9, it is said of Indra that 'he smote the Dasyus and gave protection to the Aryan colour (Aryam Varnam)' and in x, 49, 3, Indra boasts that 'he gave not up the Aryan name to Dasyu foes.' The black skin of the Dasyus is referred to more than once, and Indra, the leading guardian deity of the Aryans, is said in I, 130, 8, to have 'plagued the lawless' and 'given up to Manu's seed the dusky skin.' Again in IX, 41, 1, the river Soma Pavamana is said to 'drive the black skin far away' and in the next hymn the riteless Dasyus are referred to. The hymns have often been searched by scholars for other indications about the physiognomy of the Dasyus, but the result of the search has so far been the discovery of the dubious expression *Anasa*, which Max Müller, in opposition to Sayana, interprets as 'without nose,' *i.e.*, 'flat-nosed.'[32] The above references however are sufficient to prove that under the name of Dasyu is included a people who were not Aryans and were racially

24 *Rig-veda*, i, 51, 8; i, 176, 3; vi, 14 3.
25 *Ibid*, iv, 16, 9.
26 *Ibid*, vii, 6, 3.
27 *Ibid*.
28 *Ibid*, x, 22, 8.
29 *Ibid*.
30 *Ibid*, v, 29, 8.
31 Iyenger's *Life in Ancient India*, pp. 3 ff.
32 See *Rig-veda*, v, 29, 10.

distinct from them. As regards the composition of this people, we have very little solid ground to go upon. In the Rig-veda, I, 100, 18, Indra is said to have slain the Dasyus and Simyus, the latter probably a race allied to the Dasyus or a particular Dasyu tribe. The expression, *Pancajanah*, which is of frequent occurrence in the Vedas, has lent itself to various interpretations at the hands of Vedic scholars. But Yaska, the most ancient Vedic lexicographer, gives an interpretation which is probably much older than his own time, by which the expression is said to include the four *varnas* with the Nisada as the fifth.[33] Mr. Ramaprasad Chanda insists that the Nisadas represent the aboriginal non-Aryans who are called Dasyus in the Vedas.[34] But whatever the composition of the non-Aryans, it is clear that there was a keen and determined racial conflict between them and the Aryans in 'the age of the Mantras.'

There is strong ground also for the view that these Aryans themselves were not racially homogeneous, even leaving out of consideration the theory, held by some scholars, that an Aryan race, properly so called, never existed at all. The theory of Aryan immigration into India in successive waves was first put forward by Dr. Hoernle. "This theory supposes that after the first swarm of Indo-Aryans had occupied the Punjab, a second wave of Aryan-speaking people, * * * impelled by some ethnic upheaval, or driven forward by some change of climate in Central Asia, made their way into India through Gilgit and Chitral and established themselves in the plains of the Ganges and Jumna, the sacred Midland (Madhyadesa) of Vedic tradition." This theory has since received confirmation on linguistic grounds from Dr. Grierson and on anthropometric grounds from Sir Herbert Risley who differentiates the latter type by calling it Aryo-Dravidian[35] Mr. R. Chanda also has drawn attention to certain obscure legends in Vedic literature which bear out the theory of racial heterogeneity of the Vedic Aryans.[36] Thus, according to Chanda, there were two

[33] Yaska, III, 8—"Gandharvas, manes, gods, demons, and monsters according to some, and the four *Varnas* with Nisada as the fifth according to the Upamanyus."
[34] Chanda's *The Indo-Aryan Races*, Part I, pp. 3 ff.
[35] Risley's *The People of India*, pp. 55-56.
[36] Chanda's *The Indo-Aryan Races*, Ch. I.

sections of the sacerdotal class in Vedic India, Brahmans by descent and Brahmans by adoption who differed in their physical types. "In the Rig-veda (VII, 33, 1) the Vasisthas, who represent the first group, are described as *Svityam*, white, while Kanva (x, 31, 11), representing the second group, is *Svava* or *Krshna*, dark." Patanjali, in his commentary on Panini (on V. 1, 115) described the physical characteristics of the Brahmana as white complexion and yellow or red hair which appeared so strange to his scholiast Kaiyata that he says that Brahmans with such physical characteristics flourished in a previous cycle of existence and their descendants are rarely seen. There are also traditions to indicate that some of the Vedic tribes, *e.g.*, the Turvasas and the Yadus, came by a different route from a different region.[37] The theory of the existence of four original *Gotras* (Mula-gotrani) and the subsequent development of several other *Gotras* 'which came into existence through good deeds' would also seem to imply a racial differentiation among the Aryans.[38] Along with these indications, we have to read the significance of the fact that in several instances in the hymns certain Aryas are represented to be as much the enemy and victim of Indra as the Dasyus themselves. For instance in the *Aitareya Brahmana*, the descendants of Visvamitra together with the Andhras, Pundras, Sabaras, Pulindas, Mutibas are said to form a large portion of the Dasyus.[39] The conclusion, though highly speculative, is not improbable that tribes like the Angiras, Kasyapa, Vasistha and Bhrigu, forming the *Mula Gotrani*, were the representatives of the original Aryans in India; that they formed the nucleus of the sacerdotal caste to which there were accretions from the later-coming Aryans, and that, while these formed the bulk of the priestly body, the later Aryans

[37] *Ibid*, pp. 26 ff.

[38] मूलगोत्राणि चत्वारि समुत्पन्नानि पार्थिव।
अङ्गिराकश्यपश्चैव वशिष्टो भृगुरेव च ॥
कर्म्मतोऽन्यानि गोत्राणि समुत्पन्नानि पार्थिव।
नामधेयानि तपसा तानि च ग्रहणं सतां ॥

—*Mahābhārata*, Śānti-parva, 296, 17-18.

[39] *Aitareya Brāhmaṇa*, VII. 18.

made up the warrior class, and were distinguished not only by occupation but also by difference of race. This unconscious sense of original racial difference might possibly be the source of the curious conflict between the Brahmana and the Ksatriya which survives through the *Upanishads* down into Buddhistic and Jaina literature.[40] It is not possible to elaborate the point further in this thesis.

The well-known *Purusa Sukta* in the Rig-veda (X, 90, 11-12) is admitted to be a late hymn. We do not know what changes society underwent through intermixture and cross-breeding during the period preceding the compilation of this hymn. But the sense of racial conflicts in society survived, and this sense of race became the foundation of a theoretic classification of society. In the above hymn, four classes of society—Brahmana, Rajanya, Vaisya and Sudra—are represented as springing out of several parts of the primordial Purusa—they are clearly differentiated in origin, *e.g.*, ब्राह्मणोऽस्य मुखमासीत् वाहू राजन्यः वैश्य उरु पद्भ्यां शूद्रोऽजायत। In the *Taittiriya Samhita* (vii, 1, 1, 4-6) the same Purusa is called Prajapati, and the process of creation of all things, material and spiritual, is described on the lines of the *Purusa Sukta*. Thus from his mouth, proceed Trivrit hymn, Agni, Gayatri metre, Rathantara Saman, Brahmana among men, and goats among brutes; from his chest and arms, Pancadasa hymn, Indra, Tristup metre, Vrihat Saman, Rajanya among men and sheep among brutes; from his belly, Saptadasa hymn, Visvadevas among gods, Jagati metre, Vairupa Saman, Vaisya among men and cows among brutes; from his feet, Ekavimsa hymn, Anustup metre, Vairaja Saman, Sudra among men and horse among brutes.[41] It is easy to discover here that the earliest conception of

[40] This conflict between the Brahmanas and the Ksatriyas forms one of the obscurest chapters of ancient Indian history. The real significance of this conflict is still an unsolved problem. Some highly suggestive thoughts on this point will be found in Rabindranath Tagore's brilliant essay, entitled ভারতবর্ষে ইতিহাসের ধারা। (See *Pravasi*' Baisakh, 1319 B.S.). The superiority of Ksatriya teachers like Janaka is a feature of Upanishad literature. It is the Ksatriyas who are represented there as repositories of spiritual lore. In the Buddhist *Suttas*, wherever the castes are mentioned, Ksatriya comes first in the enumeration. See Rhys Davids's *Dialogues of Buddha*, Vol. II, pp. 103 ff. In the Jaina *Kalpa Sutra* (in Bhadravahu's *Lives of the Jinas*), it is said that Arhats, etc., are not born in "low families, mean families, degraded families, poor families, indigent families, beggar's families or Brahmanical families" (See *Jaina Sutras*, S. B. E., I, p. 225).

[41] The whole passage is quoted in Chanda's *The Indo-Aryan Races*, p. 35 (footnote). Chanda's translation, the accuracy of which I am not competent to judge, is given at pp. 34-35.

the four classes of society was that they were four different species with physiological differences such as the expression *Varna* (colour) clearly implies. It has often been observed that the theory of social classification in India is analogous to similar theories in other countries,—it is in fact the only rational classification on which all ancient society was based.[42] But what differentiates the Indian theory is this recognition of congenital and natural differences among classes,—a distinct survival of old racial conflicts, as we have already seen. In its evolution, the Indian theory was determined by an ancient 'sense of race.'

At a later stage of social evolution, we find this sense of race evaporating and leaving behind only a theory of heredity. There are famous instances to show that in the Vedic age racial intermixture was not interdicted, and marital alliances among the races must have brought about in the course of centuries a state of society in which race-conflict was no longer the determinant of social classification. When we come down to the age of the Smritis, we find that race or physiological difference is no longer the leading idea, but the difference of social habits and occupations. The idea is prominent in the *Mahabharata*, expressed succinctly in the *Bhagavat Gita*, चातुर्वर्ण्यं मया सृष्टं गुणकर्मविभागशः and elaborated in a conversation between Yudhisthira and Ajagara in the *Ajagar-parva* (Aranyaka), ch. 250.[43] In the *Srimat Bhagavat* again, in 3.12.35, the idea is carried to its logical consequence and it is asserted that if the qualities of a certain caste are discovered in a person of another caste, he should be designated as belonging to that caste

[42] See a short discussion of this point in Dr. N. C. Sen-Gupta's *Sources of Law and Society in Ancient India* (1914), published by the University of Calcutta. Alberuni notices a parallel classification of society among the ancient Persians which was restored by Ardashir ben Babak—see Sachau's *Alberuni*, Vol. I. p. 100.

[43] शूद्रे ष्वपि च सत्यं च दानमक्रोध एव च ।
आनृशंस्यमहिंसा च घृणा चैव युधिष्ठिर ॥
शूद्रे तु यद्भवेल्लक्ष्म द्विजे तच्च न विद्यते ।
न वा शूद्रो भवेत् शूद्रो ब्राह्मणो न च ब्राह्मणः ॥
यत्रैतल्लक्ष्यते सर्प वृत्तं स ब्राह्मणः स्मृतः ।
यत्रैतन्न भवेत् सर्प तं शूद्रमिति निर्दिशेत् ॥

the qualifications whereof he possesses.[44] The birth-theory of caste is elaborately refuted in a late *Upanishad*, called the *Vajra-sucikopanisad*, in which the question, को वा ब्राह्मणः (who is Brahmana?) is emphatically answered by saying न जातिर्ब्राह्मणः (There is no Brahmana by birth). The Smritis have thrust into prominence and have elaborated and settled once for all the ancient Vedic classification of society. But the idea of any racial conflict or physiological difference is conspicuous by its absence in the Smritis. They take society as it is and apply to it the ancient classification on the ground of the possession of hereditary qualities. The classification is altogether functional and not racial, determined by hereditary occupation and not by original or congenital difference. It is well-known that this standard classification was but a recognised norm and corresponded at no period of Indian history to actual conditions of society.[45]

It is important to consider at this stage the complete modification of the caste-theory from the Vedic age to the age of the *Mahabharata* and the *Smritis*. We have pointed out above that in the age of the *Mantras* there was a keen racial conflict between the Aryans and the non-Aryans. But when we come down to the later age we observe that the conflict takes on another character; it is not a racial conflict at all, but one of social habits and occupations, fixed by heredity. In the *Mahabharata*, Yudhisthira asks as to how to distinguish a non-Aryan who appears like an Aryan? Visma answers him by saying that a non-Aryan is to be known by his conduct (*e.g.*, अनार्यत्वमनाचारः क्रूरत्वं निष्क्रियात्मता).[46] This *Acara*

[44] यस्य यल्लक्षणं प्रोक्तं पुंसो वर्णाभिव्यञ्जकं ।
यदन्यत्रापि दृश्येत तत् तेनैव विनिर्दिशेत् ॥

i.e., Even a Sudra with the characteristic qualities of a Brahmana is to be called a Brahmana.

[45] Proof of this is now overwhelming. See Rhys David's *Buddhist India*, pp. 55 ff. The evidence is not confined to the *Jatakas* and other Buddhist literature. There are traces even in Smriti literature to show that the castes never kept to their proper functions. See, for instance, *Atri-Samhita*, 364-375, in which ten kinds of Brahmanas are mentioned, some among them warriors, some traders, etc.

[46] युधिष्ठिर उवाच—वर्णापेतमविज्ञाय नरं कलुषयोनिजं ।
आर्यरूपमिवानार्यं कथं विद्यामहे वयम् ॥

becomes later on the differentium in place of race. The Vedic theory of original differences among the castes is altogether thrown overboard in the *Mahabharata* where it is said that there is no inherent or congenital difference between the castes; that all men were originally created as Brahmanas, but they differentiated into diverse castes only because of their *Karma;* and that outside these castes there existed the Pisacas, the Raksasas, the Pretas, and different classes of Mlecchas who were unregulated in their conduct and action (स्वच्छन्दाचारचेष्टिता:)[47] A complete change is thus felt in the angle of vision with regard to the caste-theory. *Acara* or adherence to traditionary social regulations becomes the passport for admission to the Hindu-Brahmanical society. We know as a matter of history that between the age of the *Mantras* and the age of the *Mahabharata*, various races from outside the borders of India filtered down into the country. They all had their respective places in society, high or low, according to the degree of strictness in their observance of the *Acara*, the Brahmanas being of course its traditionary custodians. Thus it is said in the *Mahabharata* that the Sakas, the Yavanas, the Kambhojas were Ksatriyas, but they became *Vrisala* (outcaste), because of the absence of Brahmanas

भीष्म उवाच— योनिसङ्कलुषे जातं नानाभावसमन्वितम् ।
कर्म्मभि: सज्जनाचीर्णैर्विज्ञेयो योनिशुद्धता ॥
अनार्य्यत्वमनाचार: क्रूरत्वं निष्क्रियात्मता ।
पुरुषं व्यञ्जयन्तीह लोके कलुषयोनिजम् ॥

—*Mahābhārata* ; *Anuśasana-parva*, 39-40-41.

47 न विशेषोऽस्ति वर्णानां सर्व्वं ब्राह्ममिदं जगत् ।
ब्रह्मणा पूर्व्वसृष्टं हि कर्म्मभिर्वर्णतां गतम् ॥
कामभोगप्रियास्तीक्ष्णा: क्रोधना: प्रियसाहसा: ।
त्यक्तस्वधर्म्मा रक्ताङ्गास्ते द्विजा: क्षत्रतां गता: ॥

—*Mahābhārata* ; *Śānti-parva* ; *Moksadharma-parva*, 188, 10-11.

तेषां बहुविधास्त्वन्यास्तत्र तत्र हि जातय: ॥
पिशाचा राक्षसा: प्रेता विविधा म्लेच्छजातय: ।
प्रनष्टज्ञान-विज्ञाना: स्वच्छन्दाचारचेष्टिता: ॥

—*Ibid*, 17-18.

among them.[48] For the same reason, the Dravidas, the Kalingas, the Pulindas, the Usinaras, the Koli Sarpas, the Mahisas, who were Ksatriyas also fell.[49] It is highly interesting to contrast this passage with another in the *Aitareya Brahmana,* in which the Andhras, the Pundras, the Sabaras, the Pulindas and the Mutibas, the Dravidian tribes and races, are classed as Dasyus, the racial antagonists of the Aryans.[50] In fact the sense of race must have already passed away when races like the Sakas and the Yavanas from outside and antagonistic races within like the Dravidas, the Kalingas and the Pulindas could be allotted recognised places in society. Social recognition depends on one test only—how far the people conform to *Acara*?

The Smritis as we have said adopt the same ancient classification and seek to apply it to existing conditions of society. They do not refer to race-distinction at all, but only to the later criterion of adherence to *Acara.* But the legists of ancient India found that there existed large and populous classes who were not guided by traditionary social regulations at all and in whose case the test of *Acara* would fail. In these instances they invented a theory which is adumbrated in the *Mahabharata, viz.,* the theory of *Varnasankara.* The theory was that these classes came into existence by a complicated system of misalliances among the original four *Varnas,* which is elaborated in 48th chapter of the *Anusasana Parva* in the *Mahabharata.* A great play is made with this theory in the Smritis, and there is no doubt that the classes described as the result of *Varnasankara, viz.,* the Ambosthas, the Parasavas, the Ugras, the Sutas, the Vaidehakas, the Candalas, the Magadhas, the Nisadas, the Ayogavas, etc.—included tribes and

[48] शका यवनकाम्बोजास्ताः क्षत्रियजातयः।
वृषलत्वं परिगता ब्राह्मणानामदर्शनात् ॥

—*Mahābhārata ; Anuśāsana-parva,* 33, 21.

[49] द्राविडाश्च कलिङ्गाश्च पुलिन्दाश्चाप्युशीनराः।
कोलिसर्पा माहिषकास्ताः क्षत्रियजातयः॥
वृषलत्वं परिगता ब्राह्मणानामदर्शनात्।

—*Ibid,* 22-23.

[50] *Aitareya Brāhmana,* VII, 18.

peoples drawn from different races, who were hardly amenable to what is known popularly as Hindu law.

The caste-theory, thus expanded and developed from original race-distinctions, succeeded in creating a social orbit, bounded by the traditions of ancient Indian culture, within which racial distinctions were rapidly dissolved and racial conflicts smoothed out. Till the 10th and the 11th centuries, A.D., this social orbit embraced practically the whole of the Indian peninsula. A condition of racial stability and harmony was produced thereby which, as we have seen, is achieved in other countries in other different ways. Over this wide social orbit, successive socio-religious systems have operated in the course of Indian history, but without impairing its complete and well-rounded wholeness. Buddhism and Jainism for a long period covered a large portion of it, and though these systems were inimical to the pretensions of caste superiority, they did not break up the complex structure of existing society, but only modified it to a certain extent. The actual modifications brought about by Buddhism and Jainism in Aryan-Brahmanical society are still a matter for research and are not capable of being dealt with here. But it is certain that they did not break up ancient society into its component atoms, but only altered its aims, ideals and internal divisions. It has often been said that the caste-system is the bond of Hindu Society. But such a description is entirely misleading. Census officers, specially in Southern India, have experienced considerable difficulty in defining the name, Hindu. Says McIyer in the Madras Census Report of 1881—"A good deal might be said as to the propriety of the use of the word 'Hindu' as a religious classification when applied to the mass of the Southern Indian population. Regarded as a definition of religion, or even of race, it is more liberal than accurate. From the point of view of race it groups together such widely distinct peoples as the true Aryan Brahmanas, and the few Ksatriyas we possess, with the Vellas and Kallars of the South, the Nairs of the West and the aboriginal tribes of the southern hill-sides. As a religious classification it lumps the purest surviving forms of Vedic belief with the demon worshippers of Tinnevelly and South Canara. On the other hand, if it conveys no very distinct idea of a race limitation or a religious group, it serves fairly as a socio-political classification since it treats as a whole the people who recognize caste, and who are governed by one form or other of Hindu law.''[51] The fact is that the caste-theory really created a certain social orbit which had no other boundary than the traditions of ancient Indian culture. To call it Hindu is to misunderstand its true scope and significance, for historically Buddhism and Jainism which sprang out of the same culture had also their places in it.[52] In the next section of this chapter, this point will be dealt with in a fuller way.

At a certain stage of Indian history therefore a condition of racial harmony was produced in India which in England had been produced by racial blendings, in France through the effects of centralised government and in America through the subtle absorbing influence of a prevailing democratic atmosphere. The caste-theory was at the same time a solvent of racial conflicts and an agency for the unification of races. Wherever the ancient customs, traditions, and manners of society, summed up in the conception of *Acara,* spread and established themselves, race distinctions were merged, and tribes and communities of diverse origins arranged themselves harmoniously round the nucleus of caste. This integrating aspect of the caste system has been emphasised by Rabindranath Tagore who says: "Her (India's) caste system is the true outcome of the spirit of toleration. For India has all along been trying experiments in evolving a social unity within which all the different peoples could be held together, while fully enjoying the freedom of their own differences. The tie has been as loose as possible, yet as close as the circumstances permitted. This has produced something like a United States of a social federation, whose common name is Hinduism.''[53]

This social unity at one time embraced practically all the teeming races and tribes of India and it still covers about two-thirds of the whole Indian population. The caste-theory proved the sole and sufficient bond of Indian society. But its integrating

[51] Quoted in the Census Report, 1911, p. 114.

[52] There are many instances found all over India to show that people following Buddhist or Jaina modes of faith and worship have still their places assigned in Hindu society. Pundit Haraprasad Sastri in his *Discovery of Living Buddhism in Bengal* (1897) has conclusively shown that many lower orders of Hindu Society in Bengal follow a degenerate Buddhist mode of worship (*e.g.*, Dharma Puja) and in Sastri's opinion they should be included as Buddhists in the Census rather than Hindus.

[53] Tagore's *Nationalism.*

efficacy did not last throughout, for in the 10th and 11th centuries, races from outside began to invade India who not only did not conform to the ancient *Acara*, but were frankly and aggressively hostile to it. They could not even be covered by the facile theory of *Varnasankara* and thus fitted into the comprehensive system of caste. They were races, mid-Asian in origin and Islamic in religion, who owed allegiance and claimed affiliation to the cult and culture, not of India, but of Arabia and Persia.

The social unity of India was broken in upon by these invading hordes of Turks, Afgans and Mongols. They were more warlike and virile races and soon established themselves in the country as the military aristocracy. But their affinities with relatives outside were lost in the course of time and they became part and parcel of the Indian population. Earlier than the invasion of these war-like tribes, who came to plunder and remained to rule, other races who could not be taken up into the wide embrace of the ancient caste-system had also planted colonies in India,—the fire-worshipping Parsi refugees from Persia, the Arab colonists in Malabar whose descendants are known as the Moplas,[54] the Arab invaders who settled in Sindh, and a handful of Jews in the south from Syria. But they remained as more or less isolated patches, hardly affecting the course of social evolution. But the Turkish, Afgan and Mongol tribes not only infused a considerable element into the Indian population, but by conversion to Islamism, succeeded in detaching large masses from the traditional social orbit. In the Census Report of 1911, it is said that " even in Northern India, the Mahomedan population is by no means wholly of foreign origin. Of the 12 million followers of Islam in the Punjab, 10 millions showed by the caste entry (such as Rajput, Jat, Arain, Gujar, Muchi, Tarkhan, and Teli) that they were originally Hindus. The number who described themselves as belonging to foreign races, such as Pathan, Baloch, Sheikh, Saiyid and Moghal was less than 2 millions, and some even of these have very little foreign blood in their veins. Pundit Hari Kishan Kaul is of opinion that only 15 per cent. of the Mahommedans of the Punjab are

[54] See Thurston's *Castes and Tribes of Southern India* (under Mappila).

really of foreign origin." [55] In the other provinces too, specially in Bengal, the Mahammadans are mostly the descendants of Hindu converts, and there are interesting classes of people all over India, such as the Sunni Boras and the Molasalam Giriasiyas of Bombay province, the Malkhanas of the U. P., the Matia Kunbis, the Sheikhadas, the Momnas of Gujrat, who hover on the boundary line between Hinduism and Islam.

The fact thus emerges that during centuries of Mahammadan rule, it was not really race conflicts that disturbed the social unity of India, but what really happened was that the ancient social orbit was whittled down by the falling off from it of large masses who formed themselves round a different nucleus. As Risley has rightly observed, "Islam is a force of the volcanic sort, a burning and integrating force which, under favourable conditions, may even make a nation. It melts and fuses together, in which no survivals of pre-existing usages can be detected. The separate strata disappear; their characteristic fossils are crushed out of recognition; and a solid mass of law and tradition occupies their place." [56] This actually happened with the large masses of population who deviated into Islam from ancient society. Their racial tendencies were dissolved or completely subordinated to the strict regimen of Islamism. Thus we can observe that, in spite of the apparently confusing mixture of races in India, the problem of race here is neither of the same character nor of the same poignancy as in some countries of Europe. The particular mentalities of the numerous races that have settled in India and have entered into the composition of her teeming population have in fact developed gradually with the slow lapse of centuries under the moulding pressure and influence of two different systems of cult and culture, *viz.*, that which prevailed before the 11th and 12th centuries and that which encroached upon it thereafter. The mould was not race, but formative cultural system which rounded off all racial divergences.

Since the 17th and 18th centuries, India has been invaded by races from Europe also. But these races never came to stay and

[55] Census Report, 1911, p. 128.
[56] Risley's *The People of India*, p. 217.

merge themselves, as did the races from mid-Asia, in the Indian population. They retained completely their external affinities and never looked upon India as their final home and resting place. The result of the influx of these European races has been the growth of small communities of cross-breeds, the Goanese,[57] the Eurasians, the Dutch and French half-castes who hang loosely on the main body of Indian population, without really entering into its composition. Their total number is comparatively small and their influence in history so negligible that they may safely be left out of account in considering the problem of Indian nationality.

So to sum up, we have observed that, generally speaking, race operates as a selective agency in national life,—it thereby determines the type of national character and the species of culture which is the outcome of it. But different races often mix and mingle in a single geographical receptacle without combining into an organic whole. In such circumstances, the operation of the selective agency of race is either conserved by racial harmony, the result, it may be, of historical or geographical circumstances or of human institutions, consciously devised or unconsciously evolved, or disturbed and deflected by discord and jar of incompatible races. In India the racial conditions are more complex than elsewhere, partly because of her vast geographical extent and partly because of the long-continued duration of her history. India however succeeded in bringing about a certain racial stability and harmony in her own inimitable way by the subtle agency of the theory and system of caste. In its origin, the theory was grounded on race-conflict, on a primitive sense of race. But it developed through the evolving ages till the race-conflicts were worn out and the race-sense merged in an accepted comprehensive theory of social classification and gradation in which *Acara* took the place of race as a test of social status. Thus the caste-theory worked out a certain social unity in India, irrespective of racial differences, which was grounded on adherence, sometimes only nominal, to the traditionary bases of ancient culture. It produced a wide social orbit,

57 These Portuguese half-castes, called Goanese, who are numerous in Bombay and along the West Coast of India, were brought into existence through the policy of mixed marriages initiated by Albuquerque, Portuguese Governor in India, in the early part of the 16th century. "He desired to colonise the selected districts by encouraging mixed marriages with the native inhabitants"—see Smith's *Oxford History of India*, p. 335.

an organisation of ancient culture, a socio-religious system which receives accretions even at the present day from aboriginal or barbarian tribes. It was for a few centuries only, beginning with the 10th, that this social orbit underwent contraction and diminution through large masses included within it falling away and attaching themselves to the nucleus of Islam and Islamic culture. Islam itself was a fusing electric force and acted as a counterblast to racial tendencies. Its conflict lay in India at any rate in the sphere of cult and culture and not of race. If we take a wide survey of racial conditions in India at the present time, we are struck with two apparently incompatible features—the enormous multiplicity of races in India and the practical absence of race-conflict, properly so called. Society in India cannot indeed be said to be in a state of equipoise, there being sharp conflicts which disturb its even tenor and hamper its balanced development towards the ideal of national unity. But these conflicts are of a different order. The main conflict is between cults, cultures and modes of social life, and there is side by side a subordinate conflict between social classes,—the upper grades and the lower, those who were admitted ages ago into the social fold on the theory of *Varnasankara*. The lines of division, difference and conflict all over the vast Indian peninsula run right between the Hindu and the Mahammadan on the one hand and the *Acaraniya* classes of society and the *Anacaraniya* (popularly known as 'untouchable') on the other. It is essentially class-conflict and culture-conflict and not the conflict of races that strikes the student of contemporary Indian history.

Religion, Culture and Tradition—Hinduism and Mahammadism.

The practice and observance of a common religion induces a certain unity of social life which has been accounted by some political philosophers to be one of the basic factors of nationality. When, however, we descend from the ground of *a priori* political theory to historical examples, we find the unity of religion related to nationality as often as not. 'Thus the national character of the Scots is probably more due to the work of John Knox than to any other single cause.'[1] The unity of the Bohemians was wrought primarily by John Hus and the 'Hussite wars.' The Sikh community in India, founded originally as a religious federation, succeeded in developing a political and national entity in Indian history. In these cases the observance and practice of a common religion became the nucleus of a certain unity of life, which, being organised all round, produced a state of group-consciousness, the particular mental attitude implied by the conception of nationality. On the other hand, history abounds with examples to show that religious disunion has not operated to determine or obstruct the growth of nationality nor has religious unity alone succeeded in evolving it in the absence of other factors. It is said that there is no religious unity, properly speaking, in England and Germany, and yet no one has the hardihood to deny nationality to them. There are tribes and clans in Asia, professing either Islam or Buddhism, who have never been able to organise themselves into nations, although religious unity among them is wonderfully strong and sensitive. The fact is that when we speak of the binding force of religion, we use the expression, religion, in a loose and vague sense, to include phenomena, subjective and objective, embracing the widest range of variety.

Prof. Warren of Boston distinguishes two broad aspects of religious phenomena—(*i*) theoretical or speculative and (*ii*) concrete or historic. "So far as these are systems of belief merely,

[1] Muir's *Nationalism and Internationalism*, p. 38.

they constitute what may be called theoretical or speculative systems; so far on the other hand, as they are systems of tribal, or national, or voluntarily associated life, they may be styled historic or concrete."[2] It is this historic or concrete aspect of religious phenomena that carries importance and significance to the sociological or political thinker, for it blends with and cannot be dissociated from the organic life of society. It manifests itself in cultural and institutional forms, regulates the tone and temper of social and communal life, affects the innate qualities of race and sometimes, as found in ancient history, effloresces into a distinct type of civilization. An historic or concrete system of religion is in fact a highly complex product of continual interaction in various degrees between religious and social forces. "Of necessity it enters into the social life of bodies of men, constitutes a factor in the development of that life, conditions in a great measure its quality and is in turn conditioned by it. Hence originate concrete or historic systems of religion. reflecting and in some measure determining the genius of a particular people or of a particular religious society."[3] The binding force of religion must, therefore, depend for its strength as well as its nature upon a variety of factors and conditions—the innate qualities of the people, summed up by Prof. Warren in the vague expression, genius, the forms, cultural and institutional, into which the religious conception is moulded by these innate qualities, the manner, often of inextricable complexity, in which these forms influence and permeate the life of society, acting upon, while at the same time being acted upon by it, and the special kind of cohesion which results to society from this process of permeation. The bond of religion is thus not a bond of a single strand, of community of faith and belief merely, but a complicated network overspreading and interpenetrating society with countless delicate filaments. Religion expands into culture and culture into civilization.

In India, since the beginning of history, there has grown up a complex and multiform system of religion and religious culture, which still lives and flourishes among two-thirds of the population. This system has been called by western scholars like Max Müller,

[2] W. F. Warren's *The Religions of the World and the World Religion*, p. 2.
[3] *Ibid*, p. 3.

the Brahmanic system, while it is popularly known as Hinduism. It is Aryan in its origin, in its dominant tone and temperament, in its resultant social culture,—connected in fact by ties of affinity through its mythology, rites, rituals and cultural forms with the other religious systems evolved by peoples belonging to the great Aryan stock.

The system is undoubtedly indigenous to the soil. Its beginnings are lost in the mist of ages, and the period of its growth covers long centuries of Indian history. Attempts at its definition and delimitation have invariably ended in failure, and in the Census Reports will be found the practical difficulties that have always counteracted such heroic attempts.[4] Its distinguishing genius as well as its baffling quality has been a phenomenal power of absorption and assimilation. Throughout the long history of its growth and development, through the *Vedas*, the *Brahmanas*, the *Kalpasutras*, the *Upanishads*, the *Puranas* and the *Dharmasastras*, it has dissolved into itself a great deal of pre-Aryan animistic religions, something of the ethnic cults of the Bactrians, the Tartars, the Scythians and other tribes and races who invaded India at different ages and merged in her teeming population, almost the whole of Buddhism and Jainism and some portions perchance of several other religious cultures with which it came in contact in course of history. This process of assimilation is not yet arrested after the lapse of countless years and the system of Brahmanism still shows a vigour of solvent and assimilative power that strikes one as all but undying. A religious system that gathers into itself so many and diverse elements must needs be highly complex, but its complexity is essentially organic and must not be misread as "a tangled jungle of disorderly superstitions," as Sir Alfred Lyall describes it.[5] Its organic unity which lies deep beneath the bewildering variety of its superficial appearances will strike any introspective student.

In a series of profound and penetrating articles Mr. Aurobindo Ghosh has sought to discover the source of vitality and the secret of unity of this great historic system of Indian religious

[4] See Gait's *Census Report for* 1911, pp. 114 ff.
[5] Lyall's *Asiatic Studies*, 1899, Vol. II, p. 288.

culture.[6] He points out ably the reason for the failure of western scholars to appraise Brahmanic culture in its manifold totality. Most of them have found it easy to repeat the wrong estimate of Lyall and of Risley who has given currency to the phrase, 'magic tempered by metaphysics,' as a compendious and epigrammatic description of Hinduism.[7] "These misunderstandings," says Mr. Ghosh,[8] "spring always from the total difference of outlook on religion between the Indian and the normal western mind. * * * To the Indian mind dogma is the least important part of religion, and the religious spirit matters, not the dogma : but to the western mind a fixed intellectual belief is the most important part of a cult, its core of meaning, the thing that distinguishes it and makes it either a false or a true religion. That notion is a consequence of the western idea that intellectual truth is the highest verity. The Indian religious thinker believes on the contrary that all the highest eternal verities are truths of the spirit, intellectual truth turned towards the infinite must be not one but many-sided, the most varying intellectual beliefs may be equally true because they mirror different facets, form, however separated by intellectual distance, so many side-entrances which admit us into the precincts of the eternal verity."

In the earliest philosophical core of Brahmanism, represented by the *Upanishads*, this central doctrine is again and again emphasised. We find it as a leading idea in later scriptures, and a living realisation of it is regarded even to-day as the highest reach of Brahmanic spiritual culture. This doctrine or idea again is not a mere matter of intellectual perception, but it contains within itself the germ of the concrete historic evolution of the whole system itself. It is in fact the source of its assimilative power, the secret of its many-sided growth, and the real meaning of its apparently bewildering diversity and comprehensiveness. The historic result of the working out of this idea has been that Brahmanism has outgrown the ordinary acceptation of religion and has come to be a great, comprehensive, unifying principle organising a mass of social phenomena. Indian religion therefore cannot be connoted

[6] Ghose's *A Defence of Indian Culture* (published in the *Arya*, Pondichary, Vol. VI, No. 1 *et sec.*).

[7] Risley's *The People of India* (Crooke's Ed.), p. 233.

[8] The *Arya*, Vol. VI, No. 1, p. 26.

by any western definition. "In its totality it became a synthesis of all spiritual worship and experience, observed the one truth from its many sides, gave itself no specific name or limiting distinction, but only designations for its continuing cults and divisions. In its essential character, though strikingly distinguished from other creeds by its traditional scriptures, cults and symbols, it is not a credal religion, but a vast, universal, many-sided and unifying system of spiritual culture."[9]

Brahmanism, being thus not a religion of fixed dogmas and creeds, has flowed into numerous forms and institutions, according to the innate qualities of peoples or communities that have passed under its all-embracing influence. Its diversities range on the philosophical side from the lowest forms of animism to the highest reaches of pantheistic and monotheistic philosophy, on the ceremonial side from the purest soul-worship to all the pagan pomp and glitter one sees in the sumptuous temples of southern India, and on the cultural from the lowest specimens of barbarity and brutishness among the aboriginal tribes and castes to persons of the highest light and leading. Brahmanism is really a vague boundary line within which differences of race, mentality and culture are allowed their largest scope and fullest play. It has none of the communally restricting quality common to other concrete systems of religion. In its broadest aspect it is thus essentially a principle of cultural union and synthesis.

If we try to analyse this principle, we shall find that it consists mainly of three interblended conceptions of tradition, birth and country. Foreign scholars fall into the easy error of picking out certain outstanding features of the Brahmanic socio-religious system, such as caste, reverence for the *Vedas*, respect for the Brahmana, adherence to the *Smriti* conception of Acara, etc., and make them the criteria of Hinduism.[10] But nothing can be more fallacious than this, for, as Census Reporters have found out, each and one of such criteria break down in practice as a working test of Hinduism. It is the intangible and yet palpable thing called tradition, " which furnished the prescribed rule for dealing with

[9] *Ibid*, Vol. VI, No. 1, p. 36.

[10] See the Ten Tests laid down for the Census of 1911—*Report*, p. 117, and Gait's comments thereon.

the ordinary occasions of life, which is for the most part accepted without enquiry and applied without reflection and which also furnishes the appropriate institutions for providing for each class of social needs, for meeting common dangers, for satisfying social wants, for regulating social relations," "that may be said to be of its essence. It is hardly realised by foreigners, accustomed to the credal and dogmatic religion of the west, that it is not mere customs, rites and cults that Hinduism transmits from generation to generation in India. It has in fact never been characterised by any exclusive trenchancy of its intellectual, ethical and spiritual positions. Its tradition does not imply merely the eternal continuance of definite customs and institutions, the projection into the future of its material signs and symbols. The whole history of Hinduism shows on the other hand that these have been subject to the process of evolution, of selection, and of adaptation like all historic institutions of the world, and when it is said of Hinduism that "it has been closely embalmed in a mummy-like imitation of its primitive existence,"[12] the widest departure is made from the truth of history. In reality, what the Brahmanic system hands down is "not merely a set of ideas, but the whole social environment; not merely certain ways of thinking or of acting, but the conditions which prescribe to individuals the necessity for thinking or acting in certain specific ways if they are to achieve their own desires."[13]

Birth is another of its component ideas. Where the essence of religion is some definite intellectual position, such as belief in Jesus Christ as the saviour and mediator, or belief in the absolute unity of Godhead and the prophet-character of Mahammad, the accident of birth can be no restriction on an intending convert, for the intellectual truth only has to be accepted for complete conversion. But in a system like Hinduism which lays down no formula of belief and which lives by ancient tradition alone, birth becomes a highly important consideration. It is embodied in the Hindu theory of *Adhikara*. As Ghosh says,[14] "The idea of the Adhikara has to be taken into careful account if we would understand

[11] See Hobhouse's *Social Evolution and Political Theory* (1913), p. 34.
[12] See Bagehot's *Physics and Politics* (Kegan Paul's Ed.), p. 219.
[13] See Hobhouse's *Social Evolution and Political Theory*, p. 35.
[14] *Arya*, Vol. VI, No. 3, p. 163.

the peculiar character of the Indian religion." It provides for graded entrance into the traditions of the Aryan-Brahmanical religious culture only for those who are fitted for it by heredity and it excludes those who have no heritage of these traditions. The idea rests on the profound psychological truth that " the working of tradition cannot be reduced to some simple psychological phenomenon like that of imitation."[15] One, who is not to the manner born, may indeed imitate the externalities of the religious culture, but he cannot spiritually affiliate himself to it unless he has received by hereditary transmission impulses, reflexes, and instincts congenial to it. A traditionary system like Hinduism must therefore naturally insist on hereditary aptitudes. Birth thus grows into importance in this system of religion. The whole system is dominated by the idea of heredity. The Hindu must have an ancestry, a *Gotra*, a *Pravara*.[16] In all social sacraments (Samskara) he must invoke the spirits of his ancestors, as the symbol of the realisation of the individual's fitness for the sacrament by reason of long-descended hereditary qualities. The act is essentially a spiritual understanding with those 'who have engendered us according to the flesh.'

This idea of heredity may apparently seem to be a narrowing principle, a restrictive idea. But it is well-known that by faked ancestries and legends of origin, through the whole course of Indian history, various communities have accreted to Hinduism which were originally quite outside its socio-religious or cultural orbit. Examples of this are numerous and interesting.

The outstanding example of this process is offered by the teeming tribes and peoples of Southern India.[17] We do not know exactly when the Aryan leaven began to work its way into the South. The only indicative clue that has so far been discovered is a legend in the *Aitareya Brahmana* (VII. 18) where the accursed descendants of Viswamitra are said to have dwelt and mixed up with the Andhras, Pundras, Sabaras, Pulindas and Mutibas.[18] The history

15 Hobhouse's *Social Evolution and Political Theory*, p. 35.

16 See G. C. Sastri's *Hindu Law*, 4th Ed., pp. 67-68.

17 See Thurston's *The Castes and Tribes of Southern India*, published by the Government of Madras.

18 तस्य ह विश्वामित्रस्यैकशतं पुत्रा आसुः। पञ्चाशदेव ज्यायांसो मधुच्छन्दसः। पञ्चाशत् कनीयांसस्तद्वै ज्यायांसो न ते कुशलं मेनिरे।ताननुव्याजहारान्तान् वः प्रजा भक्षीष्टेति त एतेऽन्ध्राः पुण्ड्राः शबराः पुलिन्दा मूतिबा इत्युदन्त्या बहवो भवन्ति वैश्वामित्रा दस्यूनां भूयिष्ठाः।—ऐतरेयब्राह्मणम् ७।१८

of the progress of Aryan penetration into Southern India can be read dimly by reflection only in the increasingly clearer and more numerous references to tribes and places in Southern India in Sanskrit literature, which point to the conclusion that "before 350 B.C., the Aryan Northerners had become familiar with the whole country down to Tanjore and Madura."[19] The edicts of Asoka, specially those discovered in Mysore in 1892, make it clear that the whole of the upper portion of Southern India had been included in his widespread dominions.[20] How these portions of Asoka's dominions were acquired had been more or less of a problematic point, till Tamil literature partially yielded up the secret.[21] What is notable for our purpose in the references to Maurya invasions in Tamil literature of a few centuries after the events is that the tribes and peoples of the south are represented as fighting against the Vedukar and Aryar (Northerner and Aryan).[22] The 'Aryas' are described as suffering big defeats and reverses at the hands of the chieftains of the Dravidian clans.[23] It indicates clearly that even till the end of the Mauryan period the South-Indian peoples and clans realised their distinctness from the Aryans of the North. The earliest Tamil poetry shows further that immigrants from the North (Vedus) who attempted to introduce the Aryan caste-system among the tribes of the South met with a good deal of opposition[24] and the South developed its cultural life for centuries apart from northern influences. But this sense of racial and cultural distinction merged in the course of centuries and has now been transformed altogether into the distinction between caste-Hindus and casteless Pariahs (Parayana or Pancma) which is so keen and sensitive throughout the province of Madras. How did these non-Aryans of the South gain entrance into the Brahmanical circle? It was simply by connecting their origin with the system of Brahmanism through the gradual

[19] See Bhandarkar's *Early History of the Dekkan* (1884), p. 8.

[20] See Edicts discovered at Siddhapura, Brahmagiri and Jatinga Rameswara Hill in Mysore in 1892.

[21] See S. Krishnaswami Aiyangar's *The Beginnings of South Indian History*, Ch. II.

[22] *Ibid*, p. 95 and *passim*.

[23] *Ibid*, p. 96—" Narrinai 170, where the Malayalam Chief of Mullur is said to have sallied out and defeated single-handed the 'Aryas' that had laid siege to the fort."

[24] See Vincent Smith's *Early History of India* (3rd Ed.), p. 439 (on the authority of Kanakasabhai Pillai).

adoption of caste.[25] We are told for example of a powerful Andhra king of the Satavahana dynasty who "posed as the champion of Hindu religions, including both Brahmanical Hinduism and Buddhism, as against the creeds of casteless foreigners, Sakas, Pahlavas and others, and prided himself on having re-established the practice of caste-rules."[26]

Among the more purely aboriginal tribes of Central India, we observe the same process of elevation into the Brahmanical system working through the fiction of birth or caste. A curious instance of this process is observed among the Mundas and Oraons of Chota Nagpur who had in primitive times a far wider ethnic distribution in India, and whose social organisation is to this day very imperfectly Hinduised. The Mundas are divided into several exogamous septs called *Kilis*. But several of them have transformed their Kilis into Gotras by the simple transformation of names. Thus *Sandi Kili* is changed into Sandil Gotra and Nom Tuti Kili into Bhoj-Raj-Gotra.[27] Similarly the Chota Nagpur Raj family claims to belong to a mythical Rajput clan called Nagvansi.[28] These are no doubt small instances of a widespread tendency which has worked for long centuries and is not yet ceased. The non-Aryan tribes of the east also attempt to lift themselves to the plane of Hinduism on the same fiction, and the example of the Koch tribes of Assam who style themselves as Bhanga-Ksatriya or Rajbansi and claim affinity with the Rajputs is only an interesting case in point.[29]

The Rajput clans themselves are believed to be of foreign origin, although the matter is not yet settled beyond dispute.[30] But the fictions of heraldry have connected them genealogically with the great Aryan warring tribes of the *Mahabharata*. "Each race (*sacha*) has its Gotra Acarya, a genealogical creed, describing the essential peculiarities, religious tenets, and pristine locale of

[25] Many examples will be found in Thurston's *The Castes and Tribes of Southern India*.

[26] Smith's *Early History of India*, p. 210.

[27] See Saratchandra Roy's *The Mundas and their Country* (1912), p. 410.

[28] *Ibid.* Also Risley's *People of India* (Crooke's Ed.), pp. 73-74.

[29] See Risley's *People of India*, pp. 74-75, 92.

[30] See Tod's *Rajasthan* (Ambikacharan Ukil's Ed. 1899), Vol. I, Ch. 6. Tod however kept a comparatively open mind with regard to the question of the foreign origin of the Rajput clans. Vincent Smith has propounded a definite theory—see *Early History of India* (3rd Ed.), pp. 407 ff. The contrary has been held by Risley in *The People of India*, pp. 60-61.

the clan. Every Rajpoot should be able to repeat this, though it is now confined to the family priest or the genealogist." [31]

Thus we find that though historically the origins of various tribes, clans and communities in India may lie outside the pale of the Brahmanical system, they can edge themselves into it through the fiction of birth, whether by transforming their Gotra names, or by faked genealogies or by converting their tribes and clans into castes, of which Risley gives numerous illustrations.[32] Such transformations were easy, being always capable of being covered by the traditional Varnasankara theory. As soon as the foreign origin of any community is veiled, however thinly it may be, by some reference to genesis connected with the Brahmanical system, it acquires a birth-right (*Adhikara*) to admission into its socio-religious polity. Acquisition of this birth-right is a necessary precondition for imbibing its traditional culture.

The third great component idea of Brahmanism is the idea of *patrie*. No religious system in the world regards the land of its origin in the same way as Hinduism does. In other systems, the place of origin is regarded only as holy land, eminently as the place of pilgrimage : but the Brahmanical system adds to this idea and blends with it a sense of special virtue in its very soil. The Hindu is enjoined to live upon it and imbibe this special virtue as it were. The religious culture is in a real sense rooted to the soil, growing upon it and fulfilling its being by drawing the life-giving sap from it. It is by living on this soil that the Hindu maintains the purity and continuity of his culture. The limits of *Brahmavarta*, *Brahmarsi-desa*, *Madhyadesa* and *Aryavarta* are, therefore, precisely defined by Manu, and the twice-born castes are enjoined to live within these boundaries, though latitude is allowed to the Sudras to resort to any country in search of livelihood.[33] The Hindus may thus be said to appropriate the country through culture rather than by the right of conquest. The culture

[31] Tod's *Rajasthan* (Ukil's Ed.), Vol. I, p. 86.
[32] See *People of India*, p. 76.
[33] *Manu*, Ch. I, 17-24 :

सरस्वतीदृषद्वत्योर्देवनद्योर्यदन्तरम् ।
तं देवनिर्म्मितं देशं ब्रह्मावर्त्तं प्रचक्षते ॥
तस्मिन् देशे य आचारः पारम्पर्य्यक्रमागतः ।
वर्णानां सान्तरालानां स सदाचार उच्यते ॥

sanctifies and idealises the land and makes it fit for dwelling and appropriation. This curious idea, special to the Hindu-Brahmanical culture, may indeed be traced to its earliest scriptures. In the legend of the *Satapatha-Brahmana* for example (which perhaps embalms an historical incident of Aryan colonisation in the East) we are told that the sacrificial fire not having burnt over the river of Sadanira, the Brahmans did not cross it in former times, but subsequently when some Brahmans had cultivated it and 'caused Agni to taste it through sacrifices,' Mathava, the Videgha, got permission of Agni to settle to the east of the Sadanira that formed the boundary between the Kosalas and the Videhas, and his descendants were the Mathavas.[34] From Buddhist literature, we learn something of the tribes and clans that inhabited this eastern region—the Vijjis, the Licchavis, the Mallas, the Bulis, the Koliyas and the Moriyas,—and some of them, *e.g.*, the Licchavis and the Vijjis, were undoubtedly of foreign extraction.[35] But they gradually assimilated Aryan culture and were Aryanised to such an extent that they came to be regarded at least as Vratyas (*Manu*, X. 22) in Manu's age.[36] With the spread of Aryan culture, their land was included in the Vedic Aryandom. The lands to further east have a similar ancient history, their conversion to Aryan Brahmanical culture was gradual,

कुरुक्षेत्रञ्च मत्स्याश्च पञ्चालाः शूरसेनकाः ।
एष ब्रह्मर्षिदेशो वै ब्रह्मावर्त्तादनन्तरः ॥
एतद्देशप्रसूतस्य सकाशादग्रजन्मनः ।
स्वं स्वं चरित्रं शिक्षेरन् पृथिव्यां सर्व्वमानवाः ॥
प्रत्यगेव प्रयागाच्च मध्यदेशः प्रकीर्त्तितः ॥
आसमुद्रात्तु वै पूर्व्वादासमुद्रात्तु पश्चिमात् ।
तयोरेवान्तरं गिर्य्योरार्य्यावर्त्तं विदुर्बुधाः ॥
कृष्णसारस्तु चरति मृगो यत्र स्वभावतः ।
स ज्ञेयो यज्ञियो देशो म्लेच्छदेशस्ततःपरः ॥
एतान् द्विजातयो देशान् संश्रयेरन् प्रयत्नतः ।
शूद्रस्तु यस्मिन् कस्मिन् वा निवसेद्वृत्तिकर्शितः ॥

34 *Satapatha-Brahmana* (1, 4, 1, 14-17).
The passage is a long and difficult one. Eggeling's Translation of *Satapatha-Brahmana* (S. B. E. Series) may be consulted. It is clear that when the legend was embodied in the *Brahmana*, the regions to the east of the Sudanira had been colonised. Cf. "Now-a-days, however, it is very cultivated, for the Brahmanas have caused (Agni) to taste it through sacrifices." It may be some three centuries before the age of Buddha (6th c., B.C.). The origin of the legend must be older still.

35 See Rhys Davids's *Buddhist India*, Ch. II.

36 झल्लो मल्लश्च राजन्याद् व्रात्यान्निच्छिविरेव च ।—मनु । १०।२२

and the colonisation of these lands by the Aryans was co-extensive with cultural expansion. It is significant that the law-giver, Devala, prescribes fresh ceremony of initiation for visitors to the countries of the Sindhus, Sauviras, Saurastras, people of the frontier regions, of the Angas, Vangas, Kalingas and Andhras, which shows that even in his time these lands were mostly outside the pale of Aryan culture.[37]

These restrictions and prohibitions in later times seem to have lost their force, when the Aryan Brahmanical culture overspread the entire land.[38] The expansion of the idea of *patrie*, corresponding to the spread of Aryan culture, from the circumscribed region called the Brahmavarta to the whole wide continent of Bharatavarsa, defined in the *Puranas* as the stretch of space between the Himalayas and the southern seas, has been admirably traced by Dr. R. K. Mookerjee.[39] This expansion of what may be called geographical consciousness finds its ideal expression in the spread of the wonderful network of Hindu shrines and temples all over India, knitting the whole country into an ideal, cultural unit. The institution of pilgrimage was in itself a means of realisation of this ideal unity of India. "It is," says Dr. Mookerjee, "undeniably a most powerful factor for developing the geographical sense in the people, which enables them to think and feel that India is not a mere congeries of geographical fragments, but a single though immense organism filled with the tide of one pulsating life from end to end."[40] This attitude of mind of the Hindu towards the country of his birth is so peculiar as to be almost incomprehensible to a mind untrained in the traditions of Brahmanical culture. The love of country of a Hindu, trained in such traditions, is not the love of the Britisher, 'far brought from out the storied past,' rooted in a deep-lying sense of history, nor is it such patriotism as animates the nationalist in France, 'the love of a material thing, of an extended space upon the globe, of a land of plough and corn

37 The text of Devala is quoted by Vijnaneswara in his commentary on Jajnavalkya, III, 292.

38 See the quotation from *Harivamsa*, in the footnote to p. 41 of Chanda's *The Indo-Aryan Races*. The author of the passage records a fact which is more important than the causes assigned by him.

The shrines and places of pilgrimage scattered over these prohibited areas also prove the relaxation of these restrictions about visiting them.

39 See R. K. Mookerji's *Fundamental Unity of India* and *Nationalism in Hindu Culture*.

40 Mookerji's *Nationalism in Hindu Culture* (1921), p. 39.

and meadow.'[41] It is the love of the material symbol, expression and embodiment of the culture in which he lives and moves and has his being, this symbol, expression and embodiment being the country itself, Bharatvarsa from the Himalayas to the southern seas.[42]

This socio-religious system of culture, known as Brahmanism, developed in India for centuries out of its germs in the primitive Aryan culture represented by the *Vedas*, till a new departure from it was made by Buddhism. Historic causes, into which it is needless to enter here, greatly facilitated its spread over the whole length and breadth of India. It widely influenced society and mightily swayed the popular mind for ages, though almost from its very beginning it was being worked upon by the leaven of Hindu-Brahmanical ideas. In several Buddhist *Suttas*, which represent the fundamental ideas of primitive Buddhism, we find the attempt made to connect the doctrines of Buddhism with Brahmanical mythological materials.[43] These *Suttas* foreshadow the later developments of Buddhism of the Mahayana School which was in so many of its aspects a crude and ill-combined amalgamation of Buddhism and Brahmanism. It was thus easy for the ancient and dominant system of thought to absorb into itself the new tenets which had been developed out of the intellectual positions of primitive Buddhism. Buddhism moreover was essentially what Prof. Warren would call a theoretic or speculative system. It was not a great concrete or historic system like Brahmanism, penetrating

[41] See Fisher's *Studies in History and Politics*—Essay on *French Nationalism*, p. 161. French nationalism is a movement founded by a soldier-poet, De Roulede, after the Franco-Prussian War. Its present representatives are M. Barres and others.

[42] Vide *Visnupurana*, II, 3, 1—

उत्तरं यत् समुद्रस्य हिमाद्रेश्चैव दक्षिणम्।
वर्षं तद्भारतं नाम भारती यत्र सन्ततिः॥

Also *Brahmapurana*, 19, 1—

उत्तरेण समुद्रस्य हिमाद्रेश्चैव दक्षिणे।
वर्षं तद्भारतं नाम भारती यस्य सन्ततिः॥

[43] *E.g.*, the 'mythological suttas' (*e.g. Janavasabhava Suttanta*, translated in Rhys Davids's *Dialogues of Buddha*, Vol. III). In this *Suttanta* in the last paragraph of 28 and in 29, emphasis is laid on the eternity of Buddha's religion which is derived in 29 thus : Brahma Sanatkumara—Vessavan—Janavasabhava—Tathagata—Ananda—Buddhist monks and laymen—Mankind in general.

society at every pore. On its concrete side, it was a system of monarchism only, rather than a system of socio-religious polity. This fact becomes clear from a consideration of the place and importance of the *Grihya Sutras* in Brahmanism, the nidus out of which the whole *Acara* of the later Smritis has sprung, and the insignificant place held by the *Gahapati Vaggas* in Buddhism. In the corpus of early Buddhist canonical literature, we have elaborate rules in the *Vinayapitakam* for the conduct and regulation in the minutest detail of the Buddhist monastic orders, in the *Sutta Pitaka* and the *Abhidhamma Pitaka* the doctrines and metaphysics respectively of primitive Buddhism, but for rules of social polity we have only the meagre *Gahapati Vaggas* which lack any distinctive Buddhist character. Sometimes, as Kern has pointed out, they are borrowed from the Brahmanical scriptures and are at variance with Buddhistic doctrines.[44] From its very beginning Buddhism was on its concrete side a monastic institution, the laity being only its accessory.[45] The broadest distinction, according to Dr. Archibald Scott, between the Buddhist church and the Christian church consists in that the work of the latter lies outside the limits of the church: but "the lay associates of Buddhism, however numerous, were but the fringes of religious communities."[46] The same distinction may be drawn with perfect accuracy between Brahmanism and Buddhism. While the one was an all-embracing system of socio-religious polity, the other was a restricted system of cloistered monasticism. Between Hinduism and Buddhism therefore there was little occasion for a religious conflict, except in their speculative aspects, and the subtle, assimilative power of Hinduism, its elastic conception of spiritual verity, succeeded in producing a union of the speculative doctrines of the two systems which is the dominant feature of the Mahayana School.

In the 11th and 12th centuries A.D., the indigenous religious system of India was brought face to face with an historic system with which it found no way to compromise. Mahammadism could not be comprehended by tradition, birth or country. It brought with it the alien traditions of mid-Asia, did not recognise

[44] See Kern's *Manual of Indian Buddhism*, p. 68.
[45] See *ibid*, p. 72.
[46] Scott's *Buddhism and Christianity*, p. 272.

the Brahmanical theory of *Adhikara*,[47] and its face was turned towards Mecca and the Jajirat-ul-Arab. The tribes and races that penetrated into and settled in India in the previous ages could boast of no such well-moulded historic and concrete system of religion as the Mahammadan invaders brought with them into India : their religion had a great and distinguished past for nearly three centuries before its introduction into India. Hence they did not find themselves merged in the capacious system of Brahmanism. Their position in India, moreover, at any rate during the first few centuries of Mahammadan rule, was different from that in which the other foreign races had found themselves. These early foreigners had looked upon India as a sort of refuge and home, while the Mahammadans from Mid-Asia treated it in every way as a conquered country. The frontier provinces of Kabul, the Punjab and Sind had lain open for a long time to depredations by Mahammadan tribes from mid-Asia, but it was during the period between the last quarter of the 12th century and the final establishment of the Sultanate of Delhi in 1340 by Mahammad bin Tughlak, that Hindu society suffered most from Mahammadan devastation. During this period, India was reckoned more as a part of mid-Asia than as a separate entity and the Mahammadans displayed all the accentuated sense of superiority natural to a conquering race. We have unfortunately little evidence of the feelings of the Hindu population about the Mahammadan conquerors of this period, as the Sanskrit works, which might be expected to reflect them, pass over the humiliating incidents of the conquest in silence. But the fact that the earliest Hindu chroniclers of Rajputana referred to their enemies as *Asuras*, the traditional foes of the Aryan gods, not only hints at their knowledge of the foreign and semitic origin of the enemy, but also indicates the depth of their hatred.[48] The assured position of the Mahammadans as conquerers had two important effects—first, it prevented the Mahammadans from getting

[47] There is a passage in Alberuni in which the learned Arab scouts the caste-system of the Hindus. He finds the principal difference between the Hindus and the Mahammadans in this monstrous caste-system. All are equal in the eyes of God, says Alberuni. He represents the average Mahammadan mentality towards Hindu caste-system. See Sachau's *Alberuni*, Vol. I.

[48] During the period between 694 A.D. and 724 A.D., the Rajput houses of the Yadus, the Chohans, the Chawuras, and the Gehlotes were convulsed by Mahammadan invaders, chiefly Arab. Their invasions are referred to in the Chronicles and the term *Assur* or *Mleccha*, is always used to indicate the invaders—See Tod's *Rajasthan* (Ukil's Ed.), Vol. I, p. 260.

merged like the Sakas and the Huns in the Brahmanical social polity and established their separateness in India which they still maintain, and second, however paradoxical it may appear, it safeguarded Brahmanical polity and prevented its dissolution.

The establishment of Delhi sultanate and provincial governments necessarily encouraged the Mahammadan element in India which continually increased by immigration from beyond the north-western frontier, by conversion from the Hindu population and by birth.[49] But this steadily increasing element always held itself distinct from the surrounding Hindu population not only because of the imperviousness of the Mahammadan religion in its concrete and historic aspect to the assimilative power of Brahmanism, but also through the natural pride and hauteur of the ruling class. Besides the spirit of brotherhood inherent in Islam welded its adherents into one body irrespective of racial origins and gave it a sort of molecular cohesion. The distinctness of the Mahammadan population in India is maintained up to this day, the broadest division of Indian population being between the Hindus and the Mahammadans, although these are names of very wide connotation.

This separateness of the Mahammadan population was further established by the want of any necessity for compromise in the Hindu social polity itself. As conquerors and governors, the Mahammadans seized the capital cities of the empire, maintained in splendour their imperial and provincial courts, gathered taxes and revenues and built gorgeous palaces and mosques. It was purely military and administrative rule—" the system of governing by means of large camps, each commanded by a general devoted to himself, and each occupying a central position in a province."[50] It was in fact a system which carried on the traditions of mid-Asian despotism and was far removed from the constitutional monarchies and popular republics of pre-Mahammadan India. This despotic system of government had the redeeming virtue of leaving intact for the most part the traditional social and religious polity of India which was continued and carried on by the village communities away from the disturbances of political conquest and

[49] See Smith's *Oxford History of India*, 1919, p. 258.
[50] Colonel Malleson's *Akbar* (Rulers of India Series 1908) p. 6.

foreign misgovernment. Hence the Mahammadan impact did not reach deep enough to affect Hindu social polity to any large extent. During the regime of the Gaznivides, the Ghors, the Khilijis, the Tughlaks, the Saiyids, and the Lodis, though the Mahammadan element of the population was on the increase, it produced little social jar and discord in most part of the country. The religious toleration of the Moghals till the time of Aurenzeb must have been prompted no less by the existing social conditions of the country than by their personal goodness and liberality. It was perhaps more a policy than a principle.

Aurenzeb, in the plenitude of irresponsible power sanctioned by a despotic political constitution, reversed the policy of religious toleration pursued by his predecessors. This reversal of policy on the part of Aurenzeb evoked a nobly-worded protest from his Hindu subjects in which the tolerant policy of Akbar, Jahangir and Shahjahan is affectionately dwelt on. After warning the emperor of the fatal consequences of his policy, the letter of protest goes on to say: "If your Majesty places any faith in those books by distinction called divine, you will there be instructed that God is the God of all mankind, not the God of Mahammadans alone. The Pagan and the Mussalman are equally in His Presence. Distinctions of colour are of His ordination. It is He Who gives existence. In your temples, to His name the voice is raised in prayer; in a house of images, when the bell is shaken, still He is the object of adoration. To vilify the religion or customs of other men is to set at naught the pleasure of the Almighty."[51]

This noble passage has indeed a deeper historical significance and importance than appears on the face of it. It hints at the evolution of a train of ideas which had resulted from the Hindu-Mahammadan contact. We have already remarked that the relation between Mahammadism and Hinduism was different from that between Buddhism and Hinduism. In the former case, the rivalry

[51] This letter was addressed to Aurenzeb on the occasion of the imposition of the *Jijia*. There is much controversy regarding the actual authorship of this letter. Orme, who first discovered it, attributed the authorship to Jesawant Sing of Marwar. Tod obtained a copy from Udaypur in which the heading is—" Letter from Rana Raj Sing to Aurenzeb " (see *Rajasthan*, p. 395, foot-note). Prof. Jadunath Sarkar, on the other hand, attributes it to Shivaji on the authority of Royal Asiatic Society's Manuscript, No. 71. (Vide *History of Aurenzeb*, Vol. III). Rouse's translation of the whole letter is given in *Rajasthan*, Vol. 1, pp. 395-396, Foot-note.

was between an historic system and a speculative one, while in the latter it was an encounter between two historic systems, one indigenous and the other foreign. In their concrete social aspects, as we have already said, the adherents of the two systems led respectively two different modes of social life, the distinctness of the Mahammadans being assured by their position as conquerors and their system of despotic government which confined itself to the military and administrative aspects of political rule and left the social polity of the subject people intact. But in their speculative aspects, the feeling for a compromise steadily increased.

Ramananda and his disciple Kabir lived and preached in the 14th century, in the days of the Lodi Sultans. Kabir, who was a Mahammadan weaver, founded a religious sect that still survives and claims to be the children of Allah and Rama. His *dohas* or religious stanzas, which are current and popular to this day in Northern India, exhibit a tone and temper that gives the clearest foretaste of the sentiments which the Hindu subjects of Aurenzeb in the seventeenth century recommended to the Mahammadan Emperor for acceptance.[52] Kabir was the spiritual ancestor of Nanak, the founder of the Sikh sect.[53] Although the Sikh Khalsa was driven later on into sworn enmity towards Mahammadan rule by bitter persecutions and memories of martyrdom of successive Gurus, the fundamental position of Sikhism was a compromise between the speculative doctrines of Hinduism and of Islam.[54] Both the Hindus and the Mahammadans claimed the founder of the sect.[55] Coming to after-times, we observe this spirit of compromise working through Akbar's *Din Elahi*[56] which, unimportant as a new religious cult, had its place in the sequence of history of Hindu-Mahammadan relationship. The issue has been pushed to the extreme by Havell who holds that " the Brahmans

[52] The *Dohas* of Kabir have been translated into English by Tagore and Underhill and published by India Society, London, in 1914.

[53] See Macauliffe's *The Sikh Religion*, Vol. I, p. 177, where Nanak expounds his philosophy to the Mahammadan High-Priest by quoting the *Dohas* of Kabir.

[54] This mixed character of Sikhism, however, has been denied by Gokul Chand Narang in his *Transformation of Sikhism* (1912), Appendix II, where he traces the tenets of Nanak to the philosophic positions of Hinduism.

[55] Vide for instance the incidents connected with the death of Nanak described in Macauliffe's *The Sikh Religion*, Vol. I, pp. 190-191. The Mahammadans wanted to bury the Guru's dead body while the Hindus wanted to cremate it and the quarrel was avoided by the miraculous disappearance of the corpse. " The Sikhs erected a shrine and the Mahammadans a tomb in his honour on the margin of the Ravi."

[56] See Havell's *The History of Aryan Rule in India* (1918), Ch. XIX (*The Din-Ilahi*).

of the thirteenth and fourteenth centuries began to shape the metaphysics of Islam, to guide its statecraft and to reconcile racial and social antipathies by bringing it into the Hindu synthesis.''[57] Tangible historical evidence of this, however, is insufficient. According to Havell, ''Islam gave an intraspective bent of mind, and they (the Hindus) began to concentrate on the idea of the unity of Godhead'' and ''the Adwaita philosophy of the Vedanta, popularised by Sankaracharya,—the theory of the 'one without a second' was the Brahmanical statement of Mahammad's formula, 'There is no God but Allah.' ''[58] Whatever may be said of the historical justification for such statements, the fact remains that it was during the long period of Mahammadan rule that monotheistic philosophy gained the upper hand in Hinduism, whether as a revival of the philosophy of the *Upanishads* or as a result of the impact of Mahammadan religious doctrine. The historical result of this speculative development of Hinduism was that religious acerbities between the two communities were mollified until they were fanned into flame by the bigotry of Aurenzeb. We have already observed that in opposing Aurenzeb's misguided bigotry, the Hindus took their stand on this very idea of the unity of Godhead and all the speculative consequences that emanate from it, which underlay the religious movements of Kabir, Nanak, Sankara and Akbar's *Din Elahi*.

There is no doubt that the systematic persecution of Hindus by Aurenzeb left behind it as a legacy to after-times a soreness of feeling which rankles even to-day in Hindu-Mahammadan relationship. The ruined and desecrated temples all over India act even now as melancholy reminders of these bitter persecutions, long dead and buried.

We have seen that a compromise was effected between the speculative sides of Hinduism and Mahammadism during the suzerainty of the Mahammadans. But religion, as we have already remarked, has another aspect—a concrete one which seizes on and penetrates into the life of society.

On this concrete social side, there was little compromise between the two systems except to some extent in the frontier

[58] *Ibid*, p. 329.
[57] *Ibid*, p. 326.

provinces of Guzrat, Sind and the Punjab, where, through the exigencies of administration and military occupation, the two communities had to approach each other in their modes of social life. In all other provinces, the social life and organisation of the two communities was separate and at variance and in some respects even mutually repugnant. The social life of the Hindus is guided by immemorial tradition, their personal law is the growth of several centuries and their out-look on life is regulated and determined by age-long culture and its resultant mentality. The whole of this orbit of Hindu life is practically untouched (except in the provinces mentioned) by Mahammadan influence.

The establishment of British rule in India has not affected the relationship of Hinduism and Mahammadanism substantially, except in one way. The British rulers, being the adherents of a different religion, have maintained neutrality in dealing with communal and social controversies. But certain common factors, of which the exact psychological and moral values are still uncertain, have grown up between the two communities during a century and a half of British rule. Both have come to share the same feeling of political subordination, the same grievances springing out of administrative measures which affect them impartially and also the same sense of subjection to a uniform system of administration. In short, certain common political interests have come to fill the social gap between the Hindus and the Mahammadans under British rule, and if social life has an organic power of interacting through all the nerve-centres of the body politic, these political ties are bound to affect even the age-long social differences between the two communities that so sheerly divide the Indian population to-day.

The problem of Hindu-Mahammadan relationship, as it stands to-day, cannot be disposed of by any rough and ready generalisation. The Hindus constitute by far the overwhelming majority of the Indian population, the Mahammadans constituting a large and powerful minority which has for centuries maintained in India its communal distinctness. There are other minor communities like the Parsis, the Jews, the Eurasians, who lie loosely on the fringes of the Indian population, the Parsi community among them being most notable for culture, wealth and assimilation of western ideas and ideals. But these small communities put no difficulties in the way of development of Indian unity owing no less to their numerical weakness than to the fact that they have been mere flotsam and jetsam so far as the course of Indian history is concerned. The problem is really a problem between the Hindus and the Mahammadans.

A broad survey of the relationship between these two dominant communities in India will disclose interesting features. This relationship is by no means uniform all over the country ; different provinces will show different conditions. Among different strata of each community, moreover, there are unmistakable differences of attitude and feeling towards the other community. In the rural areas, the relationship is different from that in the towns and cities, and even in the rural areas, it may differ from place to place according to the economy of village life and organisation of village community. It is impossible to catch up this whole psychological network in any correct and comprehensive generalisation. But certain outstanding features may be briefly dwelt on.

(1) So far as the theoretical or speculative side of religion is concerned, there is practically little or no dissension between the Hindus and the Mahammadans. Religious conflict, properly so called, such as Germany experienced in an earlier century or Ireland labours under to-day, is conspicuous by its absence between the two communities. We have pointed out in a previous page the historic attempts that were made during the Mahammadan regime for a speculative compromise between the two religions, of which the last great example is the abortive cult of *Din Elahi* founded by Akbar. These attempts did not merely scratch the surface of Indian life, but went deeper and filtered down into the religious practices and observances of the masses. The Hindus all over India worship in their households even to-day many gods and goddesses that cannot be traced back to the Aryan Brahmanical system. Some of them may be of non-Aryan or animistic origin, but there are other deities whose existence is unmistakably due to this aspect of Hindu-Mahammadan entente. The best example of this class of Hindu household deities is Satya-Narayana whose worship, I am told, prevails in the country-side of various parts of India. We meet with this deity for the first time in the *Skanda-Purana* where the scrip-

tural legend about his advent is related.[59] But a considerable body of legendary literature about him has grown up in Bengali which shows startling divergences from the scriptural legend. This folk-literature, called *Pancali* in Bengal, composed, as appears from the colophons, by Brahmanical Hindus, represents Satya-Narayana as a Mahammadan, clothes him in the characteristic Mahammadan garb and puts Urdu speech into his mouth. I have consulted four of these *Pancalis* on Satya-Narayana, *viz.*, by Kavy Ballav, Sankaracharya, Rameswar and Kriparam.[60] In all these *Pancalis*, the deity first appears on the scene as a Mahammadan and the Hindus refuse to worship him, but afterwards he transforms himself into a Hindu deity and preaches the unity of the God of the Hindus and the God of the Mahammadans. Sankaracharya, at the end of his work, uses the Mahammadan salutation, Ámin :[61] Rameswar worships Rahim in the form of Rama and pays reverence at the beginning of his work to the scriptures of the Mahammadans ;[62] Kriparam similarly opens his work with salutation to all the prominent Mahammadan Pirs of his country.[63] Kavi Ballav at the conclusion of his *Pancali* draws a beautiful rural scene of the Hindu and Mahammadan worshippers gathering together of an evening and receiving impartially bits of the sweet food-offerings of Satya-Narayana.[64] All these *Pancalis* use the expressions, Satya-Narayana and Satya-Pir, indifferently and em-

59 *Skanda-Purana*, Reva-Khanda. There is absolutely no suggestion in the Pouranic legend of Satya-Narayana about his Mahammadan characteristics.

60 Kavi-Ballav's *Pancali* has been edited by Munshi Abdul Karim and published in 1322 B.S. by the Bangiya Sahitya Parishad, Calcutta. The other *Pancalis* also have been printed and published for use at the worship of Satya-Narayana. They are unedited and without any critical apparatus.

61 "शङ्कराचार्य्येर मत प्रवन्ध प्राचीन। अतःपर बल सबे आमिन आमिन ॥"

62 "अतःपर वन्दिनु रहिम रामरूप। चिदशेर नाथ वन्द भुवनेर भूप ॥
कोराण किताव आर कलिया संहति। सुविधा पीरेर पाय प्रचुर प्रणति ॥"

63 "प्रथमे वन्दिनु पीर आसुया मोकामे। कत शत पातकी निस्तार पाय नामे ॥
राइयामेर पीर वन्द साहाइ गोराइ। कार्य्यसिद्धि हय यदि नाम करे याइ ॥
तारपर वन्दिव पीर नवद्वीपवासी। मगदयठाकुर वन्द मने अभिलाषी ॥
मङ्गल कोटिर पीर वन्द हरषित मने। मग्‌दुमठाकुर वन्द ग्राम पलाशने ॥
एकाग्र हइया यदि सेवे सेइ पीरे। अन्धकेर चक्षु हय अन्ये किवा करे ॥
सेइ पीर वन्दि हुजि मलके करिया। पाताश्रा साहेव वन्द अवनी लोटाइया ॥"

64 "सन्ध्या काले आस्य यत हिन्दु मुसलमान।
सहरेर सकल लोक करि एक ध्यान ॥

phasise the fact that the Hindu Narayana became the Mahammadan Pir, and Kriparam calls this combined deity Pir-Narayan.[65] It appears from the legends in these *Pancalis* that the scriptural legend of Satya-Narayana in the *Skanda-Purana* was but the re-edited. Brahmanised version of the cult of a deity who crystallised in the folk-mind this aspect of Hindu-Mahammadan relationship, the theoretic amalgamation of Hindu-Mahammadan theology, the historical link whereof runs back to the reign of the Lodis in the 14th century. The point need not be laboured further, as even a casual traveller in India may observe that the members of the two communities rarely fight over purely theological questions and generally bear mutual respect for each other's susceptibilities on religious points, except when the riff-raff of both communities are excited by designing agitators over the question of cow-killing for the Mahammadan religious ceremony of Korbani.

नया छाड़ि पुरि राखि मिठाइ सिरनि।
सत्यनारायण वल्या देइ द्विजमुनि॥
मुनिन सकल पड़े पीरेर कालाम।
उठिया सकल लोक करिल सेलाम॥
पश्चाते सिरनि वान्धा दिल सवाकारे।
चाटिया खाइल हाथ मुछिलेक शिरे॥
भरमे सिरनि जदि जमिने गिरिवे।
चाटिया खाइवे से नियत हासिल हवे॥"

65 "कलिते यवन दुष्ट हिन्दुके करिते नष्ट देखिया रहिम हइल राम।"

—Rameswar.

"फकिर वलेन द्विज याह निजपुर। आमारे पूजिले तव दुःख यावे दूर॥
द्विज वलि नित्य पूजि शिला नारायण। ताहा भिन्न ना करिव यवनाचरण॥
फकिर कहेन हासि शुन द्विजवर। पुराण कोराण किछु नहे मतान्तर॥
येइ राम से रहिम नाम एक हय। त्रिभुवने नाहि दुइ जानिवा निश्चय॥
वलिते वलिते कथा अखिलेर नाथ। शङ्ख-चक्र-गदा-पद्म हइला चारिहात॥"

—Sankaracharya.

"द्विजवरे दिते वर, हरि हइलेन सत्वर, श्रीमाधव हइलेन पीर।
फकिरेर साजी जगते विराजे अद्भुत अपोर शरीर॥"

—Rameswar.

"मक्काय रहिम आमि अयोध्याय राम"

—*Ibid.*

"शुन भाइ एक मने सत्यपीर ये कारणे पृथिवीते हइल प्रकाश।
प्रवल हइल कलि यवन हइल वली हिन्दुदेर करे उपहास॥
ताहा देखि नारायण दुष्ट खल निवारण पीर मूर्त्ति हइला आपनि।

—Kriparam.

(2) But religion has a concrete or historic aspect which bears on the social organisation, culture, tradition and mentality of its adherents. There is something *a priori* impossible in the idea that two such historic systems should live in India for several centuries side by side without a good deal of mutual interaction. But this inevitable interaction was retarded, as we have already seen, by the position of the Mahammadans as the ruling class and the purely military and administrative character of their rule which could not penetrate far into the deeper life of Hindu society. But juxtaposition of the two communities necessitated social and business intercourse that could not but modify language which is its medium. The Urdu language thus came into existence and currency in northern India where the capital cities of the Mahammadan empire were situated. In this part of India too, there was some modification, due to this intercourse, in dress, social manners and standards of social respectability. Aside from such restricted spheres of mutual influence, there was throughout India little interaction of the deeper kind.

But we must not be understood to mean that the Hindu part of India led its social life as if the Mahammadan neighbours were not. In many respects, the impact of Mahammadan culture had a psychological effect on the Hindu community which it is impossible to ignore, though somewhat difficult to define. This psychological effect becomes palpable in the Indian art and architecture of the Mahammadan period. Havell, whose opinion is entitled to weight as that of an expert, says: "Islam did not alter Indian aesthetic principles or add to them, but was the unconscious instrument of giving Indian art a new impulse."[66] Indian craftsmen and architects were employed by the Mahammadan governors, who worked under the direction of Mullas dictating Mahammadan ritualistic requirements. "The exquisite refinement of contour which Indo-Mahammadan tomb-builders achieved, and their comparative reticence in surface decoration, had their counterparts and prototypes in the marvellous profiles and massive generalisations with which the Indian painter realised his ideal of divine Buddha at Ajanta; the inspiration of the Trimurti of Elephanta and of the bronze Nataraja of the Tanjore temple is evident in the

[66] Havell's *Aryan Rule in India*, p. 329.

tombs of the Pathan kings and in the dome of the Taj Mahall."[67] The art and architecture of the Mahammadan period was in fact a new development of Hindu aesthetics under the spiritual pressure of Islam. It was by no means Saracenic, but distinctly and palpably Indian.

But this psychological effect of Mahammadism hardly modified or even touched, except in certain specified areas, the material aspects of Hindu society. Although, for the most part, the two communities have been content to live side by side in peace and amity, sharing, specially after the establishment of British rule, the same joys and sorrows of life, we find even now the spirit of fanaticism springing up on occasions with the suddenness of a desert sand-storm. The phenomenon points to the existence among them of certain aspects of social life and habits which are mutually repugnant. This mutual repugnance centres among the lower classes of both communities round the question of cow-killing. It is not known for certain when the Hindus came to reverence the cow and to conceive the present abhorrence to the killing of this animal. In the Vedic times, beef seems to have been a relished article of food.[68] But at the same time the cow is treated as a symbol of many divine images. In any case, the mental attitude of the Hindus towards cow-killing has undergone a complete revulsion since the Vedic times. The Mahammadans do not share this mental attitude, and this difference leads, during the Id ceremony of the Mahammadans when cows are sacrificed for food, to riot and blood-shed specially in Northern India, quite out of proportion to the inciting cause. But it is hoped by nationalists that such elements, of strife do not strike their roots too deep and can possibly be weeded out by better understanding.

(3) This better understanding between the two communities is being promoted during the last few years by a number of factors whose existence is directly traceable to British rule and to recent changes in world-politics. It is unnecessary to dilate on the effect of British rule in this regard. Participation in common benefits and common grievances is always a potent cause of unity. But such unity may be one for mutual convenience only, tending to

[67] *Ibid.*

[68] Dr. Rajendralal Mitra has an interesting essay on beef-eating by the ancient Hindus in his *Indo-Aryans*, Vol. I.

break up as soon as the condition, which induced it, is removed. But behind this political unity, there is at present the urge of certain aspects of world-politics which it is impossible to ignore.

We have dwelt in a previous page on the attitude of the Hindu community towards the land of birth,—the Hindu sentiment which regards India not only as holy land, but also as in a special manner their own by prescriptive cultural appropriation. But this attitude, being the special outcome of Hindu culture, is not shared by the Mahammadans. During the first few centuries of Mahammadan conquest, India was looked upon by the Islamic conquerors more as a part of mid-Asia than as a distinct and separate entity. But in course of time the Mahammadans in India lost their intercourse with Moslem countries and communities outside, with the result that they began to feel themselves bound up with the land as children of the soil. But this feeling never gained the strength and intimacy of the sentiment of the Hindu, as it was crossed by the idea of Islamic brotherhood which transcended all geographical boundaries. His Highness the Aga Khan has described with clear insight the state in which this conflict of loyalties, local and religious, stands at the present time. "Twenty-five years ago," says the Aga Khan,[69] "the average Indian Moslem looked upon himself as a member of a universal religious brotherhood, sojourning in land in which a neutral government, with a neutral outlook, kept law and order and justice. His political and communal pride was satisfied by the fact that his co-religionists in Turkey, Persia, Morocco, and (nominally at least) in Egypt, enjoyed independence and national sovereignty while his allegiance was to Queen Victoria; his political self-respect was satisfied by the existence of the Sultans at Constantinople and Fez, and of the Shah and Khediva at Teheran and Cairo. The fact that the British government was the mainstay and support in the diplomatic arena of the independent Mahammadan States was naturally a source of continued gratification to him. Far be it from me to suggest that all this was actually and consciously thought and deductions made thereupon. But it is the semi-conscious and sub-conscious that give atmosphere to national life. * * * Within this generation, the whole Mahammadan outlook has changed. Forces

[69] Aga Khan's *India, in Transition* (1918) pp. 21-24.

beyond Moslem control led to the disappearance of Mahammadan rule and independence in North Africa. Persia gradually drifted into being merely a name for spheres of influence between Britain and Russia. Turkey herself, the last of the Mahammadan dominions, was drawn into the Teutonic orbit. * * * The net result is that the Indian Mahammadan, instead of holding but the outposts of Islam in the east, sees around him nothing but Moslem societies in a far greater state of decay than his own. * * * Under these circumstances, he necessarily looks upon India more and more as the hope of his political freedom and as the centre that may still raise the other Mahammadan countries to a higher standard of civilization.'' Since this was written by the Aga Khan, Turkey has passed through various reverses of fate and the Khilafat has been abolished by the Grand National Assembly, which now holds the reins of government in the country. The feeling described by the Aga Khan must have been accentuated by these historical circumstances of very recent happening. Thus as a consequence of world-politics and specially of the political changes brought about in the Mahammadan world by recent events, the Indian Mahammadan feels inclined more and more to emphasise that particular branch of his Iman (Faith) which is called *Hub-ul-Watan* (love of country). This psychological change manifested itself recently in current Indian politics in the coupling of the demand for Swaraj and for the restoration of the Khilafat, which was sought to be mutilated by the abortive Treaty of Sevres, by the Indian Mahammadans. The Hindu's spiritual love of country and the Mahammadan's Hub-ul-Watan have thus a common meeting ground, and this entente may serve somewhat to smooth the rough places that separate the social, concrete sides of Mahammadanism and of Hinduism respectively.

Language, Literature and Art.

It is necessary to conclude our survey of the basic factors of Indian life with a short reference to language, literature and art. Language is popularly believed to be the badge of race and people speaking a common language sometimes develop a fictitious sense of kinship. The popular belief was refined into a theory by Max Müller and other philologists of the old school who inferred a common descent for most of the European and Asiatic peoples from the fact that they spoke languages belonging to a common stock. But the theory now stands completely discredited, though the popular belief lingers. We have seen how passionately the Irish nationalists insisted on the Gaelic tongue as the main bulwark of their nationality, and the same insistence on language was one of the dominant notes in the conflict between the Hungarians and the Austrians some years earlier. Other minor instances may be cited where a people have called their native language 'national' and insisted on the adoption of it at schools and in law-courts as a mark of their nationality. Such historical examples show that where the factor of a common language is already present among a people, it may become an object of national feeling. It may be taken as a fictitious mark of kinship, a sign of nationhood or a protector or preserver of nationality. But the absence of the factor of common language does not necessarily imply the absence of a feeling of nationality. It is not prevented from growing in Canada by the existence, side by side, of two languages, *viz.*, English and French, and in Switzerland of several languages, *viz.*, German, French, Italian and Romansch. Similarly the possession of a common literature aids the development of national feeling. This literature may be a heritage from ancient times or a modern acquisition. As a common language may create a sense of common descent, so a common ancient literature generates a sense of spiritual and intellectual kinship. When Wordsworth tried to rouse national feeling in England on the eve of the threatened Napoleanic invasion by reminding the English people that they "speak the tongue that Shakespeare spake, the faith and morals hold that

Milton held,'' he was actually trying to touch into life this underlying sense of spiritual and intellectual kinship.[1] Modern literature on the other hand where it has a national character is mainly the product and outcome of an active spirit of nationality already existent and it does not affect its growth and development in the same way as the heritage of a common ancient literature. The same thing may be said of ancient Art and modern. The artistic and architectural relics of the past rouse a sense of pride in the common civilization, the common material life, and the intellectual and spiritual striving that acted behind it as a hidden creative force.

Now India is a vast country with a complicated history of extraordinarily long duration and there is nothing surprising in the fact that along with the other diversities of life in India, there should grow up a corresponding diversity in language. The Census Report of 1911 gives the number of languages spoken in India as 220, including 38 minor dialects, and this multiplicity of language has characterised India from time immemorial. The Vedic Indo-Aryans refer to the difference of language among the Vratyas and the unintelligibility of non-Aryan speech.[2] Since the Vedic beginnings of history, the diversity of language has multiplied more and more, with corresponding diversity of script, and the ancient Indians themselves were keenly alive to the fact as is evidenced by the various attempts at classification of languages found in ancient works on grammar and philology. A linguistic discussion is entirely foreign to the purpose of the present thesis, and what we have to consider is, in what manner the Indians themselves regarded this linguistic diversity in the past and how they take this feature of their social life at the present time. Unless we understand the psychological bearing of this factor of linguistic diversity and multiplicity in India, we cannot place it in its true relation to the problem of Indian nationality.

We shall not here attempt the ambitious task, fit only for specialists and workers in this particular line of research, of tracing the extant languages of India to the different classifications that we come across in ancient literature. These classifications

[1] Wordsworth's Sonnet entitled, 'It is not to be thought of' (composed in 1802).

[2] See *Pancavimsa-Brahmana* (XVII. 4) relating to the Vratyas, and the expression *Anasa*,' as applied to the non-Aryans in *Rig Veda*, V, 29, 10, which Sayana explains as 'of unintelligible speech.'

full of confusions as they are, between language and dialect, between local and communal diversities, between mere difference of idiom and difference of stock, represent no doubt types of speech in actual use at different times. Such languages as *Maharastri*, *Magadhi*, *Avantija*, etc., must have been local types of speech while *Sakari*, *Aviri*, *Paisaci*, etc., must have been racial or communal types. Yet curiously enough they are not regarded as definitely fixed to these localities, races or communities, that is, they are not looked upon as more or less permanent dividing lines between peoples who use them. This appears from a well-known convention of Sanskrit drama according to which different types of speech are put into the mouths of different classes of characters. The convention is thus stated in the well-known Sanskrit text-book on Rhetoric, called *Sahitya-Darpana*, vi. 157-165 :

* * * * *

पुरुषाणामनीचानां संस्कृतं स्यात् कृतात्मनाम् ॥
शौरसेनी प्रयोक्तव्या तादृशीनां च योषिताम् ।
आसामेव तु गाथासु महाराष्ट्रीं प्रयोजयेत् ॥
अत्रोक्ता मागधी भाषा राजान्तःपुरचारिणाम् ।
चेटानां राजपुत्राणां श्रेष्ठिनां चार्द्धमागधी ॥
प्राच्या विदूषकादीनां धूर्त्तानां स्यादवन्तिजा ।
योधनागरिकादीनां दाक्षिणात्या हि दीव्यताम् ॥
शबराणां शकादीनां शाबरीं संप्रयोजयेत् ।
बाह्लीकभाषोदीच्यानां द्राविड़ी द्रविड़ादिषु ॥
आभीरेषु तथाभीरी चाण्डाली पुक्कसादिषु ।
आभीरी शाबरी चापि काष्ठपात्रोपजीविषु ॥
तथैवाङ्गारकारादौ पैशाची स्यात् पिशाचवाक् ।
चेटीनामप्यनीचानामपि स्यात् सौरसेनिका ॥
बालानां षण्डकानां च नीचग्रहविचारिणाम् ।
उन्मत्तानामातुराणां सैव स्यात् संस्कृतं क्वचित् ॥

[The following points should be noted in the above passage.
Different types of speech are mentioned here :

Type	Speech	Used by
LITERARY STANDARD ...	Sanskrit for	Men of position and learning. Insane persons, Sick persons } occasionally.
LOCAL DIALECTS ...	Mahārāstri ...	In songs by women (Gāthāsu).
	Māgadhi ...	Attendants in royal household.
	Ardha-māgadhi ...	Servants, Princes, Dignitaries.
	Eastern Dialects (Prācya) ...	Buffoons.
	Avantijā ...	Knaves.
	Dākṣinatyā ...	Warriors, Citizens.
	Balk Dialect ...	Northerners.
	Drāviḍa ...	Southerners (of the Daccan).
COMMUNAL DIALECTS ...	Sābari ...	*Sabaras*, Sakas, Carpenters.
	Āvirī ...	*Avirs*, Men of lowest status.
	Paisācī ...	Blacksmiths.
OTHER DIALECT ...	Souraseni ...	Women of position. Women-servants of position. Boys. Astrologers of low class. Insane persons. Sick persons.

N.B.—I have not been able to classify *Souraseni*. Was it a local or a communa dialect ? I am not a Sanskritist enough to be able to answer this question.

Cf. प्राकृतसंस्कृतमागधपिशाचभाषाश्च सूरसेनी च । षष्ठोऽत्र भूरिभेदो देशविशेषादपभ्रंशः ॥

..........................Rudrata

Also

मागध्यवन्तिजा प्राच्या सूरसेन्यर्द्धमागधी ।
बाह्लीका दाक्षिणात्या च सप्तभाषाः प्रकीर्त्तिताः ॥

Manu thus defines *Brahmarṣi-deśa*

कुरुक्षेत्रञ्च मत्स्याश्च पञ्चालाः शूरसेनकाः ।
एष ब्रह्मर्षिदेशो वै ब्रह्मावर्त्तादनन्तरः ॥ I, 19

The word 'Surasenakā' occurs here. But it still leaves the question unsettled. Surasenā might be the name of a place or of a community or a tribe.]

In this famous convention of the Sanskrit drama, if anywhere, we find the attitude of the Indian people towards the factor of language curiously reflected. A language may be racial or communal in character and origin, but its racial or communal implications are not insisted on. It is not as a 'badge of race' that language is regarded, but rather as the outward symbol of a certain standard or type of culture. Hence a dominant race of people has never, as in European history, tried to impose its own language, as the mark of its predominance, on other races and peoples in India. Different languages have at different times risen to the rank of literary standards, but their rise has been absolutely independent of the political status of the people or community among whom they respectively originated. Their pre-eminent position has been due almost solely to the fact of their being the vehicle of some particular system of religious culture commanding a large number of adherents, recruited from different races and communities. This literary standard has then been called the original source of all the other languages.

The origin of Pali, the standard language of the Buddhists of the Hinayana school, is obscure. In a well-known passage in *Pancavimsa Brahmana*, xvii. 4, it is said that the Vratyas of the eastern regions call difficult what is easy to pronounce. Scholars have detected in this a reference to the universal peculiarity of the dialects in and round the ancient province of Magadha in which conjunct consonants are resolved and hard consonants liquefied. Now the Prakrit dialect, called Ardha-Magadhi in Sanskrit books, is said to have been the dialect used by Buddha in his discourses. The literary version of this dialect became Pali; that is at any rate the theory commonly held. This manner of evolution of Pali indicates the process of growth of the other literary standards: they stand each for a cultural system and not for racial predominance. Just as Sanskritists hold Sanskrit to be the original language from which the other languages are descended as dialects, so Kaccayana in his Pali Grammar assigns the same position to Magadhi.

It is thus clear that diversity of language in India has not the same implication in respect of the question of nationality as it has in countries where the attitude towards language is different. Where language is regarded as the bulwark of a racial or national ego, linguistic differences necessarily constitute deep dividing lines of sympathy and antipathy. But this seems to have never been the case in India from the earliest times.

But the necessities of intercourse among the different parts of India seem to have brought the question of a *Lingua Franca* to the fore very early in her history. It is a common idea among persons unacquainted with Indian history that India had no common medium of communication before the establishment of British rule, which, among other gifts, bestowed also the gift of the English language as a means of inter-provincial communication among educated Indians. Nothing can be farther from truth, for there is cogent evidence that, at different periods of Indian history, some kind of common language or other existed which was understood for all practical purposes all over the country. The existence of such a common medium of intercommunication is one of many proofs that India was never a mere geographical group of countries or a loose congeries of races.

An outstanding feature of Indian life in the 6th century, B. C., as reflected in Pali literature, is the existence of a very populous class of wandering religieux, called *Paribbajaka* in Pali. They are divided into numerous sects, recruited from different localities, races and communities, and they constantly perigrinate all over the country. There is a good deal of free intercourse among the members of these different sects at way-side rest-houses, 'debating-halls,' sometimes erected for their use, and elsewhere, relating not only to topics of ordinary life but also to higher philosophic subjects.[3] They are frequently represented as holding such intercourse, and, although many incidental details are given, there is no suggestion anywhere that difference of tongues constituted any difficulty to them. As Rhys Davids says, "It is clear that there was no obstacle, arising from diversity of language, to intercourse,—that not merely as regards ordinary conversation about the ordinary necessities of daily life, but as regards philosophical and religious discussions of a subtle and earnest kind. The common language thus widely understood—used from the land of the Kurus in the West to Magadha in the East, northwards at Savatthi and Kusinara in the Nepal hills and southwards in one direction as far as Ujjen—could not have been Sanskrit."[4] Rhys Davids's conclusion is that this common language was some standard dialect, like the English of London in Shakespeare's time. The life of Southern India however is not represented in Pali literature.

We may next consider the evidence of the edicts of Asoka. They are scattered in places situated both in Northern and Southern India from the Nepalese Terai and the extreme North-Western frontier (Shahabajgarh) to Hyderabad and Mysore. That these edicts were meant to be read and understood by people in general

[3] See Rhys Davids's *Buddhist India*, Ch. IX.
[4] *Ibid*, pp. 146-147.

appears from statements in the edicts themselves,[5] not to speak of their general purpose and manner of publication. But in vocabulary and general grammatical forms, the language employed is the same (with some provincial peculiarities), although both Kharoshthi and Brahmi scripts are used to make this common language intelligible to the eye in different provinces.[6] The language could not have been the court language of Pataliputra, confined to a part of the country and a circumscribed circle of people, but must have been a widely diffused means of communication.

Let us next come down by several centuries to the time of Hiouen-Tsang's travels in India in the early part of the 7th century A. D. It appears that in this century, throughout Northern India, either there was a common medium of inter-communication or the dialects did not differ greatly. Hiouen-Tsang observes that the people of Mid-India are pre-eminent in the quality of their speech, and that the people of the neighbouring territories and "foreign-countries" speak only degenerate forms of the Mid-Indian type.[7] Of the people of Kamarupa (Assam) which lies in the extreme east, Hiouen-Tsang says that their speech differs a little from that of Mid-India.[8] The existence of a common *lingua* or sufficient approximation for the purpose of mutual intelligibility among the dialects of Northern India is also corroborated by the fact that Harshavardhan, the contemporary king, used to call annually a Convention of Buddhist Monks for the purpose of religious and philosophic discussions.[9] But as the learned pilgrim proceeds south, he observes a clear difference in tongue.[10] Yet among the Buddhist monks interchange of thoughts and ideas is not impeded by differences of language. Hiouen-Tsang himself mixed freely with monks in all parts of the peninsula, heard legends and stories from them and exchanged thoughts and ideas. Evidently some type of speech, perhaps a kind of colloquial version of Pali, was common among the Buddhist monks in all parts of India.

[5] *E.g.*, the expression, 'For this purpose has this pious edict been written that it may long endure, and that my subjects may act accordingly' (Rock Edict, V).

[6] See Vincent Smith's *Asoka*, p. 144—"The language was invariably a form of Prakrit."

[7] Watters's *On Yuan Chawng*, pp. 152-153.

[8] *Ibid*, Vol. II, p. 186.

[9] *Ibid*, Vol. I, p. 344.

[10] See *Ibid*, Vol. II, p. 193 (Oda—Orissa), p. 196 (Ya-to), p. 209 (Andhra).

We cannot enter further into the long vista of linguistic researches that the facts referred to seem to open up. It is enough to show that even in ancient India, with all its diversities, common media of inter-provincial intercourse actually grew up in different forms at different ages. During the Mahammadan period, the same phenomenon re-appears,—a common language grows up gradually which serves as *lingua franca*. We do not know the exact extent to which Hindustani or Urdu was used between the provinces under the Mahammadan regime, but its use must have been far more wide-spread than it is now. The question, as old as the 6th century B.C., confronts the Indian of to-day. Common languages have grown up and decayed in India, as all languages must grow and decay, but the standing need for a lingua franca has always remained. It is a long stretch of time from the simple, bright, alert age which saw Lord Buddha in the Sramana's seamless robe, moving high and low among good unsophisticated people, to our own time when society is deeply complicated by so-called civilization. But the persistent need endures, and urges Indians to find out again for themselves the necessary bond of a common language. With the spread of English education in India, some knowledge of the English language has been diffused among a certain section of the Indian population. It was among this 'English-educated' section that political aspirations first grew up and found organised expression in the establishment of the Indian National Congress. At the annual meetings of this all-India assembly, political discussions used to be carried on in the English language, and until lately the claim of this language to be the future lingua franca of India seemed to be absolutely indefeasible. As Prof. Gilchrist says, "From Macaulay's day up to the present the existence of English as the common medium of expression has been an axiom of Indian education."[11] An interesting debate which took place in 1915 in the Imperial Legislative Council on the question of teaching through the medium of Indian vernaculars shows that till lately the desire for diffusion of a knowledge of the language among the people had been almost unanimous among educated and politically-minded Indians.[12] It was regarded as an asset of supreme value in the development of nationality in India. But a change is now

[11] Gilchrist's *Indian Nationality*, p. 66.
[12] Gilchrist gives a summary of the debate at pp. 67 ff. of his book.

clearly perceptible in the prevailing attitude towards the English language. The claims of Hindustani or Urdu, which is still widely diffused in Northern India, have been set over against those of the English language. The change is clearly reflected in the proceedings of the Indian National Congress, which, confined till recently to the English language, are now largely carried on in Hindustani or Urdu, though this change is not universally approved, specially by the Tamil, Telegu and Malayalam-speaking people of Southern India and the Bengali and Assamese-speaking people of the east. Between the two rival claimants for the position of India's modern lingua franca, it is not for us to decide. The decision moreover is not likely to be of greater value than Roger de Coverley's famous decision that "much may be said on both sides." But the main objection to the English language is that it is not 'national,'—that is, not a product of the genius of the people as Hindustani or Urdu is, and must needs therefore give something of a foreign turn to thoughts and feelings conveyed in a foreign mode of expression.

Side by side with the movement in favour of a common language, there is a movement for a common script. The necessity for it is thus expressed by Mr. Govinda Das: "Many complicated scripts are further anti-national forces. They make for division where there need be none. If, for instance, Marathi, Guzerati, Hindi, Urdu, Maithili and Bengali were all to be printed and written in one script, how very much easier it would become for people to understand each other and read each other's literature." [13] Mrs. Annie Besant also speaks to the same effect and recommends the adoption of one form of writing which, in her opinion, would remove the great bar to nationality presented by diversity of languages in India.[14] But she leaves out of account the question of the non-Aryan Tamil, Telegu and Malayalam languages. The opinion has been mainly divided between Devanagri alphabet and the Roman, and the *Nagri Pracarini Sabha* at Benares is identified with the cause of the former. The main difficulty of a common script is that of comprehending both the Aryan and the non-Aryan languages, and experiments are

[13] Govinda Das's *Governance of India*, pp. 244-246.

[14] See Annie Besant's Address on *What is a Nation?* (Adyar Bulletin, May-June, 1918).

being made to invent such a script of which Mr. Rama Ayyar's *Taraka Lipi* may be cited as an interesting instance.[15]

In speaking of India's heritage of ancient literature, it is necessary to use a good deal of caution. We have said that in India standard languages have grown up in close connection with systems of religious culture. Hence different languages are held to be 'sacred' by different sections of the people—Sanskrit is the sacred language of the Hindus, Pali of the Buddhists, Prakrit of the Jains, Gurumukhi of the Sikhs, etc. The sacred literature embodied in each of these different languages forms respectively the bond of intellectual kinship among adherents of the particular religious system of which the language is the vehicle. Thus it cannot be said that India has an ancient national literature in any proper sense. In recent times, there has been no doubt a remarkable growth of the sense of history among the Indians, and it has affected deeply the intellectual attitude of educated people towards the sectional and denominational character of their ancient literature. The whole of it, without denominational distinctions, is regarded as the expression and achievement of Indian genius from an historical point of view. But this outlook on ancient Indian literature is confined to the so-called intelligentsia and it is determined not by the spirit and influence of the literature itself, but by its historical value and significance. The speeches by Indian nationalists from the platform of the Indian National Congress, which it is unnecessary for us to cite, are strongly illustrative of this outlook. In a later chapter, we shall deal with the point further and show how this quickened historical sense affects development of literature in the modern vernaculars.

The artistic achievements of India in the past are now well-known. The researches of Fergusson, Havell and others have thrown a flood of light on India's architectural monuments, which embody different styles, modes and constructive principles prevalent at different ages, and indicate periods of growth, decay and renaissance. Less durable than these architectural monuments, immortalised in rock, stone and marble, are the

15 See N. M. Rama Ayyar's booklet on *Taraka Lipi* which is a new shorthand script for all Indian languages, Aryan and non-Aryan. Mr. Ayyar is a tutor at the National College of Commerce, Madras.

achievements of the art of painting. But as many of these were mural paintings, as in the caves of Ajanta, Bagh and Siguriya, they have lasted down to our day in defiance of time. Thanks to the efforts of the School of Art in Calcutta, we now possess also a collection of other ancient Indian paintings of the Rajput and Mogul schools. Amidst all their differences of form and diversities of style, they show a certain unity of tradition which has been revived in our day by Abanindranath Tagore and his disciples in Calcutta. The bearing of this artistic renaissance, which is as yet confined to one particular group of Indian painters, on the subject of Indian nationality will be dealt with elsewhere.

The Problem of Nationality.

The 'Unities' and the Psychological View-Point.

After the foregoing estimate of the basic factors of Indian life, let us turn to a general consideration of the problem of nationality. Nationality has come to occupy an increasingly important place in recent discussions of political philosophy. The ancient philosophers of the city-state and the mediæval builders of imaginary commonwealths knew nothing of it. From a cloud no bigger than a man's hand, it threatens now to overspread the entire horizon of world-politics.

It is in the social and political speculations that foreran the French Revolution that we find the first vague recognition of this political entity. The existence of a nation, says Renan, is a continued plebiscitum.[1] Rousseau's doctrine of *Volonte Generale*, which re-appears in recent politics as an atavistic form in the Doctrine of Self-determination, may be taken as the first definite recognition of a new basis of state, the existence of an underlying, continuing plebiscitum. Since the time of Rousseau, the consciousness of its existence has grown steadily and the tendency to make it the basis of state organisation has expressed itself in Europe with greater or less success throughout the nineteenth century in successive historic events—the independence of Greece, the independence of Hungary, the unification and 'resurrection' of Italy, release from Turkish empire of the Danubian Principalities, the rise of Bulgaria and Thessaly, the union of the German states, the revolt of Poland against Russia, national movements in Ireland by the Young Ireland Party, the Fenians and the Parnellians. Behind all these strifes and struggles of the century, there is a new force working, the urge of a growingly clear consciousness that wherever the forces of history have established such a union among a

1 "The existence of a Nation is (if the metaphor be permissible) a continued plebiscitum, as the existence of the individual is a perpetual affirmation of life."—Renan on Nation in Lalor's *Ency. Pol. Science* (quoted by Dr. Willoughby in his *Examination of the Nature of the State*, 1911, p. 12).

people that it feels unanimously the call to a separate political destiny, its distinctness must be established and maintained.

The ancient and mediæval world of the west had different types of political association—the tribe, the city-state, the clan, the small regional state, the league, the federation, the empire and the world-state. But the modern western world which was ushered in by the French Revolution has developed a new type, *viz.*, the nation. It is an entirely new unit of human aggregation, a new form of political life. " To build a strong and durable body and vital functioning for a distinct, powerful, well-centred and well-diffused corporate ego is its whole aim and method "[2] The emergence of this new principle of political reconstruction which marks the striking difference, explained elsewhere, between the Treaty of Vienna and the Treaty of Versailles has necessitated a more and more searching examination of the origin, character and limits of the political entity called the nation and the proper sphere for the application of the principle of nationality.

It is not possible for us within the limits of our subject to launch upon an exhaustive examination of the origin of the nation. The nations of Europe had their origins during " the long period of dissolution and reconstruction which we call the Middle Ages."[3] Two theories have been suggested to account for their growth—by Pollard[4] and Wells[5] respectively.

European history shows the first appearance of modern peoples on its stage in the role of wanderers, having but the slightest connection with the soil.[6] When these wandering peoples after the confusion of wars and migrations settled down under systems of political government, historically the beginnings of nations were made. The fact of territorial settlement, according to Pollard, was the germ of nationality, while according to Wells, it was rather that community of will which was inherited by their settled life from previous nomadic condition. As wandering peoples, their main bond of association had been relationship of blood, real or fictitious, but when they staked out

[2] Aurobindo Ghosh's *Ideal of Human Unity*, p. 119.
[3] *Per* Sidgwick : *Development of European Polity*, p. 187.
[4] See Pollard's *Factors of Modern History*, Ch. I.
[5] See H. G. Wells's *The Outline of History*, pp. 387-388.
[6] See Pollard's *Factors*, etc., p. 17.

areas of conquest and colonisation, territorial proximity replaced the relationship of blood as the bond of society. "It is this association of men with different parts of the earth's surface which begins the process of differentiating modern nations from one another, and drives vertical national lines down through the horizontal cosmopolitan lines."[7] Pollard traces this process through the substitution of personal relationship by the territorial, implied in the Feudal system, the growth of the conception of territorial sovereignty, the transformation of personal groups such as the 'hundred' and the 'tithing' in England into geographical divisions, the development of the law of the land instead of the law of persons,—in short the whole phenomena of what he calls 'territorialism.' Wells, on the other hand, seems to suggest that the modern feeling of nationality is directly descended through a long course of evolution from a trait of the nomadic life of the wandering peoples. "The primitive civilizations were," says Wells, "communities of obedience, obedience to god-kings or kings under gods was their cement; the nomadic tendency on the other hand has always been towards a different type of association which we shall call here 'a community of will.' In a wandering fighting community the individual must be at once self-restrained and disciplined. The chiefs of such communities must be chiefs who are followed, and not masters who compel."[8] The antagonism between the method of obedience and the method of will is, according to Wells, a world-wide phenomenon, and to the victory of the 'method of will' in Europe, the inevitable characteristic of political organisation developed by originally nomadic peoples, must be attributed the transition from the old world of 'non-elective divinity of kings and of their natural and inherent right to rule' to the modern order of nation-states.

Whatever may be the true origin of the nation,—and researches into it cannot yet be said to be complete or exhaustive,—it is clear that nations, wherever found, are historic growths. A present nation pre-supposes a past, and cannot be brought into existence in a day like a state or an empire by contract, revolution, or conquest. Not only its political character, its institutions, its social polity, but the very fact of its nationhood must be the last

[7] *Ibid*, p. 19.
[8] Wells's *Outline*, p. 387.

term of an evolutionary series. It could not exist at all or develop its fundamental bond of association without the working of forces acting and reacting through all vicissitudes of its history.

But the difficulty of the political thinker is that, so far as the growth of nations is concerned, history has begun during comparatively modern times. The nation-making epoch is still in progress and the examples which the philosopher must make the basis of his discussion are comparatively few up to date. At the same time, the principle of nationality has been completely accepted in modern politics which demands urgently from statesmen and politicians the immediate determination of tests and standards whereby nations can be told and described. The examples generally belong to one zone of civilization, *viz.*, the European, and hence generalisations made therefrom are likely to be sectional and therefore inaccurate. The European ensemble of the nation may be true and natural in Europe, where a common heritage of cultural consequences of ancient and mediæval history has moulded a substantial sameness of mentality, but would be altogether unsuitable in another area, *e.g.*, Asia, where cultural and political history has run an entirely different course. During the Russo-Japanese War in the early years of the present century, Japanese patriots were constantly adverting to the vast difference in cultural and political outlook between Europe and Asia.[9] "The task of Asia to-day," asserted an eminent Japanese writer, "becomes that of protecting and restoring Asiatic modes."

Among the countries of Asia, Japan has finally established herself in, what is called in political parlance, 'the comity of nations.' "Placed at a maritime coign of vantage upon the flank of Asia, precisely analogous to that occupied by Great Britain on the flank of Europe but not necessarily involved in its responsibilities, she sets before herself the supreme ambition of becoming on a smaller scale, the Britain of the Far East"[10] Yet the spring of nationality in Japan is far removed from the sources of national feeling in any European country. Japan does not suffer indeed from the countless diversities of life and culture

[9] The best work representing the mental attitude of Japanese thinkers of this period is Takakasu Okakura's *Ideals of the East*, which begins with the significant declaration Asia is one.'

[10] Curzon's *The Problems of the Far East* (1896).

which India has inherited from her hoary past, yet the conception of nationality in Japan is not exactly the political conception with which European writers on political philosophy have familiarised us. It has its roots in and draws its sap from the inner spirit of Shintoism—a living and continuing realisation of unity and identity with the worshipped ancestors of the Emperor and the people.[11] Territorialism has little to do with the growth of this feeling, though, as the student of Japanese history knows, the break-up of tribes and clans in the islands necessitated the transition from the clannish and tribal system of government to the local and territorial.[12] But the feeling of nationality in Japan grew really out of the realisation of the oneness and sameness of the people for 'ages eternal,' the transmitted spirits of the ancestors making this vital continuity. The constitution, law, religion and domestic life of the people are all determined by this ancestor-worshipping spirit of Shintoism.[13] The present constitution of the Japanese Empire was promulgated in 1889, and in the preamble of the constitution, the Emperor declared : "Having by the virtues of Our Ancestors ascended the throne by a lineal succession unbroken for ages eternal : remembering that Our beloved subjects are the very same that have been favoured with the benevolent care and affectionate vigilance of Our Ancestors, etc."[14] The expression shows accurately Japanese nationality at its two poles—loyalty rooted in ancestry and patriotism derived from ancestry—the Eternal Mikado and the 'very same' people. In some respects, the attitude of a people towards the mother country is a test of nationality. We have had occasion previously to comment on the attitude of the Hindus towards the country of their birth.[15] To them, the country is the embodiment and symbol of their special religious culture,—to the Japanese, as Dr. Nitobe puts it, "it is the sacred abode of the gods, the spirits

11 See Stead's *Japan by the Japanese* (1904)—Essay on Ancestor-worship by Prof. Hozumi, pp. 281-305. Also Henry Dyer's *Dai Nippon* (1905), Ch. III., Risley's remarks in *The People of India* (Crooke's Ed.), pp. 296-298, on Japanese nationality.

12 See Knox's *Imperial Japan* (1905), pp. 44-54. "Since the Great reform of the Taika era, inspite of the fact that the clan system continued for a long time afterwards, the basis of administrative division of the country gradually changed from being personal to being territorial." (Hozumi)—Stead's *Japan by the Japanese*, p. 297.

13 This has been ably explained and dealt with by Prof. Hozumi (see *Japan by the Japanese*, pp. 281-305).

14 See *Ibid*, pp. 290-291.

15 See pp. 67-70 of this book.

of our forefathers."[16] The two orders of ideas are different and they both differ substantially from the sense of nationality that animates the bosom of the Englishman or the French. Japanese nationality is thus a reflex of the Japanese religion of Shintoism. A-European test or standard of nationality would clearly be inapplicable here.

The prevailing conceptions of political science have been arrived at by different methods. The modes of thinking and reasoning employed have been so divergent and various that some scholars have felt a good deal of hesitation in giving to political speculations the name of science at all. One of these modes is the Historico-comparative Method which "aims through the study of existing politics and those which have existed in the past to assemble a definite body of material from which the investigator by selection, comparison and elimination may discover the ideal types and progressive forces of political history."[17] It is by a loose application of this method that western political philosophers have arrived at the ideal conception of the Nation. Thus according to the recent classification by Israil Zangwill, nations are Simple, Complex, Compound or Hybrid according to the condition in which the normal 'unities,' *e.g.*, of race, of language, of religion, etc., subsist in them, all these types tending to the ideal type of Simple Nationality.[18] The definitions of the Nation are numerous, as every tyro in western political science knows, and all these definitions are based on combinations of certain factors which prominently spring to view in the life-histories of European nations and which have not inaptly been called the unities.' Thus common language is a unity, common racial descent is a unity, common religion is a unity and so on; and a nation is said to be the psychological sum of these unities, although the calculus of each philosopher may differ. It is an interesting study in confusion which mars the political science of the west to observe the divergent conceptions that have been held of the relation of these so-called 'unities' to nationality. In whatever way this

[16] Quoted in Dyer's *Dai Nippon*, p. 35.

[17] Garner's *Introduction to Political Science*, p. 26. Garner calls it the Comparative Method and considers the Historical Method to be a particular form of it, p. 28.

[18] See Zangwill's *Principle of Nationalities* (Conway Memorial Lecture).

relation may be conceived, it is falsified by the facts of history. Ramsay Muir, after considering them one by one, [19] thus sums up his conclusion of the matter, "Nationality then is an elusive idea, difficult to define. It cannot be tested or analysed by formulæ, such as German professors love. Least of all must it be interpreted by the brutal and childish doctrine of racialism. Its essence is a sentiment." [20] The fact is that the so-called Historico-comparative Method of political philosophy has many inherent defects and they vitiate any political conception arrived at by that method. The facts with which political science has to deal have not the 'interchangeable variability' of matter : the essential diversities being infinite, its generalisations cannot attain the quality of universal applicability like the laws of the physical sciences. History moreover is always in the making and has not yet been reduced to the perfection of a science which makes prevision possible. Thus the incompleteness and uncertainty of history, coupled with the inevitable narrowness of the scope of comparison in the social sciences, renders the Historico-comparative Method essentially defective. A conception arrived at by it can be only relatively true. In dealing with the conception of nationality, Muir tacitly recognises this difficulty and says : "It is a conception and a mode of political organisation, peculiar (until these latter days) to Europe, unless we are to see in Japan a unique instance of its independent growth. It arose in Europe under the special circumstances of the mediæval period ; and because the experience of the earliest successfully established nation-states showed that the conception was extraordinarily well fitted for the encouragement of the great western ideas of Law and Liberty, and also because the potentiality of nation-states existed in a remarkable degree all over Europe, it has expanded itself during the modern age over almost the whole of the continent." We have already seen that Japanese nationality that Muir speaks of sprang from a different principle altogether.

Let us consider also the validity of the 'unities' as tests. They have been differently enumerated by different writers. We shall take for our purpose one of these enumerations, preferably Prof. Muir's :—(*i*) the occupation of a defined geographical area with

19 Muir's *Nationalism and Internationalism*, pp. 30-45.
20 *Ibid*, pp. 46-47.

a character of its own, (*ii*) unity of race, (*iii*) unity of language, (*iv*) unity of religion, (*v*) common subjection, (*vi*) community of economic interest, and (*vi*) possession of a common tradition. Now each of these factors is by itself a mere bond of association helping to mark off one group of people from another, say, in the same way as the members of a Shakespeare Society may be marked off from any other association by their common interest in Shakespearean study. The essential thing to consider is its psychological value in relation to the complexus of feeling, called Nationality. It is unnecessary for us to take them one by one, as it would be doing over again what Muir has admirably done,[21] and a critical estimate of them will land us in the same position as Muir's who says: "No single factor, neither geographical unity, nor race, nor language, nor religion, nor a common body of custom, nor community of economic interest, seems to be indispensable to nationhood; and even the possession of common traditions, though the most powerful of binding forces, need not prevent the inclusion within a nation of elements which do not fully share these traditions. Some, at least, of these ties of affinity the people that claims nationhood must possess, but no one of them is essential, or can be used as a certain criterion."[22] Now the position taken up by the learned professor implies that there may be all sorts of diversities in the life of a people, but if there are some of these factors present, *i.e.*, if there be some ground of unity which the people can seize upon, they have a chance of developing a sense of nationality. It amounts to saying in other words that consciousness of nationality among a people is a growth which must somewhere have a root which may be any of the 'unities' enumerated above. This obviously does not go very far in explaining or accounting for the feeling of nationality itself, though it points the way to a line of thought and speculation upon the subject which MacDougall has tried to explore. "Prof. Muir," says MacDougall, "has the merit of recognising the essentially psychological nature of his problem."[23]

Let us try to make the position clear by concrete examples. Before and during the last European War, the national feeling in

[21] *Ibid*, pp. 31-45.
[22] *Ibid*, p. 50.
[23] MacDougall's *Group Mind*, p. 99.

Germany was excited by an appeal to a supposed theory of the racial purity of the Germans of which Houston Chamberlain was the loudest mouthpiece and stoutest champion. The mentality of the German people at the time was such that the feeling of nationality actually throve on the supposition, however false, of the purity and unity of the Teutonic race. But this 'unity' might not have succeeded in evoking any national feeling in a country where the psychological conditions were not the same. At the present time, the Czecho-slavs are developing a sense of nationality by recalling the traditions of the long defunct Bohemian kingdom, the martyrdom of Hus and the bravery of Ziska. In their case, the popular mind has seized upon 'the factor of the possession of common traditions' as the ground for the development of nationality. Since the establishment of the Gaelic League, Ireland has been insisting on the unity of language as the basis of their nationality, and similar examples may be easily multiplied by any student of contemporary history. In these cases the characteristic mentality of the people seeks only for some congenial factor of unity as a convenient spool on which to wind the complex feeling of nationality. It is significant in this connection to consider the modern phenomenon of 'irredentism.' A dispersed people, yet feeling and realising their essential unity, seeks to establish itself on one of the unities, *viz.*, the occupation of a definite geographical area, and it is this longing that serves to rationalise the Zionist movement among the Jews,[24] the cry of *Italia Irredenta* [25] and 'Poland for the Poles.'

We observe then that people with an awakened consciousness seek as the basis of nationality for one sort of 'unity' or more in preference to others in accordance with the characteristic trend of the popular mind. The reason for this preference is to be looked for in the fact that the entities expressed by the terms, country, race, language, religion, etc., have different values and implications to different peoples. We have already seen, what the mother-country stands for to the Hindu mind is different from what it is to the English, French or Japanese mind; the Hindu conception of religion again differs wholly from any western conception of it; race does not imply to an Indian mind exactly what

[24] See Hosmer's *Jews* (Story of the Nations Series).
[25] See Hearnshaw's *Main Currents of European History* (1917), p. 242.

it implies to a westerner and a race-conflict, that ultimately resolves itself into what Carlyle somewhat cynically remarked as the perennial question between two human beings, *viz.*, 'Can I eat you ?' 'Can you eat me ?' is altogether incomprehensible to a Hindu. The psychological responses evoked by appeals to country, race, language or religion would vary in degree and kind among peoples nurtured in different cultural traditions.

The reason for the inadequate appreciation of this aspect of the so-called 'unities' by western writers and philosophers is not far to seek. The traditions of culture and the results of history fix in the popular mind the peculiar colour or the subtle nuance that hangs round the conceptions of political philosophy. They cannot be treated as categorical verities, unchangeable by degrees of latitude or longitude. As perceived by the popular mind, they are not fundamental abstractions, devoid of all colour and unaffected by all mental peculiarity. But they call up long trains of associations and act like words of incantation somewhat in the manner that Macaulay attributed to the proper names of Milton's poetry. But so far as European political philosophy is concerned, the terms, race, language, religion, etc., have been practically fixed. "Europe," says Dr. Tagore, "is one country made into many," and this aspect of European history and culture was emphasised years ago by Freeman in his *Unity of History* and recently by Marvin in his *Unity of Western Civilization* (1915). "European history, from its first glimmerings to our day, is one unbroken drama, no part of which can be rightly understood without reference to the other parts which come before and after it. We are learning that of this great drama Rome is the centre, the point to which all roads lead and from which all roads lead no less. The world of independent Greece stands on one side of it; the world of modern Europe stands on another."[26] The result of this unity of European history and culture is that the basic conceptions of western political philosophy are fixed and settled both as to their contents and their limits. But Asia has no part or share in this unity nor can it boast of any such unity of history and culture as Europe, and hence the political conceptions of Europe

[26] Freeman's *Unity of History*.

when transported into Asia suffer a kind of 'sea-change,' as difficult to define and almost as impalpable. In estimating the nationality of an Asiatic people, the test of the 'unities' which may work well enough so far as European peoples are concerned lose their value as standards, for they themselves require to be valued afresh. Japan has been recognised and accepted as a nation by Europe. But the Japanese nationalist will probably attribute the feeling of nationality to Shintoism rather than to any of the 'unities,' laid down in European political philosophy. It is not the unities of race, language, religion, tradition or geographical location that he values, but the almost physical unity of the Japanese people, continuous from generation to generation, through the past, the present and the future, that is the logical consequence of his Shinto faith.

The problem of nationality is thus not so simple as it may outwardly appear. The so-called 'unities' are at bottom material factors in the economy of the life of a people. Whether the popular mind will act upon or react to any of these factors depends upon the quality of the popular mind which again is the resultant of history and culture. European history and culture certainly produce that quality of mind which can readily seize upon any of these unities: the peoples of Europe know and understand the force of race and may be touched by it into a consciousness of nationality; they realise the value and importance of geographical boundaries in the vicissitudes of European history, and readily seize upon the unity of geographical location as a ground of nationality; they feel the power of language as a national barrier and the value of possession of a common tradition, of suffering and striving together, of common subjection to a foreign conqueror, of common efforts for political amelioration, as an incentive to the growth of nationality. All this knowledge, understanding, realisation and feeling comes of historical experiences undergone by previous generations and of culture handed down and conserved from age to age. But the history and culture of an Asiatic country like India contains, it may be, none of those accumulated experiences that give that knowledge, understanding, realisation and feeling,—in short that special mentality,—which may fit the popular mind to seize upon any of these factors called the 'unities.' It may reach out towards something new, something beyond the scope of the historical experiences which western political philosophy generalises upon.

One of the 'unities,' India undoubtedly possesses and has possessed throughout the longer part of her history: it is the unity of geography. A glance at the map of India shows that it is a clean-cut geographical unit, so securely bounded by the mountain and the sea as to be incapable of 'shading off' round its borders. It is trenchantly marked off from the rest of the world and constitutes a complete territorial whole. This outward unity of India has been emphasised by Vincent Smith [27] and others, though the school of writers, whom we have designated before as the Anglo-Indian school, has sometimes sought to deny or minimise it. Nor is this geographical unity merely a dead appearance on the map, for the Indian mind in the post-Vedic times succeeded remarkably in grasping this unity and realising its consequences. Now, territorial unity leads to certain psychological consequences —first, it gives rise to the idea of inclusion of this territory under one rule or in one state which marks the inevitable transition from tribal or clannish chieftainship to territorial sovereignty, and second, it develops the idea of *patrie* or fatherland, the connection of human efforts and activities with a definite geographical area: "having a common region of birth people living therein connect the work, the institutions, the ideals, and the purposes of their lives with that region" [28] thus diversifying the unity of history into numerous regional histories. These consequences do not issue exactly from the factum of territorial unity, but from the psychological conception thereof by the popular mind.

In the ancient literature and history of India, we can discover clearly the traces of these psychological consequences which develop in the post-Vedic age. The Vedas reveal no doubt a state of society which has not yet outgrown completely the habits of previous wandering stage. The people are not yet firmly rooted to the soil. Thus the king is referred to as the king of the people, Jana or Vis,[29] the subordinate chieftains are called *Vispatis* (lords

[27] Smith's *Early History of India* (3rd Ed.), p. 5—" India, encircled as she is by seas and mountains, is indisputably a geographical unity, and, as such, is designated by one name."

[28] Nivedita's *Civic and National Ideals* (1918), p. 57.

[29] See the references collected in R. C. Mazumdar's *Corporate Life in Ancient India* (1918), p. 42.

of people),[30] heads of families are called *Kulapas* (protectors of family),[31] and chiefs presiding over circles of Kulapas are called *Brajapatis* (lords of circles),[32] though we find mention of an officer called *Gramani* (Village lord) [33] whose functions are undoubtedly connected with a defined area of land. In Vedic literature too names of places are frequently derived from the names of tribes inhabiting them. All this points to the conclusion that the organisation of life and polity in the Vedic times did not rest so much on a territorial basis as on the tribal. But we discover at the same time a genuine love of the soil and its physical features,—its fauna and flora, its rivers, mountains and valleys, its teeming life and ceaseless bounty—such as is expressed in the *Nadi-Sukta* of the Rig-veda [34] and the *Prithivi-Sukta* of the Atharva-veda.[35] This love of the soil deepened and expanded till the conception of the country as sanctified land emerged in the *Puranas* and the epics. It roused a geographical consciousness, so to speak, a realisation of the territorial basis of the life of society. Thus in the *Puranas* and in the epics we find elaborate descriptions of the country, its shape and physical features, its cities and provinces, its fauna and flora, which cover the whole extent of the peninsula from the northern mountain to the southern seas.[36] The conception of 'fatherland' was thus definitely fixed in the Indian mind and was expressed by the name Bharatvarsa for the whole country. It was regarded as the *Karmabhumi*, the land with which all the efforts and activities of the Indians must be specially connected.[37] With this growth of the feeling of what Ramsay Muir would call 'territorialism,' the old idea of tribal and clannish chieftainship was also transformed into the idea of territorial sovereignty and empire. Thus the formula for anointing a king in the ceremony of Rajasuya shows the survival of the old idea of tribal monarchy (*e.g.*, **महते जानराज्याय महते जनानां राज्याय**), the term 'Rajya' always

[30] *Rig-veda*, i, 37, 8; i, 12, 2; i, 26, 7; i, 164, 1, etc. (see Macdonell and Keith's *Vedic Index*).

[31] See M. and K.'s *Vedic Index*.

[32] *Ibid*.

[33] *Ibid*.

[34] *Rig-veda*, x, 75.

[35] *Atharva-veda*, xii, 1.

[36] See *Visnu Purana*, II, 3; and other Puranas like Garuda, Vayu, etc., *op.cit.*, and also Varaha Mihira's *Vrihat Samhita*, Chapter XIV; *Mahabharata*, *Visma Parva*, *Passim*.

[37] See *Visnu Purana*, II, 3, 1, ff.

denoting not territory, but dominion.[38] But the transition to territorial kingship is clear where in the *Aitareya Brahmana*, monarchy at its highest is defined as embracing an empire up to the natural boundaries, establishing one administration in the land up to the seas.[39] In later literature, kingdom (Rajya) is always denoted on the territorial basis. It is superfluous to mention the attempts that were made in the long course of Indian history to build up in India all-embracing empires, answering to the conception of the *Aitareya Brahmana* of monarchy at its highest.

The emergence of the idea of *patrie* and the idea of territorial monarchy shows conclusively the grasp by the Indian mind of the fact of the geographical unity of the country. This unity might have been the basis for the growth and development of a feeling of nationality in the same way as the conception of Italian unity became in Italy in the forties of the last century, if the Indian mind had been constituted differently from what it is. To the European mind therefore it seems as though, in the words of William Archer, "from the dawn of history India has suffered from what may be called an arrested predestination." [40] Instead of developing the feeling of nationality in its European sense, Indian mind ran off at a tangent towards the conception of a religious and cultural unity for India that finds so unique an expression in the extensive establishment of shrines and institution of pilgrimages.

The besetting vice of western political philosophy has hitherto been the scant attention given to the psychological implications of political problems. Psychology, as Marvin says, is the characteristic science added to the hierarchy in our period : "it has crowned biology and is exercising a profound influence on philosophy, literature and even politics." [41] There has recently arisen,

[38] See *Satapatha Brahmana*, v. 4, 2, 3, etc.
See references to the word 'Rajya' collected in Mukerjee's *Fundamental Unity of India*, p. 74.

[39] Aitareya Brahmana—

* * * * *

साव्र्वभौम: साव्र्वायुष आन्तादापरार्द्धात पृथिव्यै समुद्रपर्यन्ताया एकराडिति ।

This is the vow taken by the king in a special form of consecration ceremony.

[40] See William Archer's *A Vision of India* (published in *The Daily News and Leader*, January, 1914)—" From the dawn of history, India has suffered from what may be called an arrested predestination. She was clearly predestined to unity, yet she could never permanently attain it. Geographically she was marked off from the rest of the world more trenchantly than almost any other region not absolutely an island."

[41] Marvin's *Recent Developments of European Thought* (1920), p. 20.

specially in France, a school of social thinkers who seek to explain social phenomena and interpret social institutions through psychological laws.[42] Whatever criticism may be levelled at the method of this school, there is no doubt that it is bound to exercise an increasing influence on the discussion of political problems. The problem of Nationality has recently been attacked by MacDougall from the psychological stand-point of this school.

After criticising Muir's analysis of Nationality, MacDougall asks : "What then is the essential condition for lack of which any such people would fall short of nationhood ?" His answer is —organisation : "not material organisation, but such mental organisation as will render the group capable of effective group life, of collective deliberation and collective volition." [43] The learned professor then goes on to discuss the formative factors of this mental organisation and collective mental life and character of a people, *viz.*, homogeneity, free communication and leadership.[44] It is beside our purpose to launch upon a criticism of MacDougall's views on this point, which in fact lend themselves easily to criticism, but we propose only to indicate the psychological point of view from which alone the problem of nationality can be fruitfully interpreted. Thus we can estimate the real value of the so-called 'unities,' only when we throw this psychological aspect of the problem in its proper perspective. MacDougall is nearer the mark than any other writer when he exposes the futility of attempts "to discover the true secret of nationality in such considerations as geographical boundaries, race, language, history, and above all economic factors." [45] "They (political philosophers) do not see," continues MacDougall, "that each and all of these conditions, real and important though they are and have been in shaping the history and determining the existence of nations, only play their parts indirectly by affecting men's minds, their beliefs, opinions, and sentiments, especially by favouring or repressing the development in each people of the idea of the nation." To this a rider needs to be added that they will so affect, only *in the manner* in which men's minds will understand them and *to the extent* to which they are fitted by history and culture to appraise and appreciate them.

[42] See Garner's *Introduction to Political Science*, p. 25, and foot-note, No. 2.
[43] MacDougall's *Group Mind*, p. 100.
[44] *Ibid*, Chapters VII, VIII, IX.
[45] *Ibid*, p. 163.

Now the 'mental organisation' that MacDougall speaks of, whatever be its ultimate formative factors on psychological analysis, cannot be regarded as an immutable quality. We have too often seen peoples in the course of world's history, for whom nationality seemed to be a wholly impossible dream or a hopelessly lost cause, developing by imperceptible degrees a collective political personality. Even after the last European War, we find the age-long story of the growth of nations repeated. Even so far as Europe is concerned,—a continent where before the War the national aggregates seemed so integral, so fixed in their places in the table (with the minor exception of the fluctuating Balkan States),—there is no knowing among statesmen at the present time what possibilities, in the way of disintegration of old nations and the formation of new ones, the era to come may not reveal. These changes undoubtedly are due to the mutations of the 'mental organisation' of peoples. The progress of history introduces new forces which play effectively on the factors which go to constitute it, tending to break it up or change its direction or confirm and consolidate it. The loose elements of group mind may be organised by new forces acting upon them, thus creating a nation where previously there was none, the contrary case being also equally possible. When this fact is realised, it becomes a message of hope for potential nations struggling to be. The lack of the so-called 'unities,' which fate may deny to a people, need not be a disappointing consideration. As we have pointed out in the Introduction, failure to realise this fact is responsible for many of the futilities on the subject of Indian nationality preached by the Anglo-Indian school as well as by its opponent, the old party of the Indian National Congress.

The question of the development of Indian nationality is therefore not a question of artificially bringing about the 'unities' —developing a common language, a common religion, a common culture or tradition for India, but of mental organisation. In order to understand rightly the direction which this organisation must take, we have to consider a number of psychological factors. These factors are not immutably fixed quantities, but rather they are tendencies which have come into existence in response to history and culture and are liable to change through the operation of similar causes. It must be understood however that a general statement, thus framed, obscures by its very generality the inward complexities of the problem. There is a prodigiously close connection between the successive states of mind, collectively considered, of a people, and the outward appearances of their history which cannot be stated merely as that of cause and effect. As Ribot says, "In the social and political order, effects and causes are not presented under the form of a simple series as in the physical order; we rather find a reciprocity of action between them. The character produces the institutions and they in turn form character; thus after several generations, the two are but one, the institutions are but the character rendered visible and permanent."[46] But a realisation of the mutability of a people's collective psychology, which history constantly emphasises, is a corrective of the error of what Dr. Stein calls 'sociological determinism through blood.'[47] In Germany recently this error was clothed with all the seductive charms of neo-romantic mysticism by Houston Stewart Chamberlain, the great Anglo-German 'mesmerist in penmanship, thought-reader of history.'[48] He attributed all the modern culture of Europe to the operation of one plastic cause, *viz.*, the German 'race.' Among a certain class of writers, there is a tendency to make a fetish of the fixity of certain racial qualities, which gives rise to such false and facile generalisations as for instance the religiosity of the Indian people or the love of liberty of the British. The latter pretension has been effectively exposed by Prof. Pollard in his recent work on the *Factors of Modern History*.[49] There is no doubt that race is responsible for certain innate qualities of a people, but speculations on the operation of these qualities require to be guarded against the excesses of logic. Hence modern philosophers try to be careful to avoid the error of sociological determinism. Thus MacDougall limits the operation of race during historical times to "giving a constant bias to the evolution of the social environment," while Stein calls race, "a regulative idea, perhaps also only a heuristic principle, but surely no constitutive

[46] Ribot's *Heredity* (English Translation, 3rd Ed., 1875), p. 109.

[47] See Dr. Stein's *Philosophical Currents of the Present Day* (Translated by Sisir Kumar Maitra, 1918), Vol. I, p. 179.

[48] *Vide* Houston Stewart Chamberlain's *Foundations of the 19th Century* (in German) and criticism by Dr. Stein in *Philosophical Currents*, Tr., Vol. I, pp. 161 ff.

[49] See *Factors*, pp. 73 ff.

factor of history."[50] Just as the individual mind grows and changes, so does the collective mind of a people, and the presence of the element of heredity in either is equally felt, though it may be extremely difficult to define it in all the elusive subtlety of its operation. This principle of heredity appears in tendencies, constantly changing their direction and constantly being modified, though ultimately rooted perhaps in the depth and darkness of the undiscerned beginnings of history.

It is an impossible demand on a writer on the subject of Indian nationality to enumerate like beads on a rosary the psychological factors that would constitute the mental organisation necessary for the evolution of nationality in India. In the previous chapters, we have made an attempt to understand the basic factors of Indian life. We shall have to consider later on the new forces that arise out of their conjuncture and the external forces that impinge upon them on all sides. It must be understood that we cannot achieve mathematical precision or attain any arithmetic summation and that political science " is still probably the most incomplete and undeveloped of all social sciences."[51] The problem of Indian nationality also is a unique one,—specious historical analogies do not solve it, current conceptions of political philosophy do not suit it, external appearances of Indian life and history serve often but to obscure it. We have to scrutinise the dim historical and psychological background before we pass on to the lighted foreground of the present time.

[50] Stein's *Philosophical Currents*, Tr., Vol. I, p. 185

[51] Garner's *Introduction to Political Science*, p. 19.

Historical and Psychological Background—the Basis of Indian Nationality.

In the Introduction, we pointed out that the past has two uses—objective and subjective. By observing the history of India from the objective point of view, we may indeed arrive at certain basic factors of Indian life. Race, Religion, Culture, Social Tradition, Language, Literature and Art have developed certain conditions of existence through the forces of history. We have observed that these conditions do not answer to the normal 'unities' of nationality as understood in western political science. They stand on a special footing in India which is hardly to be comprehended by mere historical analogies. But with this discovery, the problem of Indian nationality does not end, but it is here that it really begins.

The question which is vital to the problem is—how these basic factors affect the Indian mind. The problem of the evolution of nationality is in fact intimately bound up with and dependent on the 'historical and psychological background' that we touched upon in the last chapter. This background is created by the subjective attitude of the people towards the basic factors of their life, their own conception of their past. India, says Mr. Cousins, lives in the imagination of the Indians. It is by their own reading, understanding and interpretation of their history that they will or will not attain and realise the conception of nationality.

The history of India is admittedly vast and complicated. "Those who attempt to write on India," said Dilke, "may indeed stand appalled at the complexity of the situation which has been brought about by her past history."[1] Attempts have been made by Indian scholars to reduce this complexity to the working of some inward philosophic principle. Rabindranath Tagore, for instance, would have us believe that the root-principle of Indian history is the principle of Synthesis. According to him, "The

[1] Sir Charles Wentworth Dilke's *Problems of Greater Britain*, p. 405.

realisation of unity in diversity, the establishment of a synthesis amidst variety,—that is the inherent, the *Sanatana, Dharma* of India."[2] Aurobinda Ghosh on the other hand finds this principle in Spirituality, and he traces through the entire history of Indian life, culture and civilization the many-sided working of this principle.[3] Now, it is obvious that both of them fix their standpoint in Hindu culture and view the whole course of Indian history therefrom. They attempt to attune all the later developments of Indian history to the dominant notes of the culture of pre-Mahammadan period. It is again from this standpoint mainly that Nivedita perceives the possibility of Indian nationality when, as the creed of the Indian nationalist, she lays down the following—"I believe that the strength which spoke in the *Vedas* and *Upanishads*, in the making of religions and empires, in the learning of scholars and the meditation of saints, is born once more amongst us, and its name to-day is Nationality."[4] This idea of Indian nationality as the modern reflex of ancient Hindu culture betrays an entire misconception of its real basis.

Let us consider briefly the main factors of the problem which we have so far tried to define and interpret. Take Race first. Whether the amazing variety and multiplicity of races in India afford any argument against the possibility of Indian nationality depends entirely on the sense in which race is understood in India and the force with which the race-idea works on the popular mind. European history shows many instances of race-conflict which arises, often so sharply and suddenly, through attempts at self-assertion by a people who feel themselves to be one on account of historical kinship. Examples of similar race-conflict are not altogether unknown in Indian history. The Vedic conflict between the Aryans and the non-Aryans is the most ancient example : a much later one is the conflict between the 'Vedus' and 'Ariar' on one hand and the Dravidian tribes and clans of the south on the other, during the Mauryan period, which has been recently

[2] Tagore's *Greater India* (1921), p. 31.

[3] See Aurobinda Ghose's *A Defence of Indian Culture* (The *Arya*, Pondicharry, Vol. vi, Nos. 1, *et seq.*).

[4] See Nivedita's *A Daily Aspiration for the Nationalist* (A. Ghose's *The Ideal of the Karmayogin*, p. 112).

discovered by Krishnaswami Aiyangar from Tamil literature.[5] But all these racial conflicts were smoothed and flattened out by the pressure of a common Brahmanical culture. When this culture had taken root in the Indian mind, the race idea was completely subordinated to the idea of *Acara* : there was no longer any conflict between the Northern Aryans and the Southern and Eastern non-Aryans, but between those who adhered to the Shastric *Acara* and those who did not. Hence arose the age-long problem of the so-called 'untouchable classes' in India, the enmity between the *Acaraniyas* and the *Anacaraniyas*. When foreign elements were introduced into the Indian population in the 11th and 12th centuries, which remained distinct and unassimilated, the attitude towards them was determined not by the sense of race, but of difference in culture, tradition and religion. One of the most clearly marked races of India were the Marathas under the leadership of Chatrapati Shivaji, and such a race in Europe would have claimed self-assertion on the racial ground. But the Marathas asserted themselves in Indian history, not so much as a racial entity aiming at racial predominance, as the chosen champion and defender of the faith, as Ramdas's noble exhortation to his royal pupil Shivaji would clearly imply :[6]

"Gods and Cows, Brahmans and the Faith, these are to be protected ; therefore God has raised you up. * * * * Why live when Religion has perished ? Gather the Marhattas together, make religion live again : our fathers laugh at us from heaven." Behind the rise of the Rajputs and the rise of the Sikhs, there was the urge and impulsion of the same feeling—the defence of religion and culture from Mahammadan aggression and not the desire for establishment or aggrandisement of a racial ego.

Religious conflict too must be understood in India in a wholly different sense. It is not a conflict between doctrines, between purely theological ideas about authority in religion, such as divided so sheerly in Ireland for example the Protestant Ulstermen of the North and the Catholic Irishmen of the South and put such formidable obstacles in the way of Irish unity. The conception of

[5] See Aiyanger's *The Beginnings of South Indian History* (1918), Ch. II.

[6] See Rawlinson's *Shivaji the Marhatta* (1915), pp. 113-122 (quoted in Smith's *Oxford History of India*, pp. 431-432).

Religion in India has been wholly different and its plastic and comprehensive character served to confine the conflict of doctrines and theological ideas to purely academic ground. The life of society was practically untouched by it. It was the bigotry of Auranzeb that for once in Indian history brought this conflict out of the *Parishads* of Vedic India,[7] the Debating Halls [8] (*Samayappa-vadaka-sala*) and Monasteries of Buddhist India, the *Ibadat-Khana* of Akbar,[9] into the noisy blood-red field of battle. It was in opposition to Auranzeb's iconoclastic bigotry, which, as we have seen from the Hindus' letter of protest to the Emperor referred to elsewhere, was an abrupt departure from the liberal policy pursued by his predecessors, that the Marhattas rose under Shivaji and the Sikhs fought under the Gurus. There are anecdotes even about Shivaji to show that he respected the *Quoran* and paid deference to the religious susceptibilities of the Mahammadans. Even Khafi Khan, deeply prejudiced as he was against Shivaji, referring to him always in opprobrious terms, bears testimony to this trait of his character.[10] In this respect Shivaji probably did no more than represent the prevailing attitude of the Hindu community of his age. But at the same time it cannot be said that, although there was practically little of purely religious conflict of the crusading kind between the Hindus and the Mahammadans, except for a brief spell under Auranzeb's suzerainty, there has never existed or does not exist conflict of any other kind between the adherents of the two rival religious systems.

This conflict lies mainly in the sphere of culture and mode of social life that result from the concrete aspects of religion, and it

[7] See *Vrihadaranyakopanishad*, VI, 2.1—

श्वेतकेतुर्ह आरुणेयः पाञ्चालानां परिषदमाजगाम ।

It appears from this reference that the Parishad was an academic institution attached to a clan, to which learners after completion of preliminary studies used to resort.

[8] See Rhys Davids's *Buddhist India*, p. 142. See also *Potthapada Sutta* (*Digha Nikaya*, P.T.S., Vol. I, p. 178).

[9] The Debating Hall (Ibadat Khana) was built by Akbar at Fatepur in 1575. The theological discussions carried on here are referred to by Badauni. (See Lowe's *Translation*, Vol. II.)

[10] See the passage quoted in Smith's *Oxford History of India*, p. 433. "He attacked the caravans which came from distant ports, appropriated to himself the goods and women. But he made it a rule that wherever his followers went plundering, they should do no harm to the mosques, the Book of God, or the women of any one. Whenever a copy of the sacred Kuran came into his hands, he treated it with respect, and gave it to some of his Mahammadan followers."

expresses itself in the name *Mlechha* applied by orthodox Hindus to the Mahammadans It is difficult to estimate the exact psychological value of this conflict. But nationalists in India are confident that it does not absolutely prevent a rapprochement which the growth of common interests in different spheres of social and political activity tends to bring about.

As regards traditions too, there is a certain cleavage between the two communities. Hindu traditions are all intimately bound up with Indian history and culture ; while Mahammadan traditions are moored to the culture and traditions of countries outside India. This aspect of Islamic tradition was expressed and emphasised by the recent Pan-Islamic movement with which the educated Mahammadans in India appear to be in deep sympathy. It can hardly be denied that there exists among them a non-geographical sense of Moslem brotherhood which a few years ago led to a movement called Hijrat—an abortive attempt at exodus from India into Afghanistan and Persia by the Mahammadans of Sindh and the Punjab who felt that the British Government in India was inimical to Islam. This movement of the Mahajarin which is a matter of recent history and which failed so tragically is a curious indication of the existence of anti-national tendencies among a large section of the Mahammadan population, whose dream is to revive the old glories of Islamic brotherhood, irrespective of geographical limits. On the other hand, as we have said at the beginning of this chapter, there is a tendency among the Hindus to seek inspiration for Indian nationality in the traditions of ancient Hindu culture. The reconciliation of these divergent tendencies is the problem of problems to the Indian nationalist.

Again in respect of the variety of language, India has been called a modern Babel. But language has never been regarded in India as a bulwark necessary to safeguard the distinctness and separateness of a people. The reason why differences of language do not offer any obstacle to national unity in a country like the United States or Switzerland, while peoples like the Poles, the Czechs and the Irish insist so passionately on language as a mark of nationality, is to be sought for in the attitude of these peoples respectively towards the factor of language as a separatist agency. There are no historical examples to show that literary or linguistic phenomena were ever seized upon by the Indian mind as racially dividing lines. The problem of a common language is no doubt one of the insistent problems of the day. If such a language comes into general use and currency, it may no doubt affect the popular mind and tend it towards a feeling of unity. But its absence does not necessarily mean in India the perpetuation of racial or communal differences, in as much as the attitude towards language of the Indian is not the same as that of the Czech or the Pole or the Irish.

We thus find that a different psychological background is created by the factors of race, religion, culture, tradition, language and literature in India from what such factors would create in the case of other peoples, and this difference is produced by the subjective attitude of the people towards these factors,—the sense in which they understand them and the way in which they interpret them. In this background we discover elements of conflict as well as of union, tendencies which make for nationality and tendencies which prevent it. But it is at the same time a purely negative ground while the feeling of nationality is a positive feeling, a very conscious exertion of the group mind.

Within living memory, certain psychological forces have operated to quicken this historical background in India. The establishment of British Government has had the effect of bringing to bear on Indian life and society, even on their most sensitive parts, the impact of western ideas, political, educational, cultural and social. The military rule of the Mahammadans, however prolonged, could never have interpenetrated the life of Indian society so deeply as British rule did within a short spell of its existence. Mahammadan rule, though it cannot be called national, was still indigenous,—the forces which moved it, the inspiration which enlivened it, the personnel which manned and conducted it, all belonged to the country for good or for evil. But British rule from its beginning up to date has been all foreign—much more foreign indeed and more aggressive in its foreignness than the Mogul domination. As Hall says, " It hangs, as if suspended from the

Viceroy and the Council. It has no roots in the soil of India. It is not indigenous in any way. Its vitality is derived from England, transmitted through the Secretary of State and the Viceroy. The Government of India has no existence apart from England. It is only ''Indian' in as much as it governs India, not that it proceeds from India or is composed of Indians. The truth by which it lives is that it is purely English. The whole system of the Government of India down to the last detail is alien, is exotic.''[11] Since Hall wrote these energetic lines, certain changes have been introduced in the administration of India, first by the Indian Councils Act of 1909 and then by the Government of India Act of 1919. The latter Act has formulated a policy and enunciated the aim of British rule in India. But whatever the ultimate aim of British rule, as enunciated in the latter Act, as the administration now stands, the words of Fielding Hall remain substantiallly true : it was foreign at its beginning and remains foreign to-day in spite of the introduction of a modicum of Indian element. The mutinous sepoys in 1857, both Hindu and Mahammadan, put a Mahammadan Emperor of Mogul descent on the throne of Delhi, which shows that they considered that the indigenous system of government had come to an end with the establishment of British Raj.

This obtrusive foreignness of British Government in India has, as a sort of natural reaction, driven the minds of the Indians more and more upon the resources of their own history—a fact which has become acutely pronounced of late. There is a muttering of revolt not only against the imposition of foreign government which with the Moderate Party of Indian politics takes the form of constitutional struggle to get it Indianised, while with the Extremist Party the form of Non-co-operation to bring it to a state of paralysis, but also against all forms of western civilization that have come in the train of British rule. Thus there is a harking back to older India among the present generation of Indians which invests the historical and psychological background, in front of which they stand, with a new glow of life and colour.

11 Fielding-Hall's *The Passing of Empire* (1914), p. 11.

Collaterally there has been what Nivedita calls an awakening of the sense of history.[12] There is a significant tendency among Indian nationalists to base their case for self-government for India on the glories and achievements of India's past—on the capacities for republican, monarchical and imperial government shown by the Indians of old, of which examples are found in abundance in ancient and mediæval history.[13] In the domains of literature and art there is the same tendency to recalling 'the gentle music of the bygone years.' This tendency has shown itself nowhere more clearly and completely than in the Bengal School of Painting (so keenly contrasted with the fleshly school of Ravi Varma) which seeks to reproduce the physically attenuated and spiritually luminous types and figures carved on the unearthed railings of old Buddhist *Stupas* or painted in the dim caves of Ajanta. We shall have occasion later on to explain from another point of view the significance of the rise of this new school of painting, which has already excited no little admiration among the art-critics of Europe. In the seats of learning too the same tendency has taken the form of Indian research. The start in this direction was given no doubt by the British administrators of India who found it necessary to know the language, the literature, the customs and laws of the people in order to be able to govern them efficiently. The foundation of the Asiatic Society in Calcutta in 1784 A.D. may be truly said to have laid the basis for Indian research. But it is only in recent years that Indian scholars and historians have earnestly taken upon themselves the study and elucidation of the past of their country.[14] In connection with the University of Calcutta, a band of scholars have been carrying on valuable researches into the different aspects of Indian history from the Vedic age down to the era of the Peshwas, and these researches are undoubtedly the fruit of the tendency we have just referred to. It is

[12] Nivedita's *Civic and National Ideals* (2nd Ed.), p. 23.

[13] The speeches on '*Self-government Resolution*' delivered from the platform of the Indian National Congress strongly illustrate this tendency. See also as an illustration N. C. Kelkar's *The Case for Indian Home Rule* (1917), published under the authority of the Indian Home Rule League, Poona, Ch. 1 (*The Ancient Civilization in India*).

[14] In this connection the work of the Asiatic Societies of Bengal and Bombay; Behar and Orissa Research Society, Bhandarkar Institute at Poona, and the Mythic Society at Bangalore may be mentioned.

extremely interesting to find that the Sedition Committee traced the beginnings of the Anarchist Movement in India, which came into prominence during the years 1906-1914, to the memory of Shivaji and Marhatta ascendancy stirring among the Chitpavana Brahmanas of the Deccan.[15]

There is a third psychological force which is changing the aspect of the historical background. Facility of intercommunication and intercourse among the different parts of India has been one of the most marked characteristics of British administration, if not the most marked one. Railways, Steam-ships, Post and Telegraph have put a girdle round the entire Indian continent. If Indians had realised the geographical unity of India long ago, it has become far easier for them to realise it now. This realisation of India's geographical unity has been further emphasised by the knowledge that many Indians have been able to acquire of the world beyond the Indian boundaries. Through the instrumentality of a system of government which keeps up an unbroken link between India and distant England, she has been brought into connection with the movements of world-politics, specially of European politics. Thus Indians can realise to-day, more clearly than ever efore, that they form a group by themselves marked off from the world outside, that presses upon it specially through relations of commerce and the impact of culture and learning. This realisation of their separate position, which must not however be mistaken for nascent nationality, gives rise to a vague Pan-Indian sentiment—a curiosity among the different parts of India to know and a readiness to sympathise with each other. "A generation ago," says Mr. Mazumdar,[16] "the stalwart and turbulent Punjabi the intelligent and sensitive Bengali, the orthodox and exclusive Madrasi, the ardent and astute Marhatta, the anglicised Parsi, and the cold calculating Guzrati, were perfect strangers to one

[15] See *Report of the Sedition Committee*, 1918, presided over by the Hon'ble (then) Mr. Justice Rowlatt, *Intro.*, and pp. 1-3. "Indications of a revolutionary movement were first observed (in 1897) in Western India in connection with the development of two classes of annual festivals, namely, those in honour of Hindu God Ganapati and those in honour of Shivaji, who united the people of the Deccan against Mahammadan rulers"—p. 1. See also the *Shivaji Slokas* recited by the Chapekars at the Shivaji and Ganapati festivals, p. 2.

[16] A. C. Mazumdar's *Indian National Evolution* (2nd Ed.), p. 163.

another," but the facilities of intercommunication and intercourse have brought them close together and they are able now to meet on perfectly fraternal footing on the platform of the Indian National Congress. This growth of active sympathy and fellow-feeling among Indians living in different and widely separated parts of the country, with physical and mental characteristics as widely separated and different, perhaps goes deeper than the people themselves can realise. Speaking of the multiplicity of races in India, Holderness observes that "India has stamped them with a common seal and has wrought out a recognisable type amid a great profusion of species."[17] This observation is corroborated by Risley who quotes Yusuf Ali to point to the "underlying uniformity of life from the Himalayas to Cape Comorin"—the existence of "a general Indian character, a general Indian personality which we cannot resolve into its component elements."[18] This Indian character and Indian personality struck even a casual traveller like Sidney Low when he visited India in 1905-1906. After referring to the well-known divisions in the Indian population (which he describes as 'a patch-work of humanity'), he advises the reader not to forget that a "certain consciousness of identity is beginning to make itself perceptible through the mass." Though there is very little common among them, according to Low, except that they are all Asiatics, "they are yet faintly realising the existence, or the imagined existence, of a solidarity, a unity, which marks them off from Europe and the white peoples in general." "There is an indefinite Pan-Indian sentiment in the air, highly nebulous and even gaseous at present, which might assume a tangible form under the pressure of events in the near future."[19] This new type of Pan-Indianism, which is not descended from, but which may yet be affiliated to, the Hindu spiritual conception of Indian unity, and which, to my mind, is an outgrowth of the new conditions of life brought into existence by British rule,

[17] Holderness's *Peoples and Problems of India* (Home University Series), p. 8.

[18] See *The People of India* (Crooke's Ed.), pp. 287-288.

[19] See Sidney Low's *A Vision of India* (1921), p. 348. The author writes in the preface, "The materials on which the following pages are founded were collected, for the most part, during the progress of the King and the Queen, then Prince and Princess of Wales through the Empire of India in the autumn and winter of 1905 and the spring of the following year."

puts a new value on the historical and psychological background of Indian nationality.

As a direct result of this Pan-Indianism, the peoples of India are, so to speak, borrowing each other's history. There is no doubt a common heritage of history of the Hindu and the Buddhistic periods which all parts of India can claim through cultural affiliation. The Vedic Rishis are for all India, the heroes and saints of the Pouranic and epic age, Buddha, Asoka, Kaniska and other personalities who by their greatness transcended all local and parochial limits. But during the Mahammadan period, which may fitly be described by the phrase which Sidgwick applies to the Middle Ages of Europe, " a long period of dissolution and reconstruction," the history of India, so far as the people are concerned, degenerates into a string of provincial histories. Tribes, races and peoples pass singly over the stage of Indian history without any dramatic unity of place or of action. The Rajputs are distinct from the Marhattas, the Marhattas from the Bengalis, and the Bengalis from the Sikhs and the Jats, and they feel no need for union or combination and are supremely indifferent to each other's history. But since the close of this period of dissolution, they seem to have re-found themselves in a vague though perfectly intelligible bond of Pan-Indianism. Not only do they feel that their existence in India is not independent of but relative to each other,—but they also realise that they are inter-dependent as regards their history, tradition and culture. I shall try to make this clear by one illustration only.

In physical, racial and mental characteristics the Bengalis are widely separated from the Rajputs, the Mahrattas and the Sikhs. No two peoples are more keenly contrasted than the sturdy, heroic, mountain-bred race of Rajputs and the soft-limbed, languid inhabitants on the banks of the lower Ganges whose physical degeneracy has been a constant theme of reproach since Macaulay wrote the famous passage about them in the Essay on Lord Clive. Yet from Rangalal Bandyopadhyaya's *Padmini* to the latest dramas of D. L. Roy, the events of Rajput history have exercised a peculiar fascination over the literary men of Bengal. Those who have seen these Rajput plays staged in the theatres of Bengal will bear testimony to the enthusiasm and applause with which they are received, the pride and glory with which the audience readily identify themselves with the awful self-sacrifice and tenacious forlorn bravery of the Rajput heroes. They feel that they too have a share in the undying glory of these heroic deeds. There is again no reason in history why the Bengalis should feel kindly disposed towards the Mahrattas. The oppression of the Mahratta free-booters is still referred to in nursery songs and the 'Mahratta ditch' round Calcutta still exists as a memorial to their depredations. Yet during the upheaval of popular feeling in the province in 1906, consequent on Lord Curzon's Partition of Bengal, almost every district in Bengal celebrated the Shivaji festival with demonstrative enthusiasm. There appears to be no provincial feeling towards the great hero of Mahratta history, and at least two well-known and widely-read works in Bengali literature have been written to glorify him, *viz.*, Rameschandra Dutt's novel, entitled *Maharastra Jivan-Prabhat* and Jogindranath Basu's epic on *Shivaji*. The noble achievements of Shivaji are now treasured by the people of Bengal no less than the Mahrattas themselves. The stories of the Shikh *Gurus* also have been enshrined in Bengali poetry and song, and many of these Bengali poems on Sikh history will be found in Rabindranath Tagore's *Katha-O-Kahini* which was published during the Swadeshi movement in Bengal about fifteen years ago. This illustration from Bengali literature sufficiently shows how the Pan-Indian sentiment is working towards a synthesis of Indian history. The particular mental attitude called provincial patriotism is often a great impediment to the development of a national feeling and a continual source of weakness and disorganisation. The best example of 'provincial patriotism' is offered by Spain where a Spaniard is always either an Aragonese or a Valencian or an Adulasian or a Guipuzcoan, and to this provincial patriotism Pollard attributes the comparative failure of Spain in European history.[20] Such provincial patriotism was often a source of weakness in Indian history too. But it is fast wearing off under the pressure of a growing Pan-Indian sentiment.

[20] See Pollard's *Factors of Modern History*, pp. 62-65.

A proof of its existence is found in the keen sympathy felt in India for the benighted and ill-fated Indian colonists in South Africa, Kenya and the Fiji Islands—a fellow-feeling which would be incompatible with ' patriotism of purely local growth and colour.'

The psychological value, with which this Pan-Indian sentiment invests the historical background, is easy to understand. It throws into a focus as it were the dispersed events of Indian history. Indians of different races and provinces, sharing each other's past achievements, observe a coherence and unity in their history and feel the force of common traditions. Where foreigners observe a series of provincial histories, Indians themselves observe the chequered but continuous history of one country, *viz.*, India. This realisation of the unity of Indian history by the Indian mind may be the basis of other feelings congenial to the development of common nationality.

Nationality in no country can exist as ' the baseless fabric of a vision,' raised by a wave of Prospero's wand. In dealing with the problem of Indian nationality therefore we have first to observe analytically the basic factors of Indian life, and then proceed to consider what historic background is created by the conjuncture of these factors taking their characteristic colour from the popular mind and culture. But such a background may be dead, dull, without any power to give relief to the existing conditions of life and society in which the people find themselves. We have therefore to observe further what the psychological value of this background is, in what relation it stands to the foreground of the present age, how far it sets off or gives relief to the present dispositions of the group mind, the spiritual currents and mental tendencies of the age. It is in fact in this psychological and historical background that we may hope to find the basis of Indian nationality.

PART II.

THE MEANING OF INDIAN NATIONALITY

Relation between State and Society and Political Life in Ancient India

It is sometimes said with a certain amount of plausibility that even granting the existence of a basis for the growth of a sentiment of unity among Indians in a quickened historical and psychological background, this sentiment can never attain to the feeling of nationality properly so called; that though they may realise this unity in the sphere of spirituality and culture, it cannot take the direction of developing a collective political personality; that, in other words, if this feeling of unity must be called by the name of nationality, the conception of nationality must needs be given a different meaning in India.

In order to appreciate both the elements of truth and of error in such a view, it is necessary first of all to understand what meaning has been given to nationality by political thinkers in the west, or, to adopt the language of the psychological school, what special direction must the ' mental organisation ' of a people take in order to develop nationality. We have next to consider whether the organisation of the group-mind in India is capable at all of taking this direction or is permanently prevented therefrom by the age-long workings of Indian history and Indian culture.

In modern European political philosophy, the idea of the State and the idea of the Nation are put in close connection. This connection however has not always been conceived with clearness or characterised with precision. During the hundred and odd years that have elapsed between the treaty of Vienna and the treaty of Versailles, the idea has steadily gained ground in European politics that the essential determinant in the formation of a state must be the collective will of the people included in it. This idea is reflected in the current theory of the origin of State, thus stated by Jellinek : " The inner ground of the origin of the state is the fact that an aggregate of persons has a conscious feeling of its unity, and gives expression to this unity by organising itself as a collective personality and constituting itself as a volitional and active subject."[1] The recognition of this fact constitutes the whole difference in the principle of political reconstruction adopted in the Treaty of Vienna, with its emphasis on 'legitimacy' and the 'balance of power'[2] and the Treaty of Versailles with its creation of 'plebiscite areas.'[3] The repudiation of the principle of Balance of Power and the enunciation of the principle of Self-determination, categorically made by Woodrow Wilson in his famous speech on " The Four Principles " on 11th February, 1918, indicated in fact the reign of a new order of ideas in the political world which had been consolidating itself for over a hundred years in Europe.[4] This new orientation of European politics from 1815 to 1919 has been brought about by the growing conception of an inviolable connection between the state-idea and the nation-idea. The conception briefly is that the ideal or natural state must be the objective expression of nationhood. In his *Principles of Political Obligation*, Green characterised the state as 'the nation organised in a certain way.' " The nation," said Green, " underlies the state." The idea has developed to this position that a connection has been held to exist in the nature of things between the state and nationality, the state being regarded as a sort of efflorescence of nationality. " The natural tendency of the feeling of nationality," it has been said, " is to find expression in political unity."[5] So Bluntschli, after considering 'nationality as a principle in the formation of states,' says : " To sum up, a state is natural if its form at any time corresponds to the peculiar character and

[1] Quoted in Dr. Willoughby's *The Nature of the State*, p. 119.

[2] See Hearnshaw's *Main Currents of European History*, p. 111.

[3] See *The German Treaty Text*, published under the auspices of the Institute of International Affairs, London, 1920 (Oxford University Press). Under the terms of this Treaty, certain areas like the Saar Basin, a portion of Upper Silesia, a portion of territory on the southern frontier of East Prussia, and certain other localities have been declared 'plebiscite areas,' *i.e.*, the inhabitants of these localities are to decide by vote in a specified mode and within a specified time as to the countries within which they respectively desire to be politically included. See pp. 43, 60, 66, 68, etc.

[4] See *The German Treaty Text*, p. 261, where President Wilson's speech is quoted.

[5] Willoughby's *The Nature of the State*, p. 121.

period of development of the nation embodied in it," [6] which he explains in other words by the statement that "the nation must give to the state the impress of its own character." [7] Similar views have been held by other political philosophers which it is unnecessary to quote here.

Now from this conception of a natural connection between the state and the nation, it is possible to extricate the prevailing western idea of nationality. Nationality is a political conception. [8] Its essence is a political desire, and is is this essential element that differentiates the feeling of nationality from any analogous feeling of unity, which may constitute among a people a different bond of association. Mill recognised this element when he defined a nationality to be a "portion of mankind, united among themselves by common sympathies which do not exist between them and any others—which make them co-operate with each other more willingly than with other people, desire to be under the same government, and desire that it should be government by themselves or a portion of themselves exclusively." [9] It is this kind of unity, directed and oriented towards political ends, that underlies the western conception of nationality. In his fifth lecture on the *Expansion of England* (2nd course), Seeley expresses surprise that Brahmanism, with its inherent principle of communal unity, did not germinate into nationality in India. Speaking of the Marhatta confederacy, which in the middle of the eighteenth century covered the whole of India with its ramifications, Seeley says, "It might appear that in this confederacy lay the nucleus of an Indian nationality, that Brahmanism was now about to do for the Hindus what has been done for so many other races by their religion. But nothing of the kind happened." [10] Seeley accounts for the phenomenon by the peculiar character of Brahmanism, which, being, in his opinion, 'a loose compromise between several religions' was feeble as a uniting principle. The real explanation perhaps is

[6] See Bluntscnli's *The Theory of the State*, Ch. IV, p. 107.
[7] *Ibid*, p. 107.
[8] "The nation is a political idea"—Bluntschli, p. 109.
[9] John Stuart Mill's *Representative Government*, Ch. XVI. (*Cf.* Nationality as connected with representative government.) Mill makes a confusion between Nationality and Nation. In the definition quoted, we should substitute Nation for Nationality.
[10] Seeley's *Expansion of England*, p. 262.

that Brahmanism has never had a political orientation, that the inner inspiration of the Marhatta confederacy, as already noted, was the defence of the Brahmanical religion rather than the desire for the establishment of a national state.

It is clear that a people emerges into the condition of a nation not merely by the realisation of their historical unity but also by the evolution of a feeling towards a separate political destiny for themselves. This feeling invests it with a certain status to which the right of political self-determination has been acknowledged to belong. The realisation of this right lies in the establishment of the national state,—the only 'natural state,' as it has been called, organically sound enough to resist the working of disruptive forces. Thus Bluntschli says, "the nation has a legal personality," *i.e.*, a status with a guaranteed right. It is a "collective personality, legal and political." The criterion of a nation that distinguishes it from a society is, according to him, the possession of two characteristics, (*i*) a collective will and (*ii*) power to make its will actual in the state.[12] It will be observed that in laying down this criterion, the German Professor has in mind the conception of a nation that has already realised its inherent right, for the world is full of instances of struggling nations powerless under adverse circumstances to actualise in the state their collective will. The extreme logical consequence of this conception is crystallised by him in the epigrammatic statement, 'No State, no Nation!'[13] The same idea is put by Prof. Willoughby, cured of Bluntschli's extreme emphasis, when he says, "The tendency of course is, as indicated in Mill's definition, for nations to constitute themselves as individual states, and it may be said that this demand for political unity constitutes the surest index to the existence of a national feeling."[14] This political conception of nationality, when put in proper psychological terms, means and implies that the 'mental organisation' of a people which is essential to nationhood must be in the direction of political self-determination in order to satisfy the connotation of nationality.

[11] Bluntschli's *The Theory of State*, p. 109.
[12] See *ibid*, p. 109.
[13] *Ibid*, p. 91.
[14] Willoughby's *The Nature of the State*, p. 12.

Now, it is often said that this political direction is alien from the mentality of the Indian people. However deeply a Pan-Indian sentiment of unity may take root among them, it will never lead to the growth of nationality in its accepted sense, owing to this permanent defect or virtue of the Indian mind. It may be a unity of cultural life, unity of artistic self-expression or unity of common spiritual aspirations, but it will never develop into the unity of state-life or state-organisation as in Europe. The meaning of Indian nationality therefore must be conceived afresh, apart from the political implications of the idea in European history and European political science. As we shall show, this view is grounded on a total misconception of Indian history, though it contains an element of truth which we shall at the same time try to separate and distinguish in the following pages.

India is supposed to be typical of the East, the flash-light picture of which by Matthew Arnold in the oft-quoted lines of *Obermann Once More* is believed by westerners to be substantially true to life.[15] Lane-Poole concludes his survey of the mediæval period of Indian history in the same strain and with the same lines of Matthew Arnold.[16] Political changes of vast dimensions—foreign invasions and conquests, the rise and fall of empires, the entrances and exits of royal and imperial dynasties, wars, treaties, political federations—seem to be mere superficial disturbances of the placid course of Indian life from century to century. The people at large have no part or share in these political changes except that they passively suffer from or profit by them. Politics in Indian history are thus transactions between persons or classes from which the people in general stand silently aloof. Carlyle's exploded definition of History as being at bottom the biography of great men has been held to be peculiarly applicable to the history of India. It has been too often forgotten that such a view of Indian history may after all be based on nothing more solid than our own ignorance, for researches into the social and communal

15 "The East bowed low before the blast
In patient, deep disdain ;
She let the legions thunder past,
And plunged in thought again."
Matthew Arnold's *Obermann Once More.*

16 Lane-Poole's *Mediæval India* (Story of the Nations Series), pp. 423-424.

life of the people in different parts of India at various epochs of her history have only been recently commenced and have yielded so far a modicum of result with regard to the pre-Mahammadan period only. So far as this period is concerned, we are in possession of a rich legacy of historical traditions embedded in literature,—Sanskrit, Pali and Prakrit,—which may be pieced together, with greater or less sequence, with the aid of lithic inscriptions, iconography and numismatics. The supreme virtue of these traditions is that they are absolutely unhistorical in motive: they were not intended to perpetuate the changes of state or the doings of the ruling powers, but they reflect frankly that aspect of history on which the modern historian puts the highest premium, *viz.*, the social, communal and religious life of the people. When these literary sources of history run dry in the Mahammadan period, we are thrown for our knowledge of Indian history on court chronicles, court histories and archives, supplemented by incomplete and partial accounts by European travellers. The effect of knowledge derived exclusively from such sources is not only that the social, communal and religious life of the people is shut out from our view, but also to give a substantially wrong ensemble of history. The leading figures, that move about in the lime-light and whose activities are magnified in the histories and chronicles, appear to be the sole actors on the stage and the rest of the *dramatis personæ*, whose movements are perhaps more important in the play, are kept out of view and forgotten. Thus a wholly wrong impression is created and the *mise en scene* is wrongly conceived. It seems therefore likely that the pre-Mahammadan period of Indian history will be nearer and clearer to us than the later period: at any rate this is so in the present state of Indian researches.

As regards therefore the real history of India, *i.e.*, the history of the people in the evolution of their social life and corporate activities, our knoweldge must be pronounced to be essentially defective, and this defective knowledge is responsible for the view that the mass mind of the Indian people has always been non-political, and that the Hindus of old offered in this respect the keenest contrast to their contemporaries, the Greeks,[17] and that

[17] See Talboys Wheeler's *College History of India* (1891), pp. 1-2.

their 'patient deep disdain' of all political events has been a fixed trait of their character, despite innumerable changes of history, from the time when Alexander's legions thundered past down to date. The characteristic attitude of the Indian mind towards politics or matters of state, according to this view, is most fitly described by the pathetic lines with which Goldsmith closes *The Traveller.*[18] The facile generalisation is made that the Indian has been since the dawn of history an exclusive seeker after spirituality, yearning, oblivious of other pursuits, for "that bliss which only centres in the mind." European as well as Indian writers have leaned more or less to this view which has often led them to regard Indian history as lop-sided, as disproportionately developed on the side of religious, philosophic or cultural development to the detriment of effective political action or political purpose. Even Vincent Smith makes a sort of apology in writing a political history of ancient India by stating at the end of his work that "the most important branch of Indian history is the history of her thought."[19] We shall presently see how this prevailing impression about the non-political mentality of the Indian people is created by certain half-hidden peculiarities of the evolution of Indian history.

One of the most remarkable achievements in the field of Indian research has been the recent discovery of the existence of several types of local and communal Self-Government in ancient India of which relics are still found in different parts of Southern India. Students of ancient Indian history had been long familiar with the popular assemblies and tribunals, referred to not only in the *Dharmasastras* but also in the account left to us by Megasthenes, which acted as constitutional checks on monarchy in ancient India.

18 "Vain, very vain, my weary search to find
That bliss which only centres in the mind :
Why have I strayed from pleasure and repose,
To seek a good each government bestows ?
In every government, though terrors reign,
Though tyrant kings or tyrant laws restrain,
How small, of all that human hearts endure,
That part which laws or kings can cause or cure ?
Still to ourselves in every place consigned,
Our own felicity we ask or find :"
Goldsmith's *Traveller*.

19 Vincent Smith's *Early History of India* (3rd Ed.), p. 478.

But the extensive powers and functions of these local bodies, their wide-spread ramifications all over the country, their long-enduring vitality, and their exact relations with the ancient Indian state, whether republic, monarchy or empire, has been a matter of recent discovery.[20] This has laid the basis for a new view of ancient Indian society as "primarily an aggregate of smaller societies more or less autonomous," and of ancient Indian state as a more or less loose federation of these numerous self-governing bodies. The types of association which they represent are both territorial and communal, and many of them are undoubtedly survivals in the political state of the tribal, clannish and communistic forms of self-government characteristic of all primitive societies in pre-state or ante-political condition, of which there are well-known examples in the Folk-Moot and Hundred-Moot in England and the Gens and Curia in Rome. In distinguishing these autonomous communal and local bodies in the ancient Indian state and their modern equivalents, Dr. Radhakumud Mukherjee says: "The fundamental difference is that, while in the latter case, the state as a fully developed and completely constituted body, consciously creates autonomous centres within itself by devolution and delimitation of its own functions, in the former the communal institutions, guilds and local bodies have an independent origin and growth out of fluid and inchoate conditions of tribal life and organisation. When the state comes to supervene or be superimposed upon these, it has to treat with them more or less on terms of equality and recognise their pre-existing rights by conventions and agreements which operate as charters regulating their mutual relations."[21]

Such must have been the origin of the institutions, called the Sabha, the Samiti, Pancajanah, the Parisad in Vedic India.[22] It is difficult at this distance of time to fix precisely the respective characters, functions and extent of authority of these popular

[20] The results of recent researches in this direction have been embodied in R. C. Mazumdar's *Corporate Life in Ancient India* (1918), D. R. Bhandarkar's *Carmichæl Lectures I*, Krishnaswami Aiyanger's *Ancient India*, R. K. Mukherjee's *Local Government in Ancient India* (Mysore University Studies), 2nd Ed. (1920). Dr. Mazumdar's and Dr. Mukherjee's works are systematic treatment of the subject.

[21] Mukherjee's *Local Government in Ancient India*, 2nd Ed., pp. 6-7.

[22] A brilliant treatment of these institutions of the Vedic age will be found in K. P. Jayaswal's recent work on *Ancient Hindu Polity*.

bodies, two of which, *viz.*, the Sabha and the Samiti, are mentioned in the Vedas as indispensable adjuncts to kingly power.[23] It is difficult to discover the distinction between the two, which are frequently mentioned in juxtaposition, and Zimmer's view that the Sabha was the assembly of the villagers while the Samiti was the Central Assembly of the Tribe has been contradicted by Macdonell and others.[24] Pancajanah was also in all probability a popular institution, a committee of five elders,[25] while the clannish character of the Parisad, which in its origin was a body of learned men, is attested by a passage in the *Vrihadaranyakopanisad* in which Svetaketu is mentioned as resorting for the sake of learning to the Parisad of the Pancalas.[26]

It is an important line of Indian research, which the exigencies of our subject forbid us to follow in detail, to trace the later developments of these ancient Vedic institutions. The names still survive, though the institutions themselves have undergone numerous and various changes through adaptation to the different social environments of different times. Take the Vedic Parisad for instance. From the solitary reference in the *Vrihadaranyaka*, it would appear to have been originally a clannish assembly. It was a body of learned men, enjoying a status as the depository of ancient lore.[27] It appears also that this assembly was invested with authority to state and dictate the law to the members of the clan. This law was of course the Aryan Brahmanical law, derived ultimately from the Vedas called the *Sruti* or Revelation. But this Aryan Brahmanical law grew up in different surroundings of tribal and clannish traditions, customs and usages. Thus we have different recensions of Vedic knowledge called *Parsada, i.e.*, derived from different Parisads.[28] Political and social changes of a far-reaching character

[23] The references to *Sabha* and *Samiti* in the Vedas are ably treated in Mazumdar's *Corporate Life in Ancient India* (1918), pp. 45 ff.

[24] See discussion of divergent views in Pramatha Nath Banerjee's *Public Administration in Ancient India*, p. 95 (foot-note).

[25] This appears to be Mr. Jayaswal's view (*vide An Introduction to Hindu Polity*, Modern Review, June, 1913). It is the origin of the modern *Panchayet*. Mr. Jayaswal has elaborated this view in his book entitled, *Ancient Hindu Polity*.

[26] श्वेतकेतुर्ह आरुणेयः पञ्चालानां परिषदमाजगाम ।

Vrihadaranyaka, VI. 2.

[27] Swetaketu resorted to the Parishad for instruction in higher philosophical lore.

[28] See discussion on this point in N. C. Sen Gupta's *Sources of Law and Society in Ancient India* (1914), pp. 45-47.

must have intervened between the period represented by early Pali literature and the period represented by the *Smritis*, which led to the establishment and consolidation of monarchical systems in northern India. Consequently the proper functions of the ancient clan-assemblies were to a large extent forgotten. The institution remained no doubt, but it changed its character in accordance with altered political circumstances. The Parisad was drawn into the orbit of the monarchical system and became an assembly of learned men, casually selected, to advise the king on knotty questions of law, the number of such advisers being differently given by different authorities.[29] In Kautilya's *Arthasastra*, we meet with an institution called *Mantri-Parisad*, the functions of which are closely analogous to those of the British cabinet, which it further resembles in secrecy of deliberation and in decision by majority.[30] It is the chief executive council of the king, as is indicated by the following statement of its functions : " These ministers shall have to consider all that concerns the parties of both the king and his enemy. They shall also set themselves to start the work that is not yet begun, to improve what has been accomplished, and to enforce strict obedience to orders." [31] The following citation of authorities by Kautilya as to the numerical strength of this body shows that it must have been an old institution even in his time :

" The school of Manu says that the assembly of ministers shall be made to consist of twelve members. The school of Vrihaspati says that it shall consist of sixteen members. The school of Usanas says that it shall consist of twenty members. But Kautilya holds that it shall consist of as many members as the needs of his dominion require." [32]

The Vedic Sabha had probably a similar history : from an institution of tribal self-government, it became a limb of constitutional monarchy. In Southern India, however, this institution

[29] See *ibid*, p. 46. The members of a Parishad are given by Gautama (XXVIII, 49) as *ten*; Vasistha (III, 20) and Baudhayana I, 1, 7-9, as *ten or less*; Yajnavalkya (1, 9) as *four or less*, even one, if he is really well-versed.

[30] *vide Arthasastra* (Shama Sastri's Ed., 1919), Book I, Ch. XV. (Of मन्त्राधिकारः) *re* Secrecy, तदुद्देशः संवृतः कथानामनिस्रावो पक्षिभिरप्यनालोक्य स्यात्। *Re* Majority Decision, तत्र यद्भूयिष्ठाः कार्य्यसिद्धिकरं वा ब्रूयुस्तत् कुर्य्यात्।

[31] *Arthasastra* (Shama Sastri's Tr., 1915), p. 33.

[32] *Ibid*, p. 33.

retained its old function, character and significance and was the chief instrument of self-government of the village-community, as numerous inscriptions, unearthed during several Archæological Surveys of Southern India, amply testify.[33] Both the names, Parisat and Sabha, occur in the inscriptions to denote the ruling assembly of the South Indian village-community, and their Tamilian equivalents show perhaps the recognition of their original tribal character, as the members of the Sabhas and Parisads (Tamil—*Parudai*) are also called 'gana-pperumakkal' and 'alum-ganatter,'[34] the Sanskrit word, *Gana*, being still prevalent among many non-Brahmanical classes of Southern India, applying to tribal congregations.[35] Though there is at present a certain paucity of inscriptions in Northern India referring to the village Sabhas, yet no historical conclusion can be drawn therefrom. In the *Silpa-sastras, e.g.*, Manasara, which, according to Havell, were compiled about 5th or 6th century A.D., though embodying traditions of far greater antiquity, provision is always made in the different village-plans, such as Dandaka, Nandyavarta, Padmaka, Swastika, etc., for a central place to accommodate the village-assembly (Sabha).[36] Similarly the Vedic Pancajanah develops and expands into the Five Great Assemblies, mentioned by Megasthenes as constitutional checks on the government of Chandragupta, which reappear in the Gupta inscriptions as *Pancamandali.*[37] These very same Five Great Assemblies are, curiously enough, found in three independent kingdoms of the south, of the Pandya, Chola and Chera, as being entirely vested with the powers of government, which Kanakasabhai accounts for by the fact that the founders of the three kingdoms migrated from Magadha,[38] but which may very well be due to a common heritage of the traditions of ancient Indian polity. The modern Pancayet on the other hand is directly descended, apart from connection or contact with any

[33] See Mukherjee's *Local Government in Anient India* (2nd Ed.), *passim.*

[34] See *Bhandarkar Commemoration Volume*, p. 227. (Essay by Krishna Sastri on *Fiscal Administration under Early Colas*).

[35] *Ibid*, p. 227 (foot-note).

[36] See E. B. Havell's *Ancient and Medieval Architecture of India* (1915), Ch. I "The centre of the village, at the intersection of the two main streets, was the recognised meeting-place for the Council of Elders which regulated local affairs," p. 11. See the sketch-plans given in the chapter.

[37] See Fleet's *Gupta Inscriptions, passim.*

[38] See Kanakasabhai's *Tamils Eighteen Hundred Years Ago*, Ch. IX. See also quotations from *ibid*, pp. 109-110, given in Mazumdar's *Corporate Life*, p. 54.

centralised system of political government, from the ancient Vedic Pancajanah; and it is still a power for good or evil in most Indian villages.

The importance of thus tracing the subsequent developments of the Vedic institutions of tribal and communal life lies in the fact that it throws into relief, with almost startling clearness, a highly significant feature of the ancient Indian state. The state adopts, modifies and perhaps transforms to suit its purpose the existing forms and institutions of communal and social life. Thus the state may very truly be compared to the grain of sand which entering into the flesh of the oyster covers itself with its secretions till it develops into a precious pearl. Abstracted from the life of society, its functions are extraordinarily small. There is a mass of evidence to show that it was the assemblies, which represented the communal life of the people and were in fact its vital and functioning organs, that carried on for the most part the three kinds of functions which we associate with the modern state, *viz.*, (*i*) industrial and commercial, (*ii*) administrative, and (*iii*) social or customary, including civic, educational and religious.[39] We shall briefly refer to some of the salient points of this mass of evidence, chiefly archæological in character, which has been dealt with recently by Dr. R. K. Mookerji and Dr. R. C. Mazumdar in a systematic way :—

(*i*) Since the Vedic age, there had existed all over India guilds of merchants, traders and craftsmen (*Sreni*, *Puga*, etc.). These guilds were autonomous in the sense that the members were bound by their conventional laws (Samaya) which were recognised by the state, that these laws were administered by their own tribunals and that they were practically exempt from state interference. Each guild was recognised by the state as a distinct corporation and used its own seal.[40] The guilds sometimes carried out works of public utility and even maintained military forces of their own (Sreni-vala), presumably for self-protection.[41]

[39] Mukherjee's *Local Government in Ancient India*, 2nd Ed., p. 27.

[40] See *ibid*, pp. 111 ff., where an account of these seals discovered at different places in course of Archæological Surveys, is given.

[41] The expression *Sreni-Vala* has been differently interpreted.
See discussion on the point in Mazumdar's *Corporate Life*, p. 25. I am inclined to accept Dr. Bhandarkar's interpretation.

Sometimes several guilds united in a League or called a general convention.[42] The organisation of these autonomous and semi-political guilds covered the whole country and was found as much in northern India as in the south.

(*ii*) Local Government in ancient India, in its three-fold function, legislative, administrative and judicial, was carried on by Village Assemblies. The village in fact was the self-governing unit of administration in ancient India. It was a recognised principle of inter-state law in ancient India that in times of war the village communities should be spared from molestation. The evidence of the activities of these village communities is ampler in southern India where however they reproduce the same type (even the names of its different limbs like Mahasabha, Sabha, Samuha, etc., agreeing) as found in the North.[43] Sometimes the Village Assembly develops into the District Assembly and the latter into the Divisional Assembly, and there is a reference to a great convention of twelve divisions in a Cola epigraph.[44] The survival of these assemblies even in the eighteenth and nineteenth centuries is attested by the following reference to them by the East India Company's representative at Calicut :—" The Nad or country was a congeries of *teras* or village republics, and the Kuttam or assembly of the Nad or County, was a representative body of immense power which, when necessity existed, set at naught the authority of the Raja and punished his ministers when they did unwarrantable acts."[45] The town was similarly governed in municipal matters by the Town Assembly and in one inscription the assemblies of the Nadu (Division) and Nagar are described as meeting together for the purpose of converting a village into a mercantile town.[46] We have references to other joint conferences between such autonomous

[42] See for instance the inscription dated in the 19th year of Jatavarman Vira Pandya, No. 88 of 1914 (Archæological Survey Report of Southern India, 1913-1915), referred to by Dr. Mukherjee, p. 261.

[43] This " substantial similarity of the organisation in the North and the South " is emphasised by Dr. Mukherjee in his Preface to the first edition (p. xii). "The truth is," says he, " that India is fundamentally one, physically and culturally."

[44] See *ibid*, p. 311.

[45] Quoted in *ibid*, p. 311, from *Malabar Manual*, Vol. 1, p. 89.

[46] See *ibid*, p. 304—" No. 521 of 1912 similarly records that the *Nadu* and *Nagara* of Urrattur-Nadu assembled in the Hall called Uttama-sala Mandapa of a temple and converted a village into a mercantile town."

bodies. The Resolutions passed at these Assemblies are sometimes preserved in South Indian inscriptions which show beyond the shadow of a doubt that they exercised the same powers as departments or offices of state. There still exist all over India the lingering survivals of this indigenous rural system of local self-government,[47] quite distinct from their up-to-date analogues which the British government in India has artificially created by Acts of legislature, "by devolution and delimitation of its own functions."[48]

(*iii*) The social organisation in ancient India was perfectly autonomous as regards the management and administration of its internal affairs, including punishment for infringement of its rules by the members.[49] This autonomous organisation of society is still maintained, under the protection of British neutrality, and is represented by the caste-Pancayet. But it is probably not so commonly known that the so-called mixed castes and untouchable classes often developed into social corporations from originally tribal or clannish corporations which were perfectly autonomous in their organisation. Thus Manu mentions the Nisadas (one of the tribes referred to in Vedic literature), the Sakyas, the Mallas and the Licchavis (described as autonomous tribes in Pali literature) as social classes of Ksatriya and Vratya descent respectively.[50] The strength and vitality of the Pancayet system among such social corporations of lower grades is remarkable even at the present day and is derived in many cases from the institutions of original tribal government. We have few indications of the process by which tribal organisations became social corporations, but one of

[47] Dr. Radha Kamal Mookherjee describes a *Samuham* which he saw in a Brahmin village in Southern India in an article, entitled *Relics of Indigenous Local Government in Modern India* (Dacca Review, May and June number, 1920, p. 35).

[48] *Vide* the various Local Self-Government Acts and Municipal Acts in different provinces. The *Village Self-Government Act* of 1919 created Union Boards in Bengal which resemble the indigenous village *Sabhas* of an earlier age in their judicial and administrative functions.

[49] See Mazumdar's *Corporate Life in Ancient India*, Ch. V.

[50] व्रात्यात् तु जायते विप्रात् पापात्मा भुर्जकण्टकः ।
आवन्त्यवाटधानौ च पुष्पधः शैख एव च ॥
झल्लो मल्लश्च राजन्यात् व्रात्यान्निच्छिविरेव च ।
नटश्च करणश्चैव खसो द्रविड एव च ॥

—*Manu*, X, 21-22

See also Rhys Davids's *Buddhist India*, p. 22. Nisada is mentioned in Manu X, 8.

the most significant of these is found in *Bhaddasala Jataka* which describes incidentally in its introductory portion how the Sakyas met together and discussed how they could avoid breach of clan-custom (kula-vamsa) by giving a daughter of their clan in marriage to the king of Kosala.[51] Now the civic, educational and religious needs of the different castes included in the social organisation were provided for by the caste self-government itself. During the long period of prevalence of Buddhism in ancient India, however, the educational and religious needs of the people were met by Buddhist monasteries which covered the country like a network. These monasteries too were entirely self-governing. Their transactions were called Samgha-kamma (transactions of the community). There were different kinds of Samgha-kamma, disciplinary and non-disciplinary, the manner of carrying out which, as described in the *Vinayapitakam*, clearly shows the perfectly democratic character of these institutions.[52] They were strictly outside the sphere of state interference. A doubt is raised as to this point by Vincent Smith who, relying on the Sarnath edict of Asoka, relating to the 'unfrocking' and expulsion of schismatics describes him as acting, like an Indian Charlemagne, as 'both Emperor and Head of the Church.'[53] But Smith is palpably in error, as the edict is obviously based on a text of Buddhist monastic law embodied in the *Vinayapitakam*, which it was the immemorial constitutional duty of the king to uphold as *Samaya*.[54] "The ancient Dharmasastras associate the 'castes' with other corporations. The organisation of these social corporations seems to have been modelled on the same plan as was adopted by other corporations, the guild, for example. * * *
They served as one of the regular courts in the kingdom for the trial of offenders in the first instance. * * * The most interesting thing, however, in this connection is the fact that

[51] See *Buddhasala Jataka* (No. 465—Cowell and Rouse's Translation, Vol. IV, pp. 91 ff.) See Fausboll's *The Jataka*, Vol. IV, pp. 144 ff.

[52] The rules about Disciplinary and Non-disciplinary Sangha-Kammas are given in the Mahavagga and Cullavagga of the *Vinayapitakam*. See Sukumar Dutt's *Early Buddhist Monachism* (1924). Trubner's Oriental Series.

[53] See Vincent Smith's *Asoka* (Rulers of India Series), 2nd Ed. p. 195.

[54] The text on which Sarnath, Kosambi and Sanchi edicts are based seems to be the following—" Sanghavedako bhikkhave anupasampanno na upasampadetabbo *upasampanno nasotabbo*." Mahavagga, 1, 67.

we have even at the present day reminiscences of the old organisation. There is still the chief, the executive council, the assembly, and the legal validity of the jurisdiction exercised by each of them.''[55]

The summary given above is sufficient to show the extraordinary restrictions on the functions and activities of the state which were imposed by local and communal bodies in ancient India. The state was not the law-giver, but only the administrator of existing laws which were derived both *de facto* and *de jure* from different sources and vested in different independent and autonomous bodies. Even the administration of these laws was carried on for the most part by popular tribunals, the king sometimes retaining the right of hearing appeals [56] or adjudicating between two sovereign bodies or interfering in decisions of autonomous bodies on certain specified and restricted grounds only,[57] or enforcing in particular cases the conventional law of these bodies themselves or trying cases relating to criminal offences (sahasa).[58] It is in the exercise of the right of taxation that the sovereignty of the state is chiefly manifested. It must not however be supposed that monarchy was the only form of state prevalent in ancient India, for, though the *Smritis* contemplate almost exclusively the monarchical state, we have now overwhelming evidence of the existence, side by side, of other forms, such as oligarchy, republic and democracy. It is interesting to find that the imperial government of Chandragupta sought to suppress the other forms of state and Kautilya's *Arthasastra* betrays an unmistakable attitude of hostility

[55] Mazumdar's *Corporate Life in Ancient India*, p. 172.

[56] *Vide* Sloka quoted in Asahaya's commentary on Narada, 1, 11 :

ग्रामे दृष्टः पुरे याति पुरे दृष्टस्तु राजनि।
राज्ञा दृष्टः कुदृष्टो वा नास्ति पौनर्भवो विधिः॥

Also :—

नृपेनाधिकृताः पूगाः श्रेणयोऽथ कुलानि च।
पूर्व्वं पूर्व्वं गुरुज्ञेयं व्यवहारविधौ नृणाम्॥

—Yajnavalkya, II, 31.

[57] See pp. 149-150.

[58] Vrihaspati excludes *Sahasa* from the cognizance of popular tribunals (1.28-30). They were within the exclusive jurisdiction of the king. Yajnavalkya (1.336) thus defines the king's duties :—

चाटुतस्करदुर्व्वृत्तमहासाहसिकादिभिः।
पीड्यमानाः प्रजाः रक्षेत् कायस्थैश्च विशेषतः॥

towards the Sanghas.[59] But tribal and clannish organisations of a republican or democratic character persisted vigorously and survived the break-up of Gupta imperialism.[60] The wonderful persistency of these tribal and clannish political organisations is shown by the rise, after long centuries, of the Rajput tribes and the Marhattas, towards the close of Mogul suzerainty, and it is curious to note the survivals in the Marhatta system of government of the institutions of ancient Hindu monarchy.[61]

As we have already remarked, the character of our sources of knowledge regarding the Mahammadan period of Indian history precludes us from tracing the developments and changes of these autonomous institutions with anything like fulness of outline. Important materials may be discovered with the progress of research into the Hindu empire of Vijaynagar and the administrative system of the Marhattas.[62] But we have to await the results of research to bring to light historical or archæological facts showing the existence and condition of these hoary institutions of ancient Indian polity. So far, we may infer only that the notorious character of Mahammadan rule as primarily fiscal or police administration[63] would have important bearings and results. In the first place, these autonomous bodies would cease to exercise the same constitutional check on monarchy as they were wont to do in

[59] See *Arthasastra*, Book XI (*Sanghavrittam*). Kautilya advises the king to befriend *Sanghas* well-disposed towards him, but to destroy by punishing and sowing dissensions among those that are ill-disposed. He mentions two classes of Sangha वार्त्तशस्त्रोपजीविनः and राजशब्दोपजीविनः. The latter class of Sanghas connote non-monarchical, tribal and clannish organisations.

[60] See Mazumdar's *Corporate Life in Ancient India*, p. 107. Dr. Mazumdar has started a theory that the republican forms of polity were crushed out in the neighbourhood of Magadha by Gupta imperialism, imbued with the principles of Kautilya. Dr. Mazumdar gives an account of political Sanghas which revived after this period. See pp. 113 ff.

[61] This has been pointed out by Dr. Surendra Nath Sen of Calcutta University in a paper contributed to *Sir Ashutosh Mookherjee Silver Jubilee Commemoration Volume*, III.

[62] Researches into the history of Vijayanagara were initiated by Robert Sewell who published his interesting work, *A Forgotten Empire*, in 1900. There are also several learned Essays in the Archæological Survey Reports (1907-8, 1908-9, 1911-12) on the subject by Krishna Shastri. But these researches are not yet complete. See the remarks of Vincent Smith in *Oxford History of India*, p. 300.

To Dr. Surendra Nath Sen must be given the credit for recently initiating researches into the administrative system of the Marhattas. The field is a fertile one and further spade-work is necessary.

[63] "Whether we look at the military or the civil aspect of the system (*i.e.*, Mogul government from Akbar to Auranzeb), it is clear that the Mogul administration in India was even more in the nature of an army of occupation than the camp to which the Ottoman Empire has been compared."

Lane-Poole's *Auranzeb* (Rulers of India Series, 1918), pp. 114-115.

pre-Mahammadan times: thus the rift between them and the Mahammadan State would widen more and more, and with the loss of their constitutional functions, there would be a corresponding loss of cohesion and vitality. In the second place, they would continue to discharge their functions of local self-government, as even now after the lapse of so many centuries, they are found doing in several parts of the country. In fact the traditions of mid-Asian despotism and personal rule, which were introduced into India by the Mahammadans, constituted a definite break with the ancient system and hence Mahammadan government was for the most part of its duration in a state of unstable equilibrium. But it still left the social life of the people and their communal organisation mostly intact, which in fact made the Hindu religious movements during the period of Mahammadan rule perfectly possible, in spite of occasional outbursts of blind fanaticism on the part of the rulers.

What then was the conception of the state in ancient India? As a first step to understanding this conception, we have to realise its difference from the western idea of the state. Sovereignty or "the power of ultimately determining its own legal competence" has been held to be the essential quality of the state in western political science. It is thus explicated by Dr. Willoughby[64]:—

(1) That sovereignty signifies the exclusive power of the State to determine its own rights and attributes.

(2) That sovereignty being the supreme will of the State is indivisible and inalienable.

(3) That all law is expressive of the will of the State and is in essence a command directed by a political superior to a political inferior,—from a sovereign to a subject.

So strong indeed is this conception of sovereignty as the essence of the state-idea that even that anomalous creation of politics, the Federal State, of which the United States of America is the best example, is endowed with this attribute of sovereignty by a sort of legal fiction. Abraham Lincoln took shelter behind such a legal fiction when in his first message to the Congress, he pointed out the relation between the State and the Union[65]: "The states

[64] See Willoughby's *The Nature of the State*, p. 240.
[65] Quoted in *ibid*, p. 254.

have their status in the Union and they have no other legal status. The Union is older than any of the states and in fact created them as states,"—which is undoubtedly untrue as a matter of history.

Now the expression and manifestation of this sovereignty of the state has been believed, almost as an axiom of jurisprudence and political philosophy, to be legislation. From Austin to Wilson is a long stretch of time and a considerable period of political evolution. Yet we find Woodrow Wilson echoing Austin from the other shore of the Atlantic. "Sovereignty," says Wilson, "is the daily operative power of framing and giving efficacy to laws. It is the originative, directive, governing power. It lives; it plans; it executes. It is the organic organisation by the state of its law and policy; and the sovereign power is the highest originative organ of the state. It is nonetheless sovereign because it must be observant of the preferences of those whom it governs. The obedience of the subject has always limited the power of the sovereign."[66]

As a matter of fact, the whole history of politics in western countries has turned round the locus of this theoretical sovereignty of the state. The question as to where the state's sovereignty resides or ought to reside has been the fighting issue on which momentous changes in European politics have turned. The central part of political philosophy is occupied with this discussion and when Louis XIV of France sought to clinch it by his monumental doctrine of *L'etat c'est moi*, fault was found in his arrogating a quality which should properly reside in the people and not in a person. But the sovereignty of the state was undisputed; the moot-point was about the exact location of it in the body politic.

Judged by these fundamental ideas about the state in western political philosophy, the state in ancient India would appear to be *sui generis*. It does not in fact satisfy at all the test of sovereignty. From a consideration of the facts we have dealt with above, it is evident that the state did not enjoy the exclusive power to determine its own rights and attributes. Rather these rights and

[66] Woodrow Wilson in *An Old Matter and Other Essays*. (Quoted by Willoughby, pp. 307.8.)

attributes were predetermined for it by existing autonomous corporations which divided its sovereignty. As we have already said, these corporations did not enjoy their powers of legislation by devolution from the state, but by immemorial custom. There are instances no doubt to show that in certain cases the Resolutions of the Corporations required for their validity the sanction or order of the king.[67] But political theory was different, and it is effectively proved by important exceptions. *Exceptio probat regulam.* In nearly all Sanskrit law-books, the king is enjoined to preserve the *Dharma* of Desa, Kula, Jati, and Sangha.[68] These catagories are intended to cover all kinds of autonomous corporations based on the territorial or the communal principle. This is the standing constitutional rule and we shall observe how the rule is substantially proved by the exceptions mentioned by Narada (X. 4-6). According to this law-giver, cases for royal interference with the workings of these corporations arise only under certain specified circumstances, *e.g.*, when they are hostile to the king, when they are unnatural, when they are opposed to economy, etc.[69] The passage has been clearly explained by the commentator who says that the text serves to exclude the king's duty of upholding such Resolutions (प्रतिज्ञा) as "we shall forbid the subjects to pay revenue to the king," "we shall speed along the royal road," "we shall worship at a place where there is *sakhotaka*," etc.[70] The implication of this commentary is clear. The king was constitutionally

57 See instances given in Mazumdar's *Corporate Life in Ancient India*, pp. 81-82.

58 See pp. 157-159.

69 प्रतिकूलञ्च यद्राज्ञः प्रकृत्यवमतं च यत् ।
बाधकञ्च यदर्थानां तत्तेभ्यो विनिवर्त्तयेत् ॥
मिथः संघातकरणं अहिते शस्त्रधारणम् ।
परस्परोपघातं च तेषां राजा न मर्षयेत् ॥
दोषवत् करणं यत् स्यादनाम्नाय प्रकल्पितं ।
प्रवृत्तमपि तद्राजा श्रेयस्कामो निवर्त्तयेत् ॥

70 पाषण्डादिभिर्या या संवित् मिलित्वा कृता या सैव चेद् रक्षणीया । तदतिक्रमी तु ते राज्ञा दण्ड्यास्तदा (*i*) वयं सर्व्वे राज्ञे करदानं वारयाम इति (*ii*) अस्माभिः सर्व्वदा नग्नै र्भाव्यमिति (*iii*) द्यूतं चरिष्याम इति (*iv*) वेश्यां रमयिष्याम इति (*v*) राजपथे सवेगं धावाम इति (*vi*) शखोटकस्थलं पूजयामीत्यादि प्रतिज्ञा अपि अवश्यं रक्ष्यन्तामिति तन्निरासाय वचनमिदमिति ।

bound by all the Resolutions of the corporations unless they infringed the principle of *salus populi est suprema lex.*[71]

Some interesting inscriptions from Southern India show the force of this constitutional rule.[72] In order to reward officers or endow temples or for other purposes, the king had often to make grants of land. But these grants had to be put into effect by the village assembly. The officer in charge of royal grants called the *Adhikarin* had to go to the spot, communicate the king's grant to the assembly, who would then meet together to ratify the same, put their signatures to it and would proceed as a constituted body to give effect to it. The most striking and interesting of these inscriptions is the Manalikkarai Inscription of Keralavarman (1234-35 A.D.), where the king issues a proclamation purporting to make some arrangements about the revenue, " agreeably to the understanding arrived at " in a consultation duly held among the ruling chieftains, the members of the Sabha, the people of the village and the local revenue officers of the crown.[73] It is significant of the *locus standi* of the Sabha that it had a voice even in revenue arrangements. When we remember that the autonomous corporations did not enjoy their legal status by devolution from the state, the conclusion from above considerations becomes irresistible that sovereignty of the state in ancient India was not by constitution indivisible and inalienable.

The crucial test however of the sovereignty of the state is its power of making and enforcing laws. A comparative study of the sources of law in the jurisprudence of the west and of India respectively would yield remarkable results bearing on this point. Now the expression, ' source of law ' (*fons juris*), has several meanings. As Salmond says, " We must distinguish in the first place between the ' formal ' and the ' material ' sources of the law. A formal source is that from which a rule of law derives its force and validity. It is that from which the authority of the law proceeds. The material sources, on the other hand, are those from which is derived the matter, not the validity, of the law. The material source

[71] The texts of Dharmasastras on this point are collected in Mookherjee's *Local Government in Ancient India*, Ch. IV.

[72] These inscriptions are referred to in *ibid*, pp. 238-239. Also Mazumdar's *Corporate Life in Ancient India*, p. 82.

[73] See *Indian Antiquary*, pp. 300 ff. which is quoted in Mazumdar's *Corporate Life in Ancient India*, pp. 70-71.

supplies the substance of the rule to which the formal source gives the force and nature of law."[74] From Austin downwards, writers on jurisprudence have identified this formal source of law with the sovereignty of the state : it is the sanction of the state that invests, according to them, a rule of conduct with the force and validity of a law. Now it will be observed that to ancient Indian jurisprudence this idea is altogether foreign. In the *Smritis* we find various enumerations of sources of law which signify for the most part what Salmond calls the material sources, but the question of the source of validity of the laws derived from these diverse sources is set at rest by the well-known text of Jaimini whose *Purva-mimansa* is universally regarded as the sole exegetic authority on Hindu Law :

धर्मस्य शब्दमूलत्वादशब्दमनपेक्ष्यं स्यात्। अपि वा कर्तृसामान्यात् प्रमाणमनुमानं स्यात्। विरोधेत्वनपेक्ष्यं स्यादसति ह्यनुमानं। हेतुदर्शनाच्च।

Translation.—(It may be contended) that as the words of Revelation form the foundation of Law, therefore that (such as the Smriti) which is not embodied in such words should not be regarded as authority. But (the answer is) the Smritis being compiled by sages who were also the repositories of the Revelation (from which it was handed down by tradition until recorded in writing), there arises an inference that the Smritis are founded on the Sruti or Revelation and therefore (they should be regarded as authority). But if there be conflict (of any precept of the Smriti with one of the Sruti) the Smriti must be disregarded (as spurious), also, when there is found a reason (for fabricating it, such as the covetousness of priests or the like).[75]

Thus the formal source (**मूल**) of law in ancient India was divine Revelation (**शब्द**) and this conception of formal source which gave authority and validity to the laws was stretched to cover even the large body of customary law (**सदाचार**) by the presumption of their being based on unrecorded Revelation.[76]

There is thus a fundamental difference between Indian and western jurisprudence. As G. C. Sastri says, "The idea of

[74] Salmond's *Jurisprudence* (4th Ed.), p. 117.
[75] Quoted in G. C. Sastri's *Hindu Law* (4th Ed.), p. 4.
[76] See *ibid*, pp. 20-21.

sovereign in the modern juridical sense was unknown to them (the Hindus). They had kings, but their function was defined by the divine law contained in the Smritis and they were bound to obey the self-same law, equally with their subjects. By this original theory of its origin, the law was independent of the State, or rather the State was dependent on law, as the king was to be guided in all matters connected with government by the revealed law, though he was not excluded from a control over the administration of justice. The king being theoretically the administrator of justice, his decrees must have been recognised as binding on suitors from the very earliest times. And this gradually introduced the view recognised by commentators that royal edicts in certain matters have as much binding force as divine law, should the former be not repugnant to the latter.''[77] This recognition of the king's legislative power, if it is such at all, found in the following text of Manu, VII, 13—

तस्माद्धर्म्मं यमिष्टेषु स व्यवस्येन्नराधिपः ।
अनिष्टं चाप्यनिष्टेषु तं धर्म्मं न विचालयेत् ॥

was in fact wholly incongruous with the principles of Hindu jurisprudence. This was fully realised by the commentators. Medhatithi therefore restricts this power to passing executive orders only in the illustrations that he gives. He interprets 'Dharma' in this passage as **कार्य्यव्यवस्था** such as the following orders :[78]

(*i*) To-day let all people observe festivities in the town.

[77] *Ibid*, pp. 11-12.

[78] यतः सर्व्वतेजोमयो राजा तस्माद्धेतोरिष्टेषु वल्लभेषु मन्त्रिपुरोहितादिषु कार्य्यगत्या धर्म्मं कार्य्यव्यवस्थां शास्त्राचाराविरुद्धां व्यवसेन्निश्चित्य स्थापयेन्नविचालयेत् । या तादृशी राज्ञोऽनुज्ञानतिक्रमणीया ।

(*i*) अद्य पुरे सर्व्वैरुत्सवः कर्त्तव्यः ।

(*ii*) मन्त्रीगेहे विवाहो वर्त्तते तत्र सर्व्वैः सन्निधातव्यम् ।

(*iii*) तथा पशवो नाद्य सैनिकैर्हन्तव्याः ।

(*iv*) न शकुनयोरन्ध्ययितव्याः ।

(*v*) नर्त्तिका धनिकैराराधनीया । एतावन्त्यहानि । एवमनिष्टेष्वपि ।

(*vi*) एतेन संसर्गो न कर्त्तव्यः ।

(*vii*) एतस्य गृहे प्रवेशो न देयः

एवम्विधो धर्म्म पटहघोषादिना राज्ञादिष्टो नातिक्रमणीयः ।

नत्वग्निहोत्रादि-धर्म्मव्यवस्थायै वर्णाश्रमिनां राजा प्रभवति ।

(*ii*) There being a marriage ceremony at the house of the minister, all should attend it.

(*iii*) Soldiers must not kill animals to-day.

(*iv*) Vultures should not be blinded (*e.g.*, their eyes should not be gouged,—perhaps referring to a usual form of cruelty to animals).

(*v*) Rich men should entertain dancing girls for so many days only.

(*vi*) People should not mix with this man.

(*vii*) No entrance into his house.

The passage of Manu in fact is obscure and is susceptible of different interpretations.[79] "It is significant," says Dr. Sen-Gupta, "that this slight recognition of the king's legislative powers has not been enlarged upon in subsequent times, and in all the elaborate disquisitions on the sources of law that we find among the commentators we do not see the king even once mentioned. Commentators like Raghavananda moreover attempt to explain away the text altogether."[80]

The Edicts of Asoka have not yet been studied from this constitutional point of view. The fact that most of these edicts proceed from a Buddhist Emperor does not imply that the principles regulating the functions of a king as laid down in the Dharmasastras do not apply to them. These principles were abstracted from immemorial constitutional practice and were not evolved out of the heads of the Brahmin legists, as was supposed by an earlier school of European writers on Hindu law, now thoroughly discredited, represented by Nelson.[81] A study of the

[79] See the Commentaries of Medhatithi, Sarvajna-Narayana, Kulluka, Raghavananda, Nandana and Ramachandra in Mandlik's *editio princeps of Manu, loc. cit.*

Of. Raghavananda—इष्टेषु प्रियेषु धर्मं यथेश्वमर्हंत्ययमेवं नाहंतीति व्यवस्थापयेत् । स्थापयितुस्तं प्रौढ्यादिना न चालयेत् यतः क्रुद्धो हन्ति प्रयत्नोऽनुग्रहणीयान् । Burnell's translation—"Therefore let the king never alter the rule, either the law he arranges for those he loves or the punishment for those he dislikes."

[80] Gupta's *Sources of Law and Society in Ancient India*, p. 81.

[81] See Nelson's *Prospectus of a Scientific Study of Hindu Law.*

Asokan edicts from this angle is likely to yield remarkable results.

These edicts, so far as up-to-date researches in archæology go, are *sui generis* in Indian history. Whether they were inspired by the example of Darius, as Smith suggests, is a problem for further research.[82] But a study of them from a constitutional point of view may help a good deal towards elucidating the peculiar style in which they are couched and the spirit in which they are conceived. We find few mandatory rules in them, the majority edicts of a mandatory character we find :
being of a recommendatory or preceptive character.[83] Among

(*i*) those relating to the employment of supervisory officers (Rock Edict III, V; Pillar Edict IV);

(*ii*) those relating to the regulation of the Buddhist Sangha (Sarnath Edict; Kausambi Edict; Sanchi Edict);

(*iii*) those relating to animal sacrifice and cruelty to animals (Rock Edict I; Pillar Edict V).

As regards (*i*), we have already seen that the supervisory powers of the king were sanctioned and established by constitutional principle and practice. They were incidental to the king's main duty of preserving the Dharma, and Asoka himself is anxious to explain this constitutional position in Pillar Edict VII. His efforts, as he is careful to explain, are in consonance with the conception of the king's duties and obligations as entertained by his predecessors. As regards (*ii*) also, we have seen that Asoka laid down in these edicts not his own law, but a rule of the conventional law of the Buddhist Sangha itself. The enforcement of conventional law (Samaya) was part of the king's constitutional duty, as laid down in various texts of the Dharmasastras. The most interesting of the edicts, from this point of view, are no doubt those referred to under (*iii*). Being a devout Buddhist and committed absolutely to the doctrine of non-killing, Asoka might have laid down a law penalising the killing of animals, if he had the

[82] See Vincent Smith's *Asoka*, p. 141.
[83] The edicts may be consulted in Hultzch's *Inscriptions of Asoka*, 1925, in *Corpus Inscriptionum Indicarum*, New Edition.

power to legislate. But we find him on the other hand in Pillar Edict V, imposing certain restrictions only on wanton killing of or cruelty to animals, and in Rock Edict I, preventing animal-sacrifice at Pataliputra only. (The word, *Idha*, ' here,' in this edict is important and significant.) Now the question arises,—was not the Emperor legislating in these edicts? It cannot be satisfactorily answered without exhaustive researches which the plan and purpose of the present work preclude. But there are certain indications to show that even in these edicts, Asoka was not playing the forbidden role of a legislator. Perhaps in Pillar Edict V, Asoka was only promulgating extant law as to animal-killing. The following passages from the Edict (in Vincent Smith's translation) may be read side by side with passages from the *Arthasastra* (in Shama Sastri's translation), bearing on the law *re* animal-killing which must have been extant long before Asoka's time :—

(1) *Asoka*—She-goats, ewes and sows, that is to say, those either with young or in milk, are exempt from slaughter as well as their offspring up to six months of age (*Asoka*, p. 187).

Arthasastra—He (the king) should prohibit the slaughter of females and young ones (p. 492).

(2) *Asoka*—On the 8th, 14th, 15th days of each fortnight as well as on the Tishya and Punarvasu days, and festival days, the castration of bulls must not be performed, nor may he-goats, rams, boars and other animals liable to castration be castrated (*ib.*, p. 187).

Arthasastra—(Castration prohibited) p. 492.

(3) *Asoka*—At each of the three seasonal full moons, and at the full moon of the month Tishya, for three days in each, namely, the 14th and 15th days of the first fortnight as well as on the fast days throughout the year, fish must not be killed and on the same days in elephant-preserves or fish-ponds no other classes of animals may be destroyed (p. 188).

Arthasastra—He (the king) should prohibit the slaughter of animals for half a month during the period of *Chaturmasya*, for four nights during the full moon, and for a night on the day of the birth-star of the conqueror or of the national star (?) (p. 492).

There are some other prohibitions and restrictions in the edict which may perhaps be traced in earlier law, if diligently searched.[84] There is in the same edict a long list of birds and beasts which the Emperor declares exempt from slaughter. It is interesting to compare this list with another list of beasts and birds given in *Parasara-Samhita*, VI, 2-14, the killing of which involves various degrees of penance, and also the list of animals, slaughter of which involves penalties in *Arthasastra*, Book II, Ch. XXVI. Many of the names tally.

The crux of the problem however is the prevention of sacrificial killing in Rock Edict I. But, being an order confined to a particular locality, *viz.*, Pataliputra, it cannot perhaps be considered properly as a law at all and is to be equiparated with such orders (**कार्य्यव्यवस्था**) as 'soldiers must not kill animals to-day,' that Medhathiti mentions in his commentary on Manu, VII, 13, as being within the competence of the king to pass.[85] The definition of law in western jurisprudence also is that it should be an order passed by a sovereign authority relating to a general course of conduct, unrestricted in its incidence as to time, place or person.[86]

In any case, there is some reason for thinking that the edicts of Asoka were not an unwarranted arrogation and exercise of the power of legislation by the king; that Asoka was bound by the standing constitutional restrictions on the functions of the king, and also that the fact of his being a Buddhist, made not the slightest difference in this respect.

[84] Such as burning chaff with living things in it, branding of animals, etc.

[85] This suggestion is put forward with a good deal of hesitation. I cannot be sure of my ground that the word, *Idha*, was actually meant to be so important in the context as it appears to me from a constitutional point of view.

[86] See Holland's *Jurisprudence*.

In the epics and the *Smritis*, the State is centred in and represented by the king. The virtues of kingship are extolled up to the plane of divine attributes. Yet sovereignty, as defined by Woodrow Wilson, *viz.*, "the daily operative power of framing and giving efficacy to laws" never rests in him. It is thus apparent that the conception of the state in ancient India was fundamentally different from its conception in the west.

In order however to understand the ancient Indian theory of the state, we have to rely on political philosophy which is concerned with one form of the state only, *viz.*, monarchy. It is now common knowledge that there were different forms of state prevalent in ancient India; but researches into them are not yet complete and it would be extremely hazardous to theorise on them in the present imperfect state of our knowledge. Even in the literature that bears exclusively on monarchy, we may discover curious hints and suggestions of the existence of other political forms. Thus the existence of oligarchy is admitted in the following passage in Kautilya's *Arthasastra*, which is exclusively devoted to a discussion of the monarchical form of government.[87]

कुलस्य वा भवेद्राजा कुलसङ्घो हि दुर्जयः ।
अराजव्यसनाबाधः शश्वदावसते क्षितिम् ॥

Some of these non-monarchical forms are mentioned in Book XI, entitled सङ्घवृत्तम् in which the Machiavellian means by which hostile Sanghas are to be overcome or circumvented are dwelt on, *viz.*:[88]

लिच्छिविकवृजिकमल्लकमद्रककुकुरकुरुपाञ्चालादयो राजशब्दोपजीविनः ।

There is a curious passage in the *Mahabharata*, describing the origin of kingship, in the course of which it is said that in primitive times anarchy had prevailed among people, to avoid which they met together and resolved that men guilty of certain offences should be ostracised and, having made that Resolution, they lived together

[87] *Arthasastra* (Shama Shastri's Ed.), p. 35.
[88] *Ibid*, p. 378.

adhering to it in mutual trust among all the *varnas* without distinction.[89]

अराजकाः प्रजाः पूर्व्वं विनेशुरिति नः श्रुतम् ।
परस्परं भक्षयन्तो मत्स्या इव जले कृशान् ॥
समेत्य तास्ततश्चक्रुः समयानिति नः श्रुतम् ।
वाक्शूरो दण्डपरुषो यश्च स्यात् पारजायिकः ॥
यः परस्वमथादद्यात् त्याज्या नस्तादृशा इति ।
विश्वासार्थञ्च सर्व्वेषां वर्णानामविशेषतः ।
तास्तथा समयं कृत्वा समयेनावतस्थिरे ॥

When we remember that the word *Samaya* (Agreement) is used in the Dharmasastras in a legal sense to indicate the Resolutions or Laws of corporate bodies[90] and also the character of the particular Resolution, mentioned in the foregoing verses, which is a rule of positive law, we discover in this passage an unmistakable indication of the recognition of a democratic form of polity. But among all the diverse forms of polity prevalent in ancient India, it is the monarchical form that seems to have attained the highest development.

In the *Arthasastras* of Kautilya, in the *Neeti-sastras* of Sukra and Kamandaka, in the *Dharmasastras* of Manu, Yajnavalkya, Goutama and others, in the *Mahabharata* and elsewhere, we have the political philosophy of monarchy elaborately discussed. There is a substantial agreement of ideas and principles among them which shows that the constitutional ideas they embody were well settled and persistent.

The *raison d'etre* of kingship in its origin, growth and development is held to be the preservation of social economy. The theory about the origin of kingship is that monarchy was instituted to prevent a state of disintegration in society, marked by *Matsya-nyaya*, *i.e.*, the principle of 'might is right.'[91]

[89] Mahabharata : Santiparva—Rajadharma, Ch. 67, 17-19.
[90] See p. 158.
[91] मात्स्यन्यायाभिभूताः प्रजा मनुं वैवस्वतं राजानं चक्रिरे ।
अराजकाः प्रजा सर्व्वं विनेशुरिति नः श्रुतम् ।
—*Arthasastra*, p. 22.
परस्परं भक्षयन्तो मत्स्या इव जले कृशान् ॥
—*Mahabharata* (*quoted supra*).

The king was sent by Heaven to hold in check " the good old rule, the simple plan, that they should take who have the power and they should keep who can." This original idea regulates and determines all the functions of the king. They are summed up in the expression, *Danda*, which is extolled, glorified and sanctified as being the result of divine ordination.[92] This *Danda* or power of coercion which is symbolised by the royal sceptre (*Raja-danda*) is the principle by enforcement of which people are kept to their respective status in life, and society is saved from flying apart.[93] The king is under the unavoidable obligation of protecting the people, this obligation being a contractual one in return for the revenue which the subjects pay him.[94]

The king is regarded primarily as the bond of society. He ' contains ' the people—as Kautilya expresses it, **कूटस्थानीयो हि**

[92] दण्डो हि केवलो लोकं परं चेमं च रक्षति ।

—*Arthasastra*, p. 150.

दण्डः शास्ति प्रजाः सर्व्वा दण्ड एवाभिरक्षति ।
दण्डः सुप्तेषु जागर्त्ति दण्डं धर्म्मं विदुर्बुधाः ॥
दण्डः संरक्षते धर्म्मं तथैवार्थं जनाधिप ।
कामं संरक्षते दण्डस्त्रिवर्गो दण्ड उच्यते ॥

—*et seq.*
—*Mahabharata, Santiparva,*
Rajadharma, 15.2-3.

See also *Mahabharata*, Santiparva : Rajadharma, Ch. 122, in which the origin of *Danda* is related. God is said to have incarnated himself in *Danda* :

ततः स भगवान् ध्यात्वा चिरं शूलवरायुधः ।
आत्मानमात्मना दण्डं संसृजे देवसत्तमः ॥

—Ch. 112, v. 24.

See also *Manu*, VII, 17-32.

[93] *E.g.*,

चातुर्व्वर्ण्याश्रमो लोको राज्ञा दण्डेन पालितः ।
स्वधर्म्मकर्म्माभिरतो वर्त्तते स्वेषु वर्त्मसु ॥

—*Arthasastra*, p. 9.

Parallel passages may be cited from the *Mahabharata* and *Manu*.

[94] See P. Banerjee's *Public Administration in Ansient India*, p. 73, and the references cited there.

स्वामी.[95] He is called धर्म्मप्रवर्त्तक because he maintains social order ; *e.g.*,

चतुर्वर्णाश्रमस्यायं लोकस्याचाररक्षणात् ।
नश्यतां सर्व्वधर्म्मानां राजाधर्म्मप्रवर्त्तकः ॥[96]

This social order is protected and preserved by the king's *Danda* :

राज्ञः स्वधर्म्मः स्वर्गाय प्रजा धर्म्मेण रक्षितुः ।
अरक्षितुर्वा क्षेप्तुर्वा मिथ्यादण्डमतोऽन्यथा ॥
दण्डोहि केवलो लोकं परं क्षेमं च रक्षति ।
राज्ञा पुत्रे च शत्रौ च यथादोषं समं धृतः ॥[97]

Protection (*i.e.*, of the social order) is the sum of the king's functions,—as Vasistha expresses it compendiously स्वधर्मो राज्ञः पालनम्[98]

Now it is important to consider what this function of the king amounts to. Society in ancient India, as we know, was an aggregation of several autonomous units, formed on different principles of association. Castes, guilds, village-communities, religious societies and such other corporations were the units of which society was composed. The king, as the representative of the state, preserved this composite economy of social life,—kept its different parts and organs in their settled order. The unitary cells of the body politic had each its own function and vitality and the state represented the principle of protection by coercive power which co-ordinated them for the general weal. This idea finds clear expression in *Yajnavalkya* I, 461 :

कुलानि जातीः श्रेणीश्च गणान् जानपदांस्तथा ।
स्वधर्म्मचालितान् राजा विनीय स्थापयेत् पथि ॥

So in *Vasistha*, XIX :

देशधर्म्मजातिधर्म्मकुलधर्म्मान् सर्व्वान् वैतानुप्रविश्य ।
राजा चतुरो वर्णान् स्वधर्म्मे स्थापयेत् । तेष्वधर्म्मपरेषु
दण्डन्तु देशकालधर्म्माधर्म्मवयोविद्यास्थानविशेषैर्दिशेत् ।

This fundamental idea determines in fact the character of kingship. It is neither the function nor the competence of the king to originate the law (Dharma). The Law is antecedent and

[95] *Arthasastra*; p. 322.
[96] *Ibid*, p. 150.
[97] *Ibid*, p. 150.
[98] *Vasistha*, Ch. 19.

superior to the state. The head of the state is only to see that the laws of the different corporate units of society are properly observed and to punish infringements thereof. Hence *Danda* or power of coercion is the sole power vested in him, and also the judicial powers that are its necessary concomitants. We have said already that the units of ancient Indian society were autonomous in character. The laws regulating the affairs of these units are therefore properly designated as Samaya (Agreement). Apastamba and Gautama use the word in an extended sense and designate all the rules of the Dharmasastra as *Samayacarika Dharma*,[99] which is explained thus by the commentator Haradatta :

पौरुषेयी व्यवस्था समयः। समयमूला आचाराः एवम्भूतान् धर्म्मान्।

But the word, *Samaya*, usually means what is known in jurisprudence as Conventional Law.[100] Conventional Law in fact as well as in theory stood in ancient Indian jurisprudence on a different footing : its authority was absolute and independent of recognition by the state. The king was only to see to the proper observance of the *Samaya* which is thus explained by Narada :

पाखण्डिनैगमादीनां स्थितिः समय उच्यते।
समयस्यानपाकर्म्म तद्विवादपदं स्मृतः॥
पाखण्डिनैगमश्रेणीपूगव्रातगणादिषु।
संरक्षेत् समयं राजा दुर्गे जनपदे तथा॥
यो धर्म्मः कर्म्म यच्चैषामुपस्थानविधिश्च यः।
यच्चैषां वृत्त्युपादानमनुमन्येत तत् तथा॥

So, even according to Manu, who stretches the king's power to its utmost limit, giving him power to legislate even against the fundamental principles of Hindu jurisprudence, the king's Dharma

[99] See *Apastamba, I, 1, 1*; Gautama, VIII—

षट्सु वा समयाचारिकेष्वभिविनीतः

[100] " By Conventional Law is meant any rule or system of laws agreed upon by persons for the regulation of their conduct towards each other.........In many cases conventional law is also civil law ; for the rules which persons by mutual agreement lay down for themselves are often enforced by state." Salmond's *Jurisprudence* (4th Ed.), pp. 54-55.

must be in accordance with the Dharmas of Jati, Janapada, Sreni and Kula :

जातिजानपदान् धर्म्मान् श्रेणीधर्म्मांश्च धर्म्मवित् ।
समीक्ष्य कुलधर्म्मांश्च स्वधर्म्मं प्रतिपालयेत् ॥

The same idea is found in Gautama, XI, where the king's judicial functions are referred to :

वर्णाश्रमांश्च न्यायतोऽभिरक्षेच्चलतश्चैनान् स्वधर्म्मे स्थापयेत् ।
* * तस्य व्यवहारो वेदो धर्म्मशास्त्राण्यङ्गान्युपवेदाः
पुराणं देशजातिकुलधर्म्माश्चाम्नायैरविरुद्धाः प्रमाणं
कृषिवणिकपाशुपाल्यकुसीदकारवः स्वे स्वे वर्गे तेभ्यो
यथाधिकारमर्थान् प्रत्यवहृत्य धर्म्मव्यवस्था न्यायाधिगमे
तर्कोऽभ्युपायस्तेनाभ्यूह्य यथास्थानं गमयेत् । etc.

Gautama here refers to Agriculturists, Merchants, Cowherds, Money-lenders and Artists. We know from numerous inscriptions that they had guilds of their own and the laws of these guilds were recognised as binding upon them in law-suits in royal courts. In such cases the king had to call in the aid of experts in order to inform himself about the law, so Jimutavahana says on the authority of old texts :

येषान्तु समयादेव वहुशो व्यवस्था तेषां समयज्ञै रेव
व्यवहारस्य निर्णयः कर्त्तव्यः ।[101]

Such texts may be easily multiplied. The constitutional position of the monarch as revealed in these texts throws a good deal of light on a passage in the *Mahabharata* where the king is described as *paratantra* (dependent on or led by others) in all matters, even in passing executive orders.[102]

[101] *Vyavahara-Matrika*, edited by Sir Asutosh Mukherjee in the Memoirs of A. S. B., Vol. III, No. 5, p. 281.

[102] परतन्त्रः सदा राजा स्वल्पेष्वपि प्रसज्जते ।
सन्धिविग्रहयोगे च कुतो राज्ञः स्वतन्त्रता ॥
* * * * *
यदा त्वाज्ञापयत्यन्यांस्तत्रास्योक्ता स्वतन्त्रता ।
अवशः कार्य्यते तत्र तस्मिंस्तस्मिन् क्षणे स्थितः ॥
—*Mahabharata*, Santiparva, Moksadharmaparva, Ch. 320, vv. 138-140

As we have already remarked, our information regarding non-monarchical states is up till now extremely meagre. Further researches will probably show that the political theory of these states also was the same. Perhaps an indication in this direction is found in *Mahaparinibbana Suttanta* I, 4. It is evident from this passage that one of the non-monarchical states in Buddha's time was that of the Vijjis, whom Ajatasattu, king of Magadha, wanted to invade. The king sent his prime-minister Vassakara to Buddha to confer about the matter. Buddha informed Vassakara that, while sojourning at Vesali, he had instructed the Vijjis in seven principles conducive to welfare (satta aparihaniya dhamma). One of these was that they should "enact nothing not already established, abrogate nothing enacted, and act according to the ancient institutions of the Vijjis as established in former days (appanattam na pannapessanti pannattam na samucchindissanti yatha pannatte porane *vijjidhamme samadaya vattissanti*). This shows that the power of initiating legislation of the Vijjians was as much restricted as that of a king.

We are thus in a position to realise the vast fundamental difference between the idea of the state in western and in Indian polities respectively. The principles that they represent, the organs and institutions which embody these principles, the functions and activities of the state by which they are worked out in practice, differ vastly and fundamentally. It is curious to find that even in western political philosophy, new thought-currents are setting in, the drift of which seems to be, though vague and unconscious at present, in the direction of the state-ideal of ancient India. A recently published treatise of political philosophy, entitled the *New State*, may be cited as typical of this trend of political thought. "One of the characteristics of present political theory," writes the author, "is its reaction against the state, and a salient fact to-day is the increasing amount and power of group-life—trade-unions, professional societies, citizens' leagues, neighbourhood associations, etc. * * * Group organisation is to be the solution of popular government. * * * The study of the group process * * * shows us that politics cannot be founded on representative or electoral methods, but must rest on vital modes of association."[103] What is described in the passage quoted above represents exactly the political ideas of the ancient Indians, and it is extremely interesting to observe how the wheel comes full circle and the old State in India comes back to be the 'New State' in western political thought. If an epigrammatic statement of the difference between the ancient Indian state and the modern western state were needed, we might say that while the latter is the expression and embodiment of the principle of sovereignty, the former was that of the principle of co-ordination in social life.

Now politics arise out of the relation between state and society, and the fundamental difference in the nature of this relation in India from what it is in the west accounts for the well-known attitude of the Indian mind in matters of politics. Vincent Smith says, "The political history of India cannot vie with that of Greece, Rome or modern Europe as illustrating the evolution of constitutions in city or state."[104] The learned historian hardly realises that in comparing Greece, Rome or modern Europe with India, as regards political evolution, he is leaving out of account an essential factor, *viz.*, the difference of group psychology brought about by the different manner of evolution of social and political life. The conditions which determined this evolution in India are special and perhaps unique, and it is in these conditions that we must seek for rational explanation of the fact, noted by Vincent Smith, that "Indians usually have been content with simple despotic rule." It cannot be accounted for by intellectual inertness of the Indians. The truth is that so long as the social life of the people could freely express and realise itself in corporate organisations and activities, the changes of kings, royal dynasties and forms of government mattered little to them. Politics had restricted spheres of action among the various types of association, which were practically free from state-interference. They

[103] See M. P. Follet's *The New State*: *Group Organisation the Solution of Popular Government* (Longmans, March, 1919). The Group-theory of the State has for some years past been gaining ground in European politics. What is called 'Guild-Socialism' is one of the forms of this theory. "What is clear," says Barkar, "is that the idea of the Guild—whether, as with Mr. Bellock, it is only the shield and cover of peasant proprietorship, or, as with the authors of Guild-Socialism, the essential organisation of a life in which the guild fills and permeates the whole mind, is the idea of the hour"—*Political Thought from Spencer to To-day* (Home University Series—1915), p. 233

[104] Smith's *Early History of India* (3rd Ed.), p. 377.

derived indeed a good deal of their vitality from the state, and it is quite probable that the establishment of the alien form of despotic personal rule by the Mahammadans cut off this source of energy and vigour, causing them to degenerate and decay for a long period of Indian history. But at the same time the very military and police character of this rule largely assured to them freedom from interference and allowed them room to continue their existence.

This persistent social life of the people, so firmly rooted to the soil, so umbrageous in the amplitude of its branches and foliage, and so strong and broad of girth, the growth of centuries, has been idealised as the 'Swadeshi Samaj' by Rabindranath Tagore.[105] "The government in our country, the *Sarkar*, has no relations with our social organisation—the *Samaj*," says Tagore, "so that whatever we may seek from the former must be paid for out of our own freedom. From whichever of its duties our Samaj seeks relief by getting it done by the Sarkar, to that extent will it be disabled with an incapability which was not of its essence in the past. To-day we are striving, of our own accord, to place in the hands of the Sarkar the whole duty of our Samaj"[106] this last statement being almost an echo of what Mr. Carstairs had said in connection with modern local self-government, *viz.*, "without the people, the Government can do nothing; without the Government, the people will do nothing."[107] The passage quoted from Tagore has a double significance—first, it shows exactly the old mentality of the Indians with regard to the state; secondly, it alludes to a change in this mentality which we hope to explain in the next chapter. This psychological change, hinted by the poet, has in fact an important bearing on the meaning of Indian nationality. Without deeply studying this change, we cannot understand at all what the expression means, far less summarily dispose of it by hasty generalisations about the non-political attitude of the Indian mind.

[105] Tagore's *Greater India* (*Our Swadeshi Samaj*).

[106] *Ibid*, p. 6.

[107] Cited by (the then) Hon'ble Sir S. P. Sinha in moving a Bill to extend Village Self-Government in Bengal in the Bengal Legislative Council on the 28th March, 1918. (See *Calcutta Gazette*, April 24, 1918, p. 667.)

The lesson which the Anglo-Indian school is still in need of learning is that India is not a land of saints and philosophers, which bows low before the blast of political events in 'patient deep disdain' and rises but 'to plunge in thought again.' Such India never has been in the past, and such she assuredly is not at the present time.

Present Relation between State and Society—meaning of Indian Nationality.

We now turn to an aspect of our subject which calls for delicate handling by reason of the fact that it is thickly beset with susceptibilities, born of vested interests. Historians of India like Sir William Hunter have noted that "the British won India not from the Moguls but from the Hindus." The central authority of the Moguls had irrevocably gone to pieces when the British power took a hand in the gamble for supremacy in India. The decisive battles which enthroned and finally encrowned this power were fought with the two expanding Hindu confederacies of the Marhattas and the Sikhs. The last Marhatta War dates as late as 1818 and the Sikh confederation was not finally overcome until 1849. When the brief period of confusion and unbalance which attends inevitably on a change of central government was over, the British began to establish, consolidate and expand their state in India. This state however was neither a continuation nor a development of the ancient Indian state; its nature was predetermined by the history of Europe ; its leading principles were derived from western politics ; it aimed at the realisation of political sovereignty as understood in European political theory and not at mere fiscal, military and administrative control like the Mogul system or at social co-ordination like the ancient Hindu system. The system of governance, which was initiated to encompass this aim, though changed, modified and developed from time to time to suit altered social and political circumstances, was in respect of preservation of peace and order better than anything India had previously experienced. Under this state and this form of government, immunity from the dangers of violence was secured to society ; but notwithstanding its effective protection of peace and order in society, the British Indian State stood in a different relation to it from the ancient Hindu or mediæval Mahammadan state. It neither directed its efforts towards the consolidation in their places of the component units of society and the harmonious co-ordination of the different parts of its composite structure, nor did it adopt an imbecile or indifferent attitude of *laissez faire laissez passer*. The vital governing principle of this state was sovereignty and it conceived and carried out its functions and conducted and controlled its activities in pursuance of this governing principle. Thus it evolved a complete machinery for the performance of legislative, judicial and executive functions, promulgated laws and regulations (with a due regard of course to prevailing customs and usages), established courts of law, deriving their authority from it, to administer these laws, and organised official departments and bureaus for the execution of its sovereign will. The system thus evolved, to a large extent with the willing aid and co-operation of the subject peoples, was a highly potent mechanism, satisfying completely Taylor's definition of it as 'a functional totality, the construction, regulation and energising of which is from without.'[1] It was however wholly foreign both to the political theory of ancient Indians and to the constitutional practices of republican and monarchical governments in ancient and mediæval India.

The point requires further elucidation, as it is likely to be obscured by the fact that the bulk of this governmental machinery is carried on by the hands of the Indians themselves, and recently under the Government of India Act, 1919, Indians have been placed at some of its controlling centres. But Government is merely the instrument by which the State carries out its purposes and realises its will; it is the state itself as established by Britishers in India, according to their own political theories and practices, that bears this hall-mark of an aggressive foreignness. It is a definite break with the past, altogether out of the wonted course of evolution of Indian life and society. This aspect of the British Indian State is most important to consider on account of its direct bearing on the meaning of Indian nationality.

The difference is luminously pointed by a contrast between the old state and the new in their relations with that part of the life of society where the two come in the closest contact. In the higher spheres of the machinery of the state, the forms and appliances, *e.g.*, the Legislative Councils, the Executive Councils, the

[1] Taylor'e *The Right of a State to be*, p. 30 (quoted in Willoughby's *The Nature of the State*, p. 182).

Ministries, are exotic and new, and it is only the small though growing body of men conversant with European history and acquainted with western modes of politics, living in towns and cities, who understand their points and bearings. Lower down however we find that the forms and appliances of government bear a spurious resemblance to some of the indigenous institutions of the country.

The peoples of India are mainly dwellers in villages, and the Census Report shows the proportion of the urban to the total population as only 9.5 per cent.[2] Even the towns are in most cases only overgrown villages which carry on the essential features of rural life modified to a little extent by the amenities of modern surroundings. We have seen that in ancient times most of the functions associated with the modern conception of state were carried on by self-governing corporations, known by various names as Gana, Kula, Jati, Puga, Vrata, Sreni, Sangha, Naigama, Samuha, Parisat, Samuha-samutthana. The Village Assemblies, called Samuha or Sabha, ruled and dominated the social affairs of the village and the different autonomous bodies, formed on different principles of association, held each other in check. The powers exercised by the state over these bodies were those of taxation and general supervisory control, aimed at the prevention of mutual conflict and the maintenance of social order in the interests of Dharma which it was the constitutional duty of the king to uphold. These powers would be exercised with varying degrees of strictness according to the personal character of the kings and their ministers. But in other respects they were independent of the state and incapable of being affected or modified, in their respective forms, characters and constitutions, by the state outside of which they had originated. There is no doubt that they in their turn moulded the character and constitution of the state to a large extent. The Gramani or Village Head-Man is mentioned in the *Rig-Veda* in a few isolated passages.[3] His liberality is extolled by the poet with a gratitude that probably means a lively sense of favours to come, but his character and functions are far from clear. But the institution of Gramani re-appears in later times. In the *Arthasastra*,

[2] See *Census Report*, 1911, p. 40.
[3] See *Rig-veda*, x, 62, 11; 107, 5.

the headman of the village is called Gramika, and it is ruled that when the headman is out on tour on municipal duty he should be accompanied on pain of fine by groups of villagers by turns.[4] Certain police and other duties devolve on him, though, significantly enough, he is not mentioned among the paid officers of the king.[5] His duties were probably those settled by immemorial custom and not imposed by authority, though the violation of these duties was punishable as any other violation of customary obligation would be.[6] In the *Mahabharata*, we find mention of a hierarchy of village-officers (ग्रामाधिपति), placed over the Gramika, whose duty with reference to them is defined to be to observe and report the grievances of the village : [7]

ग्रामे यान् ग्रामदोषांश्च ग्रामिकः प्रतिभावयेत् ।
तान् ब्रूयाद् दशपायासौ स तु विंशतिपाय वै ॥
सोऽपि विंशत्यधिपतिर्वृत्तं जानपदे जने ।
ग्रामानां शतपालाय सर्व्वमेव निवेदयेत् ॥

It is significant again that the Gramika is not appointed by the king, who appoints only the hierarchy of supervisors beginning with the Adhipati of Ten Villages.[8]

In Manu, the same organisation of supervision is described, and in addition we learn that it was the Gramika who had to deal in the first instance with the grievances of the village, and in case of his being unable to do so effectively, he was to carry the matter higher up to the authority presiding over ten villages, and so on.[9] The Gramika was also responsible for collection of the revenue of the village.[10] It is unfortunate that the passages quoted and referred

[4] *Arthasastra* (S. Sastri's Ed.), p. 171.

ग्रामार्थेन ग्रामिकं व्रजन्तमुपवासाः पर्य्यायेणानुगच्छेयुरननुगच्छन्तः पणार्द्धपणिकं योजनं दद्युः ।

[5] See *ibid*, Book V, Ch. III (भृत्यभरणीयम्).

[6] See *ibid*, p. 171.

[7] *Mahabharata* : Santiparva, Rajadharma, Ch. 87, vv. 1-7.

[8] *Ibid*, v. 3.

[9] See Manu, VII, 116-117 :

ग्रामे दोषान् समुत्पन्नान् ग्रामिकः शनकैः स्वयं ।
शंसेद् ग्रामदशेशाय दशेशो विंशतीशिने ॥
विंशतीशस्तु तत् सर्व्वं शतेशाय निवेदयेत् ।
शंसेद् ग्रामशतेशस्तु सहस्रपतये स्वयं ॥

[10] See Manu, VII, 118 :

यानि राजप्रदेयानि प्रत्यहं ग्रामवासिभिः ।
अन्नपानेन्धनादीनि ग्रामिकस्तान्यवाप्नुयात् ॥

to above have not been up till now critically examined. A critical examination of them would clearly show that the affairs of the village were regulated by the village community represented by its own non-official headman, and the king's power and authority were limited to gathering taxes through the headman and supervision through paid and duly appointed officers. The state and the village community thus stood in a mutual relation which strengthened and invigorated each other. But this relation was possible only because the prevailing conception of the state was different from the modern conception which makes the attribute of sovereignty essential to it.

The dealings of the British Indian State in the sphere of what is called local self-government show unmistakably how this mutual relation between the state and society at large, which in India dwells mainly in the villages and rural towns, has undergone an entire revolution through the pressure of western political ideas. After the consolidation of British rule in India, it was discovered by the rulers that the necessity and, at the same time, the difficulty of governing India "down to the villages and the people" were enormously great. They therefore initiated the system of local self-government in limited spheres of activity and with limited powers. The system has undergone great developments in course of time and has by now a history behind it which falls roughly into two periods,[11]—the period of what has been called 'de-concentration of authority' beginning properly with the Act of 1850 which sanctioned the creation of Town Committees throughout British India, and the period of decentralisation of functions beginning with Lord Ripon's famous Resolution on Local Self-Government in 1882. During the long period of more than seven decades, the system has gradually extended through the District Boards, Municipalities, Local Boards, Union Panchayets, etc., till the last link seems to have been forged in Bengal in the Village Self-Government Act of 1919, which creates the Union Board with restricted municipal, fiscal and judicial powers for a group of villages. The local bodies thus created appear no doubt like feeble analogues to the ancient self-governing local bodies of India, the Sabhas, Samuhas, Urars, Nattars and Nadu Assemblies of ancient

11 See Rangaswami Iyangar's *The Indian Constitution*, 2nd Ed, 1913, p. 115.

India. It was through these ancient local bodies that the abounding social and communal life of the people found its characteristic expression. But what is important to consider and what illuminates the foreignness of the existing state is the contrast in general character and constitutional status between the old self-governing bodies and the new.

Mr. Rangaswami Iyengar thus characterises the new bodies : " Indian local bodies, whether they be the rural unions and boards or the municipalities, mofussil and metropolitan, are similar to English local bodies in that they are public bodies discharging public functions and exercise their powers on lines and within limits defined by the legislature. They owe their origin therefore to express creation by means of specific enactments whose interpretation rests in the hands of the courts of the land."[12] It was Lord Ripon, who, in his famous Resolution of 1882, first dealt with the *raison d'etre* of these local bodies. " It is not, primarily with a view to improvement in administration," said Lord Ripon, " that this measure is put forward and supported. It is chiefly desirable as an instrument of political and popular education."[13] Lord Ripon proceeded to explain how, with the progress of civilization and material prosperity, the task of administration had become so onerous that there was a crying need for parting with some of the functions of government and transferring them to popular bodies. By this transference, according to him, " the small beginnings of independent political life " would be made and people would be induced to " undertake, as far as may be, the management of their own affairs and to develop a capacity for self-help in respect of all matters that have not, for imperial reasons, to be retained in the hands of the representatives of Government "[14] Lord Ripon thus diverted the policy of local self-government from deconcentration to decentralisation. But it made not the slightest approximation to the character of the self-governing bodies of old, whose legal status was not created by the carving out of a portion of the functions of the state, but by the fact of their being vital organs of the life of society. The state could no more create or abrogate them than it could create or abolish the physical features

12 *Ibid*, p. 121.
13 See *ibid*, Appendix IX, p. cvii.
14 See *ibid*, p. cvii.

of the territory. In moving the Village Self-government Bill in the Bengal Legislative Council, Sir S. P. Sinha (now Lord Sinha) said, "The Council is aware that the Decentralisation Commission recommended that Panchayets should be given civil and criminal jurisdiction in petty cases arising within the village; the Indian Police Commission of 1902-3 had made a similar suggestion in respect of petty criminal cases ; and village courts created by the legislature have for many years been in active operation in other provinces."[15] But as we have already seen the village assemblies of old exercised all these powers and more by immemorial custom. In one sense it may be said that the position in ancient India was just the reverse, and instead of the state giving these powers to the local and communal bodies, it was they that gave the state its powers,—for the latter enjoyed mainly the residuary powers of control and supervision, supported by its right of imposing penalty, after the autonomous bodies had taken their share.

We have elaborated the point so far because the relation between the central government and the local is in a sense a crucial test of the relation between State and Society, this relation being the actual nidus of politics. In all European countries, local bodies dealing with municipal and rural affairs, with which really the vital interests of the people are bound up, are part and parcel of the state. They enjoy their status either at common law as in England or by acts of legislature as in France or Prussia. They are either self-governing bodies or agents of the central power. But consistently with the theory of sovereignty of the state, they cannot be conceived to be functioning independently of or outside the state. But in India this inconceivable measure of freedom was enjoyed by them, and the organs of social life, originating perhaps in a pre-State or ante-political condition of society, evolved their vital functions and powers, not in the cramping surroundings of state-organisation, but in the free and fresh air of the large life of the community. Education was not the business of the state but of the community, and could pursue the even tenour of its way in spite of changes in the state unless a

[15] See Speech of the (then) Hon'ble Sir S. P. Sinha in moving a Bill to extend Village Self-Government in Bengal Legislative Council on 28th March, 1919 (*Calcutta Gazette*, April, 24, 1918, p. 668).

general condition of anarchy supervened. Social and vital needs of the people, which are looked after at the present time by District Boards and Municipalities, were supplied by different corporate bodies, the organs of social life. Administration, legislation and even judicial functions were for the most part carried on by them, the state limiting itself to the task of general control, supervision and co-ordination. The ancient *Swadeshi Samaj* had so to speak swallowed up, digested and assimilated the *Sarkar*, and it does not appear that Mahammadan rule made any essential change in this relation between state and society except in that, by stopping the free flow of currents of influence between the two, it brought about a decline in the vitality of society and its organs.

It is in this thoroughly altered relation between State and Society under British rule that we may discover, if anywhere, the inner meaning of Indian nationality. We have already remarked that a vague sentiment of Pan-Indianism is becoming more and more pronounced in Indian life and society, and if we consider for a moment the basic factors of Indian life, as they have been determined by history, we find that on the whole they offer few impediments to the gradual, harmonious development of this sentiment. It has behind it a quickened historical and psychological background. But this sentiment is barren of significance and impotent for political expression unless it has an organised direction towards a political ideal. Pan-Indianism may express itself as well in a community of spiritual life or in cultural synthesis, but Indian nationality is a different thing,—it must be Pan-Indianism oriented towards a political ideal. In this sense nationality in India, the existence of which is now admitted though tardily and hesitatingly even by the Anglo-Indian School, is a plant of recent growth. It germinates out of the impact of the British Indian State on the persistent, long-evolving life of Indian society, rooted to the forms and types of corporate self-expression, the origins of which vanish in the dim distance of antiquity.

We have pointed out in the Introduction that even so early as 1890, Sir Charles Dilke said that, amidst the amazing diversities and contrarieties of Indian life, some people were able to discover the glimmerings of the idea of nationality. Since Dilke's time, many foreigners who have observed the conditions of Indian life have borne testimony to the existence of this feeling of nationality and have felt themselves at a loss to account for it. It is a puzzling disturbing phenomenon which assumes the appearance of what is commonly called 'unrest' in India—a curious discontent with existing conditions of political life, a strange unsettlement of past modes of thinking and feeling with regard to them, which seems to some people, obsessed with the idea of the fixed non-political mentality of the Indians, to be a 'great perturbation in nature. The feeling of the rulers and administrators of India towards this phenomenon of Indian unrest is well expressed by the wondering, questioning attitude of Lord Morley who spoke thus in 1907 : "Is all this what is called unrest in India froth ? Is it deep rolling?..............................Is it natural effervescence or is it deadly fermentation ? Is India with all its heterogeneous populations—is it moved really to a new and undreamt-of unity ? It is the vagueness of the discontent, which is not universal, but of the discontent so far as we can perceive it that makes it hard to understand, harder to deal with."[16] In the course of the last fifteen years, the suspicion that a feeling of nationality is the impelling force behind this unrest has ripened into a certainty which few will now care to dispute. But this nationality has not been accepted in political transactions as yet because its meaning has not been understood and its form has not been recognised. As we have explained in Part I of this thesis, the evolution of nationality in India is psychologically by no means impossible : the psychological school of politics which is gradually coming to the fore has brought a deeper analysis to bear on the question, and according to this school, as we have already seen, as represented in England by MacDougall, the psychological concept of nationality is not necessarily restricted within the categories of Unity of Race, Unity of Language, Unity of Religion, etc. But though Indian nationality is now accepted as a fact, different meanings have been read into it by different persons who have sought, often slightly and cursorily, to interpret this newly-evolved entity in Indian life. With some, this nationality means a united striving of the Indian people, leavened by western culture and brought to a sense of unity by the uniform conditions of social and political life created by centralised British rule, towards western ideals and modes of

[16] Lord Morley's speech at Arbroath on 21st October, 1907. (See *Speeches on Indian Affairs* by John Morley, published by Natesan & Co., p. 94.)

political life. With some again, it means nothing more than the reflex of ' Indo-Oriental ' opposition to the invasion of western culture, civilization and political government. This contrariety of view about the meaning of this puzzling political phenomenon is however based on a common presupposition, *viz.*, that India had no political life of her own in the past and that it is British rule that either creates nationality by fostering positive aspirations or evokes it negatively by rousing conservative opposition.

There is a strong body of opinion which emphasises the educative aspect of British rule in India and interprets Indian nationality as the political culture which is the result of this education ; the yearning for the western mode of political life which realises the principle of nationality more or less in the organisation of state is according to it, begotten by the liberal policy of British rule as well as the study of the masterpieces of English literature. Lord Morley described the educated Indians as being " intoxicated with the ideas of freedom and nationality and self-government," promulgated by writers like Milton, Burke, Macaulay and Mill.[17] Risley states more definitely the causes which, in his opinion, have led to the development of Indian national sentiment within a certain section of the community. They are :—

" (1) The consciousness of a certain community of intellectual pursuits and aspirations, derived from the common study of the history and literature of England and from the common use, for certain special purposes, of the English language in addition to a provincial vernacular.

" (2) The consciousness of being united and drawn together by living under a single government, by taking part in the administration of a common system of laws, and by sharing in the material benefits of a common civilization." [18] Risley admits that there is no historical precedent to show that such causes can evoke a sentiment of nationality in a people, and after examining the seemingly similar case of the Gauls under Roman government and Roman influence, he dismisses it as throwing no direct light on the

[17] See *ibid*, pp. 96-97.

[18] Risley's *The People of India* (Crooke's Ed.), p. 294.

problem, for the Gauls did not develop nationality, but "ceased to be Gauls in any but a geographical sense and became Romans with a Gallic tinge."[19]

Now it is true that the systematic and practical carrying out of the principles of western education embodied by Macaulay in his famous Minute has resulted in the growth of a politically-minded class who are smitten with a deep yearning for western modes of political life. The best representatives of this class are found in the old generation of Congress-men whose political views have been briefly described in the Introduction. But the fallacy of mistaking such a fine cultured sentiment, existing among a microscopically small group of educated and learned men only, is too self-evident. As Risley puts it in a telling way, "A mere top-dressing of idealism will not make nationality."[20]

A different interpretation has been put upon Indian nationality by another school which seems to hold the field at the present time. This interpretation is just the contrary to that we have noticed above. Indian nationality is regarded as the result not of the psychological *action* but rather the *re-action* of British rule. It means the gesture not of willing submission to, but of conscious revolt against, the aggressive occidentalism that the British rule and its characteristic institutions represent. In his recent speeches and writings, both in Bengal and in England, Lord Ronaldsay, ex-Governor of Bengal, has strongly supported this interpretation by elaborate references to the views expressed by the most prominent nationalists of the day. A compact statement of this view is given by Innes which deserves to be quoted at length.[21] After referring to the well-known physical, racial, linguistic and religious diversities of India, Innes goes on to say, "From these considerations we can derive a comparatively definite idea of what may be meant by Indian Nationality." India, according to him, "is not a nation at all in the sense in which we distinguish the nations of Europe." "In the eyes of an oriental, it would be much easier to distinguish and class at sight a Bengali Brahmin, a Sikh, a Gurkha, and a Marhatta, than a Frenchman, an Englishman, a

[19] *Ibid*, pp. 295-296.

[20] *Ibid*, p. 300.

[21] See Arthur D. Innes's *A Short History of the British in India* (1905), pp. 9-10.

Spaniard, and an Austrian." "But," says Innes, "the distinction between East and West is more than between nation and nation or between creed and creed. People who have no sense of unity will become united to resist a more intensely alien foe. The Marhatta is more akin to the Pathan than to the Englishman ; as the Englishman is more akin to the Frenchman than to the Marhatta. There are Indian habits of mind as there are European habits of mind. We cannot quite formulate the distinction as one between orientalism and occidentalism, for the Chinaman is an oriental who is hardly if at all more akin to the Indian than is the European....................The primary facts to be grasped are two : the Indo-orientals, Pathans, Rajputs, Bengalis, or Marhattas, may be opposed to each other as Frenchmen and Germans or English may be ; but the opposition is insignificant in comparison to that subsisting between all of them and the European ; just as the type-distinctions of European nations become insignificant in comparison to that between all of them and the Indo-oriental." This interpretation, as we shall see, has the merit at least of skirting the border of truth, though it misses widely the real core of the meaning of Indian nationality. Western culture moreover affects directly an insignificantly small part of the vast Indian population.

The fact has been brought to light by recent researches that, despite the diversities and contrarieties of racial and cultural forms prevailing in India throughout her long history, there was a substantial general uniformity from age to age in the relation of society to the state. When we have made all possible allowances for differences of forms of government and of personal equations in the case of monarchy, the truth remains that the idea of state-sovereignty in the western sense was absent in India. It was so in theory and practice in ancient India and in practice only in mediæval India under Mahammadan rule. Exceptions and aberrations may no doubt be pointed out, for the history of India is immeasurably rich in contents, but the persistent norm was there all the same. India had in the past, with perhaps lapses and periods of eclipse, an overabundant vitality. It expressed itself in her art and architecture, her literature, her forms of local and communal government, her religious and philosophic culture, her purely academic speculations in diverse fields, variety of religious movements, and even, as recent researches have proved, in her maritime activities and colonial expansion.[22] What were the characteristic organs through which this vitality was able to function ? The answer comes from a thousand significant inscriptions which archæologists have unearthed and a hundred hitherto obscure passages in ancient literature which scholars have unravelled. The history of India is not merely the biography of heroes and great men. The truth is gradually dawning, with multiple revolutions like the Vedic *Ushas*, that Indian history is essentially the history of corporate activities. They linger on even into the present era, self-suppressed and little noticed, with a vitality that refuses to be entirely crushed out. Researches have proved that in the ancient period of Indian history they had evinced extraordinary vigour of life, perhaps because of the influence received from the state ; in the mediæval period, evidence *ex silentio*, which however is not wholly reliable and may be contradicted by future researches, seems to point to an ebb in this vigour of life, probably on account of the withdrawal of state influence ; while in modern times they are threatened with extinction under the pressure of the idea of state-sovereignty. This explains why the poet of India laments in the passage, quoted in the last chapter, that " to-day we are striving of our own accord to place in the hands of the Sarkar the whole duty of our Samaj."

The religious *Samgha* was a form of corporate life. We know from different sources that it used to provide for the educational and intellectual needs of the people. The monasteries that were established all over India under the auspices of the Buddhist Samgha gradually developed into great centres of learning. Those at Amaravati,[23] Nalanda,[24] Odantapura,[25] Vikrama-

[22] The researches of Foucher, Stein and Radhakumud Mukherji (see *History of Indian Shipping and Maritime Activities*) have thrown a good deal of light on this obscure chapter of ancient Indian history.

[23] The ancient name of Amaravati was Sri-Dhanya-Kataka. The Pubbaseliya (Eastern Hill) and Aparaseliya (Western Hill) Schools of Buddhism originated here. The inscriptions show that it was a famous place of learning. (See *Report of the Archæological Survey of Southern India*, Vol. I. 1883, pp. 100 ff.). It is also referred to as such in Thibetan literature. See also Rhys Davids's *Sects of the Buddhists* (J.R.A.S., 1891, footnote).

[24] Described in Houen-Tsang's *Life*, called *Siyuki* (Tr. by Beal) and in I-Tsiang's Account (Tr. by Takaksu).

[25] Mentioned in Thibetan literature as a famous seat of learning.

sila[26] and Jagatdala[27] grew to the proportions of universities with their full complement of libraries, schools of studies, lecture-halls, professors and students flocking from all parts of Asia, far and near. Among them the fame of the University of Nalanda has been immortalised by Houen-Tsang and I-Tsiang ; the former speaking of it in his famous Book of Travels in the same strain of endearment as Matthew Arnold used to speak of Oxford. During the Mahammadan regime also, when the Samghas were suppressed by sheer brute violence,[28] we find the school of Sankaracharya's followers reincarnating in the Maths the corporate spirit and learning of the Buddhist monastic centres. There were other seats of education at Guru-griha, the chief of which in Bengal, at Nadia, learning at Guru-griha, the chief of which in Bengal, at Nadia, flourished throughout the Mahammadan period. All these educational institutions were brought into existence by the urge of the inner intellectual life of the people and not by charters and acts of legislature.

Similarly affairs relating to the material welfare of the people were initiated and regulated by local self-governing bodies throughout India, irrespective of all the prevailing diversities of life. Two inscriptions discovered at Uttara-mallur, assigned to the 10th century A.D., testify to the extensive functions and the efficient organisation of the local village community which may well be taken as the measure of all the rest.[29] It was divided into six committees with definite functions and definite rules about the election of members, their qualifications and disqualifications, etc., which are striking in their curious appearance of modernity. The

[26] Described in Thibetan literature (see S. C. Vidyabhushan's *Medieval School of Indian Logic*, Appendix C).

[27] Referred to as a Mahavihara in many colophons of Thibetan versions of Sanskrit Buddhist works.

[28] Magadha was the most flourishing seat of Buddhistic learning on the eve of Mahammadan conquest. It was, even before the conquest, harried several times by the Mahammadans. Their violence seems to have been chiefly directed to monasteries and monastic communities. Taranath describes a raid by 500 Turuskas on the University of Vikramasila in the time of Kamala Rakshita in 10th cent. A.D. (See Vidyabhushan's *Logic*, p. 151, footnote.) The account is no doubt based on old legends. Kutubuddin's general, Mahammad, stormed Behar and carried out a wholesale massacre of monks in 1197 A.D. (See Raverty's *Tabakat-i-Nasiri*, p. 552.) Vikramasila is said to have been finally destroyed by Bakhtiar Khiliji about, 1203 A.D., when Sakya-Sri-Pandita of Kashmira was at its head. (Vidyabhusan's *Logic*, p. 151—on the authority of S. C. Das's *Thibetan-English Dictionary*, p. 869 and Waddell's *Lamaism*, p. 16.)

[29] See Mukherjee's *Local Government in Ancient India* (2nd Ed.), pp. 167 ff.

23

organisation of the village community which continued its existence, however feebly in comparison with its past, through all the vicissitudes of Indian history was noticed in Southern India by the revenue officers of the British Government even so late as the first quarter of the last century. We have already referred to the verse in Manu in which the Gramika is made the agent for the collection of the king's revenue (VII, 118). The practice seems to have continued throughout the Mahammadan period till it was discontinued by the British authorities. There was a famous controversy between Sir Thomas Munro and the Madras Board of Revenue between 1818 and 1824 about the recognition in revenue matters of the self-governing village communities. The decision went against them and in favour of the now existing Ryatwari System.[30] Even to-(day in different parts of the country, relic of the communal organisation of rural life are found in a better or worse state of preservation, and these relics are scattered widely all over India.

The economic life of the people was carried on by the numerous trade-guilds all over the country that wielded great powers in relation to the state in ancient India and lived on through the Mahammadan period. India still remains the land of home industries, in spite of the introduction of western forms of industrialism in the more important cities.[31] But it appears now from the results of research that Indian home industries had separate organisations of their own of which remnants are still to be met with. The high value put in the markets of the world on the products of Indian industry in bygone times is now a matter of common knowledge and it is not a violent presumption to think that they were brought to this high state of refinement by organised activity rather than by individual genius. But the readers of Romesh Chandra Dutt and other Indian writers on Indian economic history need not be told how the commercial jealousy of the East India Company in the early part of the last century brought whole companies of handicraftsmen, specially weavers, to a state of destitution and utterly dissolved their guide-life,

30 See R. C. Dutt's Article on *Indian Land Question* in the Indian Review, Oct., 1902 (reprinted by Natesan & Co., in *Land Problems in India*, p. 7).

31 See Radhakamal Mukherji's *Foundations of Indian Economics*.

Contemporary evidence on this point like William Bolt's *Considerations on Indian Affairs* is not wanting.[32]

Among the Hindus, the organisation of social life on caste-basis was regulated by the caste Panchayets, which still survive among the lower orders of Hindu society. The organisation however was not a close corporation and we have famous instances of tribes, originally out of the pale of Hindu society, changing their character into castes and finding places for themselves in its wide and elastic organisation. The curious process of the conversion of tribes into castes is still going on, which gives point to Prof. Gilchrist's dictum that "caste is practically an instinct of Hindu life."[33] It is difficult to conceive of such a revolution in Hindu society as brought about the break-up of the Japanese caste-system in the seventies of the 19th century, because caste here is not a mere social arrangement. "We should rather conceive of it," says Risley, "as a congenital instinct, an all-pervading principle of attraction and repulsion, entering into and shaping every relation of life,"[34] the withdrawal of which would create a like disaster in Hindu society as the withdrawal of some elemental force like gravitation or molecular attraction would produce in the material universe. The researches of Risley and the Census officers have established the fact that caste in modern India is not simply the continuation of the ancient Vedic principle of social gradation and classification. There are at least seven distinguishable types of caste, *viz.*, tribal, functional or occupational, sectarian, cross, national, migratory and castes formed by change of occupation.[35] This variety of types, originating in different ways, points to the inference that the instinct which brings them into being must

[32] This book was published in London in 1772, *i.e.*, seven years after the East India Company's acquisition of the Dewani of Bengal. The author describes himself as "Merchant and Alderman, or Judge of the Hon. The Mayor's Court of Calcutta." The book is now rare. The expressions of the Company which began in Seraj-al-Dowlah's time are vividly described in Ch. XIV. Bolts cites the evidence of an English gentleman of his acquaintance who was "witness to the fact of above seven hundred families of weavers, in the districts round Jungulbary, at once abandoning their country and their professions" (p. 194). *Nagads* or silk-winders were forcibly carried away wholesale to English factories (p. 194). Bolts says, "Many manufacturers of all denominations have, by unparalleled oppressions, been driven from their callings and country" (p. 206). Bolts however was not free from prejudice against the East India Company.

[33] Gilchrist's *Indian Nationality*, p. 127.

[34] Risley's *People of India*, p. 278.

[35] See *ibid*, pp. 75-94.

have had its roots in a fundamental principle of the life of society which we may call the group-principle.

Now the social features we have just dwelt upon are common to all India irrespectively of all local, racial and cultural diversities, and they constitute indeed that "underlying uniformity of life from the Himalayas to Cape Comorin" which Yusuf Ali has pointed out and Risley admitted. We have said elsewhere that the growth of active sympathy and fellow-feeling among the Indians, facilitated by the appurtenances of the British system of government, perhaps has deeper roots than the people themselves can realise. It has in fact its roots deep down in this long-persistent, long-enduring 'uniformity' of Indian life which is now scarcely perceptible because of the over-laying activities of British state-sovereignty. We can understand this point only by getting at the inner meaning of the contrast between the character of local government in ancient India and that under the British Indian State. And there is at the present time a blind, half-conscious effort to hold fast to this rapidly-dissolving fundamental uniformity of Indian life by a readjustment of the relation between the state and society on old lines, and its name to-day is Nationality.

That such is the real meaning of Indian nationality will appear from the utterances of prominent nationalists of the day, when they are read between the lines and turned inside out. It is perhaps invidious to make quotations from living nationalist leaders whose personalities are wrapped up in the bitter controversies of the hour. The highest idealistic formulation and expression of their aspirations will be found in the following passage which I take the liberty of quoting from a recent nationalist journal. Speaking of the achievements of India's past, the writer says : "These memories still linger in the national mind and life, but the spirit is gone. Forms overcrowd, the ideals have lost their living hold on national consciousness. * * * The time is come for a vaster, richer, more comprehensive and synthetic self-assertion of India in all her fields of thought, life and activity." [36] This 'synthetic self-assertion of India' is the

[36] From the *Standard Bearer* (a fortnightly journal published from Chandernagore), May, 1922, now defunct.

Indian nationalist's aim, and its political implication, and direction are not far to seek. It is keenly felt by nationalists that this self-assertion is compatible only with a state which must be different from what exists at the present time. This ideal state is described as Swaraj. The popular lectures on Home Rule by the late Bal Gangadhar Tilak, who was as much a scholar as a nationalist and political leader, betray this very conception of Swaraj—the revivified ideal ancient Indian State that left the people absolutely free to evolve their own genius in all spheres of life and activity. "The Rishis," says Tilak, "who laid down the law of duty betook themselves to forests, because the people were already enjoying Swaraj or People's Dominion, which was administered and defended in the first instance by the Kshatriya kings. * * * It does not matter who the sovereign is. It is enough if we have full liberty to elevate ourselves in the best possible manner. This is called the immutable Dharma, and Karma Yoga is nothing but the method which leads to the attainment of Dharma or material and spiritual glory. We demand Swaraj, as it is the foundation and not the height of our future prosperity."[37] Tilak then goes on to say that this Swaraj does not imply a denial of British sovereignty or British rule, by which he probably means such British connection as countries of dominion status within the British Empire retain. In another speech, Tilak explains more explicitly what this People's Dominion is, "The village Panchayets, the Councils of Pandits or Elders to advise the King or Emperor, and such other kindred institutions were in existence for long. The king was not the final authority in matters of law. * * * The words *Swarajyam, Vairajyam*, were actually seen in the sastras."[38] Swaraj is therefore to Tilak and other nationalists a new modernised version of the old, old Indian conception of the state. "The meaning of Swarajya is the retention of our Emperor and the rule of the English people, and the full possession by the people of the authority to manage the remaining affairs."[39] As we have already seen, changes of central government in ancient and mediæval

[37] *Bal Gangadhar Tilak—His Writings and Speeches* (Enlarged Edition, published by Ganesh & Co., Madras, 1919), pp. 245-246.

[38] *Ibid*, p. 226.

[39] *Ibid*, pp. 147-148.

India affected little the course of development of the real life of the people and it is this that explains the mental attitude taken up in this definition of Swarajya.

The conception of Swaraj is thus clear. But the difficulty of arriving at a correct definition of it has constituted the crux of modern Indian politics. Speculations have been rife since almost the beginning of the Indian National Congress about the exact form which the ideal, future state of India is destined to take. But it has been too often forgot that this state can only be determined in its character and functions by the evolution of nationality itself. Schemes concerning the constituent parts, arrangement of powers, distribution of functions of this future state must therefore be sent along with the figments of imagination of Plato and his brood of imaginary commonwealth-builders to the Limbo :

> " Whither aerial vapours flew
> Of all things transitory and vain." [40]

It was perhaps a wise act on the part of the Indian National Congress at its 35th session at Nagpur to have left the expression *Swaraj* without any qualifying or descriptive epithet in the statement of the Congress Creed. Perhaps the Group-theory of State will help towards a final solution of the problem.

---

[40] Milton's *Paradise Lost*, Book III.

PART III.

PRESENT TENDENCIES TOWARDS DEVELOPMENT OF NATIONALITY.

It would be almost a truism to say that a subjective feeling like nationality cannot be gauged by any standardised measure. In spite of the presence of certain factors seemingly incompatible with its existence, the stir of a feeling of nationality in the group mind of India can no longer be ignored. Perhaps India will never develop into a 'simple nationality' as defined by Israel Zangwill.[1] The particular form, which it will ultimately take and for which the character of evolution of Indian history has predestined it, is a 'divine event' of the future, vain for us to discuss. It is open to us only to observe the existence of the feeling and to trace, if possible, its development in the phenomena which lie around us in the Indian world of to-day. We have tried to elucidate the inner significance of this feeling which is rooted to a deep-lying historical basis. But it is at the same time a novel force in the collective life of the people, evoked, as we have said, by the peculiar conditions, established by British rule, in the traditionary relations between society and state. The all too common supposition that its working is confined to a circumscribed circle of educated and cultured persons and hence not truly national in character is gradually melting away like many another baseless supposition about India. These cultured and educated persons, being trained to the power of expression by their culture and education, are naturally the most vocal exponents of nationality at the present time. But it would be wilful blindness to existing conditions to hold that the so-called masses are unaffected by and beyond the reach of this feeling by reason of their illiteracy and other irremediable shortcomings. Such a reason might be considered valid if the feeling were the result of western culture only, but it rises from a deeper source, from an experience of incongruity in existing political conditions which 'goes home to the business

[1] See Zangwill's *The Principle of Nationalities* (Conway Memorial Lecture).

and bosoms ' of the classes and the masses alike. It is impossible to prove the existence of national feeling among the masses by actual facts and figures and a difference of opinion about it is difficult to meet. In the debate in the House of Commons on 5th June, 1919, on the second reading of the Government of India Bill, it was a moot-point between Sir H. Craik, Member for the Scottish Universities, and Herbert Fisher, President of the Board of Education. In the course of his speech, Fisher said truly, " The old image of India as being silent, stationary, unperplexed, and unvexed by all the agitations of political life, if it was ever true, has now long ceased to correspond to the realities of to-day."[2] To an impartial observer, it is apparent that the feeling of nationality in India today is ' in widest commonalty spread,' though it is a clear and conscious feeling with some, while dim and half-conscious with others, springing however from a common source of experience of life.

It is a newly-evoked force in India. The turns and complications of its workings are difficult to trace for want of perspective and of clear perception of the direction of events. We can at most show the indications and tendencies, though even these are often extremely difficult for a contemporary to distinguish. Incidents, which wear to the eye of enthusiasm a highly promising and forward-looking aspect, may turn out after all to be barren of possibilities, while some hidden beginnings may develop potentialities to be unfolded only to the eye of the future historian. But with all these limitations on our view, we may note certain dispositions of phenomena that may indicate the way in which nationality, understood in the sense we have tried to explain, is developing in India at the present time.

We have spoken of the cultured nationalists of India, some among whom are leaders of great masses of people. The very growth and existence of such a class has a value, both interpretative and causative, in the development of nationality. They represent a new type of character, Pan-Indian in sympathies, activities and modes of self-expression. They point not only to

[2] I have not had an opportunity to consult Hansard. The quotation is from the *Indian Annual Register*, 1920. (edited by H. N. Mitra, Shibpur, Calcutta), Part II, p. 194.

the existence of a wide-spread sentiment that springs from a clearly conceived idea of India as an indivisible and indissoluble entity, but they also help the development of this sentiment among the masses by rousing the spirit of imitation. Bagehot was the first to draw attention to the force of imitation as a causative factor in the formation of national character. "National character is formed," says Bagehot, "by the confluence of congenial attractions and accordant detestations,"[3] and a leader and great man crystallises them in the example of his own personality. An elaborate analogy is drawn by him between the manner in which the character of literature of a particular age is formed and the manner in which national character is formed. As a dominant personality in the literary world, like Pope for example in English literature of the eighteenth century, sets the fashion to imitative authors and determines the literary character of the age, so a leader and great man "sets the tone which others take and the fashion which others use." Great men are models to ordinary people who try to imitate them and are thus infused with their personal likes and dislikes, and a new type of character comes to be settled thereby to which the masses try to conform. MacDougall cites several instances of this process which leaders of men set going. "Would Germany now be a nation, but for Frederick the Great and Bismarck ? Would America, but for Washington, Hamilton and Lincoln ? Would Italy, but for Garibaldi, Mazzini and Cavour ?"[4] The exact nature of this process is thus described by Bagehot : "A new model in character is created for the nation ; those characters which resemble it are encouraged and multiplied ; those contrasted with it are persecuted and made fewer. In a generation or two, the look of the nation becomes quite different, the characteristic men who stand out are different."[5] We can therefore no more ignore the influence of individual character in a 'scientific view' of history than we can the influence of the sun in a scientific view of nature.[6]

In the contemporary history of India, we see a small but highly influential group of leaders and great men who stand for Indian

[3] Bagehot's *Physics and Politics* (Kegan Paul's Ed.), p. 105.
[4] McDougall's *Group Mind*, p. 137.
[5] *Physics and Politics*, p. 206.
[6] *Ibid*, p. 96.

unity, for fostering indigenous arts and industries to the exclusion of western imports, for unity between the Hindus and the Mahammadans, for filling up the gaping cleft in Hindu society between the *Acaraniyas* and the *Anacaraniyas*, etc. The examples of these men and their social and political propaganda produce that outward seeming of unity which has a tendency, curiously enough, to substantiate itself into reality. The words of the poet describe exactly this subtle psychological transformation :—

> " How we
> Track a livelong day, great Heaven, and watch our shadows !
> What our shadows seem, forsooth, we will ourselves be.
> Do I look like that ? You think me that : then I am that."

The vexed problem of Hindu-Mahammadan unity in India may be solved only by this highly curious psychological process.

An impetus to the development of Indian nationality is thus given by the examples and precepts of leaders and great men who are coming to the fore in modern India. In many of them, their racial and provincial characteristics appear in clear relief : in a leader like the late Bal Gangadhar Tilak, the practical Marhatta characteristic that Elphinstone and others have noted,[7] *viz.*, the wish to justify the means by the end, appears distinctly ; in the eloquent orations of the late Surendranath Banerjea, the Bengali characteristic is clearly seen in an exalted emotional expansion ; in Mohandas Karamchand Gandhi perhaps some will notice a calculating coldness inborn in one of the Guzerati trading caste ; but these provincial or parochial characteristics are not the dominant points about them : they all stand for Indian unity and a larger-interprovincial life.

This larger life that is fast developing in India, with the Indian National Congress as its great focus or resonator, becomes the seed-ground of Indian nationality. The state attempts to take up this life in a way that is necessarily inconsistent with Indian

[7] See Elphinstone's *History of India*, 9th ed., p. 600—

" A Marhatta thinks of nothing but the result and cares little for the means if he can attain his object. * * * The Rajput is the most worthy antagonist—the Marhatta the most formidable enemy; for he will not fail in boldness and enterprise when they are indispensable, and will always support them or supply their place by stratagem, activity and perseverance."

ideas, Indian sentiments and the trend of Indian political history. It is not with a mere craving for western political institutions that nationalists of modern India are smitten to-day, though such craving undeniably exists among a certain section of the educated community. It is a much larger feeling,—the yearning for what has been called 'the synthetic self-expression of India.' It takes a political form and direction, because it is felt that the establishment of Swaraj alone can make such self-expression possible,—that ideal state, different from all western types, which leaves, what Tilak calls, the People's Dominion intact. The satisfaction of this yearning is therefore impossible for the rulers and administrators of India to guarantee by readjustments of the points and bearings of the administrative machinery, for it is the existence of this machinery itself that Indian nationalists revolt spiritually against.

Are there indications to show that this seeking after national self-expression exists in India to-day? It is indeed by such indications only that we can follow the development of Indian nationality, and it would be difficult to deny their existence in certain tendencies of art, education and culture as well as politics in India of the present day.

A most interesting indication is found in the realm of the modern art of Indian Painting. The ancient mural paintings in the caves of Ajanta are the common artistic heritage of India. They represent a flourishing school of art in 7th or 8th century A. D. that points back to much earlier beginnings. The widespread influence of this school is attested by the surviving fragments of decoration in the caves of Bagh and the rock-cut chambers of Siguriya. Paintings, distinctly Indian, have also been discovered in the Himalayan regions (*e. g.*, Kangra valley) and outside India which show the continuity of the artistic tradition which passes on into the later Rajput School. This Rajput School of Painting existed side by side with another, known as the Mogul School of Painting, which lasted down into the 17th century, reaching its zenith of perfection in the reigns of Jehangir and Shah Jahan. "The Mogul style," says Dr. Coomaraswamy, "though built up with the materials of many different traditions is most undeniably original, in the same sense that the Mughal culture in India is as a whole original." [8]

Now the collection of ancient and mediæval Indian artistic specimens by the School of Art in Calcutta, under the direction and guidance of E. B. Havell and A. B. Tagore, has brought to light the remarkable fact that a persistent tradition representing 'a fundamental spirit and turn of the æsthetic sense native to the mind of India' links the paintings of Ajanta with the Rajput School, separated as they are by several centuries and wide differences of cultural environment. The figures in the Ajanta caves transmit their æsthetic spirit as well as a little of their technique through the Himalayan School, represented by the Vaisnava paintings from Kangra Valley, to the Rajput school, represented by the drawings of symbolical *Ragas* and *Raginis* and the eternal Radha-Krishna legend at Jaipur. Nothing is clearer than this tradition,—yet so intimately is it intertwined with the innate qualities of the Indian mind that it cannot be defined more simply than in the following words of Aurabindo Ghose : "The sensuous appeal is there, but it is refined into only one and not the chief element of the richness of a soul of psychic grace and beauty which is for the Indian artist the true beauty, *lavanya* : the dramatic motive is subordinated and made only a purely secondary element ; only so much is given of character and action as will help to bring out the deeper spiritual or psychic feeling, *bhava*, and all insistence or too prominent force of these mere outwardly dynamic things is shunned, because that would externalise too much the spiritual emotion and take away from its intense purity by the interference of the grosser intensity which emotion puts on the stress of the active outward nature. The life depicted is the life of the soul and not, except as a form and a helping suggestion, the life of the vital being and the body." [9] James Cousins, an Irish poet of the Celtic Revival and a sympathetic student of the modern Bengal school of painting, seeks to express the same idea by calling the Indian national direction in art *evocative* in contra-

[8] Lecture on *Mughal and Rajput Painting* to the Indian Society of Oriental Art, Calcutta, 1910, reprinted in Coomarswami's *Art and Swadeshi* (Ganesh & Co., Madras), p. 77.

[9] *Defence of Indian Culture* (*The Arya*, Vol. VI, No. 9, p. 553).

distinction to the *invocative* direction of European genius.[10] Its emphasis is on soul-life which it attempts to visualise by spiritual suggestions, unencumbered by the attractions of merely physical grace or likeness. The traditionary reliance therefore of the artistic impulse in India on religion "was not a reliance on something extraneous as it is in the west, but on something integral, something as essential to the Indian artist as visualisation to a dramatist or motor-power to a sculptor."[11]

This tradition had entirely stopped in the different schools of art, established in Calcutta, Bombay and elsewhere under the auspices of British Government. The modes that used to be insisted on at these schools were the well-known western modes, the best application of which to Indian subjects was made by Raja Ravi Varma. But the growth of the spirit of nationality in India expressed itself in a desire to take up at the point where it had been broken the evolution of the traditionary spirit of Indian art. This desire is clearly expressed by Dr. Coomaraswamy who says, "The arts of India must retain their Indian spirit, or become altogether worthless. The springs of art are in life itself, and when the life of the people is revitalised and reinspired, this new life will be reflected in Indian decorative art. The applied arts cannot be isolated and located as a thing apart from the national life, and the future of Indian art depends on the future of nationalism among us."[12] He finds the indication of this re-vitalisation and re-inspiration of Indian life in the Bengal School of Painting.

This school, founded by E. B. Havell and led by Abanindra Nath Tagore, is daily increasing the circle of its adherents and admirers. It continues the Ajanta-Rajput tradition of art which is decidedly not racial or parochial, but distinctively Indian, in as much as it is seen to flourish in 9th century A.D. at Ajanta in Western India in the Cave-Viharas of the Buddhists as well as in 16th century at Jaipur in Rajputana in orthodox Hindu surroundings. It is thus representative of a phase of the development of Indian nationality,—its spiritual striving for a new synthetic self-assertion. The significance of the work of this school lies, to quote

[10] See Cousins's *The Renaissance in India*, p. 35.
[11] *Ibid*, p. 52.
[12] Coomarswamy's *Art and Swadeshi*, p. 52.

again the words of Coomaraswami, in its "distinctive Indianness." [13]

In the more practical sphere of culture and education, we may perceive a somewhat similar tendency though not so clearly articulated as in the domain of art. As we have already remarked, education was never a state-controlled system in India, and at different periods of history seats of culture and learning had spontaneously grown up all over India, pursuing diverse courses of evolution according to all the diversities of religious, social and cultural life. They were liberally patronised by the state, no doubt, according to the various tastes and inclinations of the ruling authorities, a fact evidenced by the well-known examples of patronage extended to Buddhist monasteries by cultured princes like Harshavardhana and the encouragement of literary academies called *Sangams* by South Indian kings.[14] But the state never attempted to impose a system upon them or reduce their diversities to a uniform pattern. They drew their strength and vitality from the life of the community itself and were rooted to and bound up with it.

There are certain tendencies, though at present very indefinite in their character, which indicate a desire for relaying the foundation of education and culture on the various and diversified life of the community at large. Their negative aspect is expressed by the present revolt against the state-controlled system of education. It is urged that education should be "on national lines and under national control." The word 'national' is used in this connection in a vague, loose and ill-comprehended sense to mean that education should correspond to the real intellectual needs of the people, to the requirements of training in the traditions of their historic culture and communal life, and to the mental qualities and tendencies which have been developed in the course of history. The objection to the state control of education is briefly that such control is not national, an argument which is perfectly consistent in India, but which would seem absurd in a

13 See *ibid*, p. 129.

14 See an interesting account of the Tamil *Sangams* in Krisnaswami Aiyangar's article on *How Learning was honoured among the Ancient Hindus* in the *Calcutta Review*, Vol. 2, No. 1 (Jan. 1922).

country used to the idea of sovereignty of the state and recognising education among the state's proper functions. The *Guru-kula* at Kangri, Hardwar, seeks to continue an ancient system in the changed atmosphere of the present age and to organise a type of education, associated with the Brahmanical system, which is at least as old as the University of Takkasila, famed in the Buddhist *Jatakas*.[15] In several *Jataka* stories, we find legendary accounts of princes going to Takkasila for learning, residing in the household of the teacher, and either paying a fee or doing personal service in return for instruction.[16] It is the same system as described by Manu. The *Guru-kula* at Kangri is a modern attempt at the re-establishment of the old Indian system on an organised basis. In the communal universities of Aligarh and Benares, we may trace an attempt to re-shape according to up-to-date western ideas the old standing principle of educational organisation in India by which each system of religion had to develop its characteristic educational agencies—Viharas, Maths, Tols, etc. Experiments on a lesser scale than Aligarh and Benares are being made at the present moment all over India, such as the newly-founded Viswabharati at Bolpur, guided by Rabindra Nath Tagore, the National University at Adyar, under the auspices of the Theosophical Society of India, etc.—which are all outside the sphere of state-control.

In the domain of literature, the tendency is at present less pronounced, though the output of nationalist journals, pamphlets and ephemeral productions of that sort is not a negligible feature. But literature of the kind that is distinguished by the quality of permanence has not yet been infused with true national feeling. Of course, all literature must smack more or less of the soil and show something of the form and pressure of the time. But a

15 The *Jatakas* Pali birth-stories of Buddha, which have been edited by Fausboll, though compiled later, represent various interesting features of life and society in northern India through the medium of legends that must have come down from 6th century B.C. The most interesting feature is the existence of a sort of University at the extreme north-western border of India. Students from all parts of India are said to resort to this University for education. If it was a flourishing centre of culture and learning in 6th century, B.C., its origin must be referred to post-Vedic times to which the *Upanishads* belong.

16 Cf. *Tila-mutthi-Jataka* (Oxford Translations by Cowell, Rouse and others—Vol. II, p. 193). Also, *Asadisa Jataka* (Vol. II, p. 60), *Campeyya Jataka* (Vol. IV, p. 28), etc. See also the story of Jivaka in *Mahavagga*, viii, I (S.B.E.) The story of the Prince in the first named *Jataka* shows that the system of instruction at Takkasila was the *Guru-griha* system.

great literary work of truly national import such as, say, Victor Hugo's *Les Miserables* which works into the texture of its imaginative fabric the moral and spiritual forces of the collective life of a people of a particular age, is still a far-off possibility. Some of the novels of Rabindra Nath Tagore (*e.g.*, *Gora* and *Ghare Vahire*) represent this attempt of the literary imagination at the appropriation of social and moral forces working at the heart of society as materials for imaginative construction. But the attempt is as yet extremely rare, confined to provincial themes, and powerless to touch the higher plane of Indian nationality. We leave out of consideration the patriotic songs, in different vernaculars, in which the conception of India as a whole is embodied in invocations to the Mother, of which the great exemplar is the immortal 'Vande Mataram' song of Bankim Chandra Chatterji. But though their place must necessarily be in the outskirts and suburbs of literature, they point perhaps to the inchoate beginnings among the Hindu millions of India of a new cult of Motherland, similar *mutatis mutandis* to the classical cult of *Dea Roma*.

In general standards of culture too, there appears to be growing up a tendency in favour of Indian ways, manners and habits of life, though necessarily modified by the material necessities and cultural amenities of partially westernised surroundings. The type of personality that is favoured in India to-day is the type that has assimilated the culture of India as well as of Europe, and is able at the same time to give expression to it in a characteristic Indian mode. Sir M. Visvesvaraya has well pointed out in his recent book, entitled *Reconstructing India* (1918), that it is necessary to Indian union that 'certain standards of taste, thought and sentiment' should be recognised. He recommends for this purpose a comprehensive scheme of Indianisation to be devised and carried out on the American principle of education and training for citizenship. But whether such a scheme is ever consciously devised or not, there is no doubt that all over India, in spite of all provincial diversities, common standards of taste, thought and sentiment are being unconsciously built up. The fact must be apparent to any one who does not wilfully lose the wood in the trees. All these indications in the spheres of art, education and culture point to the unmistakable development of Indian nationality which has found its political expression in our day in the so-called Non-co-operation Movement, initiated by M. K. Gandhi.

The personality of the leader sums up the whole spirit of this movement. Living in the humble style of a poor Indian, wearing a piece of home-spun and hand-woven loin-cloth, describing himself with pride and pleasure as a weaver and farmer, thoroughly Indian in manners, habits and ways of speech, he is a living embodiment of the spirit of India's synthetic self-expression and self-assertion. The movement that he has initiated is essentially a nationality-movement of signal power and promise. We are not concerned in an academic thesis with its political aspects which are enveloped in a thick atmosphere of passions, prejudices and controversies, but with those other aspects of it which directly bear upon our subject-matter, *viz.*, the development of Indian nationality. Approval or disapproval is entirely out of place from our point of view.

A glance at the different items of the Non-co-operation Resolution passed at the Special Session of the Indian National Congress in Calcutta in September, 1920, as amplified and adopted at the 35th session of the Congress at Nagpur in December of the same year,[17] will show that the Swaraj or the undefined ideal state it aims at is to be secured by a special policy and in a special manner. The Indian people are urged to dissociate themselves from the existing educational institutions, from British law-courts, from the Legislative and Executive Councils, from Government service, from honours and titles bestowed by the State, from foreign trade relations—in short from all the more important activities and functions of the state. Students of modern European history are aware that this policy of dissociation from the existing state by a people striving to establish a different one in its place was inaugurated by Francis Deak in Hungary. The policy there was so strikingly successful that the imagination of the Irish nationalists was captured by it powerfully in the beginning of the 19th century. In 1905, Arthur Griffith published a series of

[17] See *Indian Annual Register* (published by H. N. Mitra, Shibpur, Calcutta), 1921, Part III.

articles in an Irish nationalist journal in which there were elaborate discussions on the so-called 'Hungarian Policy' and its applicability to Ireland, and it was not long before it was adopted under the casually acquired name of Sinn Fein. The policy is being tried for the third time in the world, in the course of less than a century, in the wholly different conditions of India under the name of Non-co-operation. The implications of this policy require to be carefully understood.

In a country where the state is the outward organised expression of nationality, which, in other words, enjoys a nation-state, a policy of Sinn Fein or Non-co-operation means the automatic disruption or septic dissolution of national life itself. In a country again, which lives under a state, but where there is no principle of nationality present, as where a ruling power governs a miscellaneously made-up territory or a heterogeneously composed population, the policy means only the reign of chaos come again, for the state in this case is the only bond of society. But in a country where there is a ruling state, which is not national, set over a subject nation with which its relation is discordant and jarring, the policy may indeed be successfully pursued under favourable conditions. In fact in the first two cases, the inauguration of such a policy appears to be unthinkable except as the freak of some interesting political pervert. Both Hungary and Ireland must have developed nationality to a large extent to be able to put the policy in operation without dissolution of society.

Viewed at this angle, the progress of Non-co-operation movement in India without social dissolution is no doubt an indication of the development of nationality. If the only bond of Indian life were the existence of the British Indian State, the loosening of it by a policy of Non-co-operation would only spell ruin and disaster. It becomes therefore a test, a measure and an indication, as it were, of Indian nationality in a real sense.

We are precluded by the academic purpose of our writing from expressing opinions on current political topics. The progress of Non-co-operation in India is no doubt a tempting topic and one on which divergent views may be held according to the personal inclination, the means of observation and the angle of vision of the writer. But if the movement has made any peaceful progress at all, it is *pro tanto* a measure of the development of nationality in India.

We have observed that the nidus out of which all politics germinate is the relation between State and Society. The state that has been established by the British people in India has undoubtedly been productive of much good to the people,—and perhaps along with it some fatal evil too. It is an open secret that people regard the Sarkar with mixed feelings which shift between the two extremes represented by the epithets, 'satanic' and 'benevolent.' But whatever the good or the evil which British rule has brought to India, the fact that it has altered the traditional relation between the State and the people affects the whole political experience of the Indians. They observe the old communal system of education and culture replaced by a uniform state-controlled system and readily take up the cry of 'national' education. They observe the old guild-life of the country broken up and replaced by western forms of industrialism and try to revive cottage industries and bring back the *Charka* (spinning wheel). They observe the old familiar mode of parochial justice routed out by the cumbrous though sure process of the British law-courts and long to revive the village communities and popular tribunals that dealt substantial, if somewhat hesitating, justice. They observe the Sarkar arrogating all the powers and obligations of the local and communal bodies, of which memories still linger, and attempt to restore the *Swadeshi Samaj* to its proper functions. In all this, a common experience of life quickened by an awakening sense of history gives to the people's thoughts and feelings a distinctly political orientation. The question has often been asked—what ails India? The diagnosis is not so difficult as some would wilfully make it to be. India may truly be said to ail from unsatisfied desire for self-expression whose other name is Nationality.

writer. But if the movement has made any peaceful progress at all, it is *pro tanto* a measure of the development of nationality in India.

We have observed that the nidus out of which all politics germinate is the relation between State and society. The state that has been established by the British people in India has undoubtedly been productive of much good to the people,—and perhaps along with it some fatal evil too. It is an open secret that people regard the Sarkar with mixed feelings which shift between the two extremes represented by the epithets "satanic" and "benevolent." But whatever the good or the evil which British rule has brought to India, the fact that it has altered the traditional relation between the State and the people affects the whole political experience of the Indians. They observe the old communal system of education and culture replaced by a uniform state-controlled system and readily take up the cry of "national" education. They observe the old guild-life of the country broken up and replaced by western forms of industrialism and try to revive cottage industries and bring back the *Charka* (spinning wheel). They observe the old familiar mode of parochial justice ousted out by the cumbrous though sure process of the British law-courts and long to revive the village communities and popular tribunals that dealt substantial, if somewhat hesitating, justice. They observe the Sarkar arrogating all the powers and obligations of the local and communal bodies, of which memories still linger, and attempt to restore the *Swadeshi Samaj* to its proper functions. In all this, a common experience of the quickened by an awakening sense of history gives to the people's thoughts and feelings a distinctly political orientation. The question has often been asked—what ails India? The diagnosis is not so difficult as some would wilfully make it to be. India may truly be said to ail from unsatisfied desire for self-expression whose other name is Nationality.

ERRATA OF SANSKRIT PASSAGES

Read	For	Page	Line
*मूलगोत्राणि	मूलगोचाणि	46	31
*अङ्गिरा: कश्यपश्चैवं वशिष्ठो	अङ्गिराकश्यपश्चैव वशिष्टी	,,	32
*सताम्	सतां	,,	34
बाहू	बाहू	47	17
ऊरू	उरू	,,	,,
चातुर्वर्ण्यं	चातुर्व्वर्ण्यं	48	21
*यज्ञविघ्नघ्न	यज्ञभेक्षघ्न	,,	33
*ब्राह्मणो न च ब्राह्मण:	ब्राह्मणो न च ब्राह्मण:	,,	34
*ब्राह्मण:	ब्राह्मण:	,,	35
ब्राह्मण:	ब्राह्मण:	49	3
जातिर्ब्राह्मण:	जातिर्ब्राह्मण:	,,	5
यज्ञचर्या	यज्ञच्चर्या	,,	28
°व्यञ्जकम्	°व्यञ्जकं	,,	28
°योनिजम्	°योनिजं	,,	37
विद्यामहे वयम्	विद्यामहेवयम्	,,	38
*°विंशे या	°विंशे यी	50	22
*ब्रह्मणा	ब्रह्मणा	,,	27
*बहुविधा°	बहुविधा°	,,	31
*प्रणष्टज्ञान°	प्रनष्टज्ञान	,,	33
*ब्राह्मणानामदर्शनात्	ब्राह्मणानामदर्शनात्	51	30
*द्राविडाश्च	द्राविड़ाश्च	,,	32
*ब्राह्मणाना°	ब्राह्मणाना°	,,	34
*शबरा:	शबरा:	64	40
*दस्यूनां भूयिष्ठा:	दस्युनां भूयिष्टा:	,,	,,
*°र्यदन्तरम्	°र्यदनन्तरम्	67	36
*ब्रह्मावर्त्तं	ब्रह्मावर्त्तं	,,	37
*स्वं स्वं	स्वं स्वं	68	25
*प्रयागाच्च	प्रयागाच्च	,,	26
*आसमुद्रात्तु	आसमुद्रात्त	,,	27
*°दासमुद्रात्तु	°दासमुद्रात्त	,,	,,
*°र्बुधा:	°र्बुधा:	,,	28
*°कीर्त्तित:	°कथित:	,,	32
*°द्व्रात्या°	°व्रात्या°	,,	42

* Denotes Foot-notes.

Read	For	Page	Line
°पुत्राणां श्रेष्ठिनां	°पुत्राणं श्रेष्ठिनां	87	19
शावरीं	शावरां	,,	22
द्राविडो द्राविडादिषु	द्राविड़ो द्राविड़ादिषु	,,	23
संस्कृतं	संस्कृतं	,,	28
*ब्रह्मर्षिदेशो वै ब्रह्मावर्त्तो°	ब्रह्मर्षिदेशो वै ब्रह्मावर्त्तो°	88	33
जनराजाय	जानराजाय	108	32
*सार्वभौम:	स.र्व्वभौम:	109	34
*°राष्ट्रात्	°राष्ट्रात	,,	,,
*एकराडिति	एकराड़िति	,,	,,
*चाक्षुषेय:	चाक्षुषेय:	135	37
*मालोक्य:	°मालोक्य	136	36
*यद्रूयिष्ठा:	यद्रूयिष्टा:	,,	37
*ब्रूयुस्तं	ब्रूयस्तं	,,	,,
व्रात्याल्लिच्छवि°	व्रात्याल्लिच्छवि°	140	38
*द्रविड	द्रविड़	,,	39
*नृपेणा°	नृपेना°	142	32
*प्रतिकूलं च	प्रतिकुलञ्च	146	27
*बाधकं च	बाधकञ्च	,,	28
*°दनाख्यायप्रकल्पितम्	°दनाख्याय प्रकल्पितं	,,	31
*प्रहृत°	प्रहृत°	,,	32
*शाखोटक°	शखोटक°	,,	36
*पूजयाम इत्यादि	पूजयामित्यादि	,,	,,
*व्यवस्थे°	व्यवस्थे°	149	27
*स्थापयेन्न विचालयेत्	स्थापयेन्नविचालयेत्	,,	,,
*सर्व°	सर्व्व°	,,	29
*मन्त्रिगेहे	मन्त्रीगेहे	,,	30
*सर्वै:	सर्व्वै:	,,	,,
*एतावन्त्यहानि	एतावन्त्यहाणि	,,	33
*एवमनिष्टेष्वपि	एवमनिष्टेऽपि	,,	,,
*एवंविधो धर्म:	एवम्विधो धर्म	,,	36
*प्रशान्तो	प्रशन्तो	150	31
°व्यसनाबाध:	°व्यसनाबाध:	154	21
*सर्वं	सर्व्वं	155	34
*राज्ञा दक्षेन	राज्ञादक्षेण	156	31
चतुर्वर्णा°	चतुवर्णा°	157	3
सर्वधर्माणां	सर्व्वधर्म्मानां	,,	4
धर्मौ	धर्मौ	,,	11
वेतानुप्रविश्य	वेतानुप्रविश्य	,,	27

* Denotes Foot-notes.

Read	For	Page	Line
°विशेषैर्दिशेत्	विशेषैर्दिशेत्	157	29
°मुपस्थानविधिश्च	°मुस्थानविधिश्च	158	23
°वणिक्°	°वणिक°	159	10
वहुशो	वहुशो	,,	20
ग्रामाणां	ग्रामानां	167	16
सर्वमेव	सर्व्व मेव	,,	,,
*°रनुगच्छन्तः	°रननुगच्छन्तः	,,	28
*स्वयम्	स्वयं	,,	34
*ग्रामदशेशाय	ग्रामदरेशाय	,,	35
*स्वयम	स्वयं	,,	37

---

* Denotes Foot-notes.